Incorrigible Kids

A Probation Officer's Story

A Novel by Richard Galbraith

Table of Contents

I Can Fly

I've never met a person who grew up wanting to become a probation officer. That career had never entered my mind when I was in school or when I was starting my adult life and getting married. Judy and I had mapped out our lives before we got married. We would make the world a better place in our own modest way. I would teach teenagers while Judy did free-lance writing so she could always be home with the four kids we were going to have. We would never be as wealthy as our parents, but with all their possessions they had demonstrated that money doesn't buy happiness. We chose a path that would allow us plenty of time to enjoy the simple pleasures while improving the minds of more than a hundred children each year.

The plan got off to a good start. Judy had two feature articles published in the newspaper's Sunday supplement. That led to an ongoing position as a stringer covering community events on the north side of town.

I was confident that my Mathematics Major and Master of Education degree that included a full year internship in a reform school would make every high school want to hire me. I had interviews with three different districts. All of them started off well, but faltered after a critical question: "What is your coaching experience?" or "We need a coach for freshman football.

Can you handle it?" With each rejection, I grew more frustrated and depressed.

As Labor Day approached, the openings for math teachers evaporated. I was getting desperate. Spending a year as a substitute teacher, with no health insurance and erratic pay, wasn't a viable option. Taking a job at my father's car dealership would be an humiliating setback. So when I saw a want ad from the County Juvenile Court with a salary that matched that for a beginning teacher, I applied for it.

At that interview, I showed more enthusiasm than I felt and got a job offer as a Juvenile Probation Officer with a new unit that was being set up specifically for incorrigibility and other status offenses (runaways, truants and chronic curfew violators). This "Family Crisis Unit" was presented as an innovative team of eight elite officers that would focus on crisis intervention and diverting clients from the court system into community resources and family counseling. It sounded good. I signed on as soon as I got the offer. The job would pay the rent and put food on our table while I was helping the kids.

The first day on the job cast doubts on the claim that we were the "elite".   Four of us were new hires, complete rookies. None of us, including our supervisor, had reached the age of thirty. Bert had been with the department for six years and was freshly promoted to head our unit. Only three other officers, with a combined five years of experience had volunteered for the Family Crisis unit: Alan, Mark and Susan. They all seemed nice and dedicated. Linda was our most credentialed member, freshly graduated from A.S.U. with a Masters in Social Work. Jack and Heather had both spent the past year as substitute teachers in the inner city. I started feeling that I would enjoy their company as we entered this adventure together. We were to be on a first name basis among ourselves, but always use the formal Mr. or Ms. when with clients or in court.

The first two weeks were our official training period. Most of the time was spent reading: Arizona laws, judicial procedures, guidelines for case histories and reports and information about approved residential facilities and foster homes, plus the case files of the fifteen long-term probationers assigned to our caseloads. (The standard caseload was forty to sixty juveniles. Our smaller numbers were supposed to provide ample time for intensive supervision and counseling.) We were briefed by the Department's psychologist and completed all the Human Resources paperwork. I spent two mornings sitting in with an experienced P.O. during intake interviews. Even that involved very little interaction. Despite being mostly boring, this training impressed me with how difficult and potentially dangerous the job would be, but did nothing to boost my confidence in my ability to handle to sticky situations that I could expect to encounter.

At the end of the two weeks, we four new hires were sworn in as officers of the court, and deputy sheriffs. As deputies, we would have the power of arrest anywhere in the state and the right to carry a firearm, though we would have to supply our own pistols. I appreciated receiving the badge and the power it represented, but I couldn't see myself walking around with a gun and holster. Anyway, the department's policy was for probation officers to call in the local police if there was a need for an arrest. Only one Juvenile Probation Officer regularly carried a gun, a .45 which he wore conspicuously in a hip holster. I had already decided to give him a wide berth.

The time had come to sink or swim. I headed out to my first real duty with trepidation. I needed to get acquainted with the probationers I had inherited. Two of them lived in the Dupa Villa Projects. Armed with their case files and a note pad, I drove to the projects just east of downtown. They were a shabby collection of 500 low-rent apartments – a neighborhood where my regulation white shirt and tie would be conspicuous. I wasn't worried about getting mugged during daylight. I did fear for my car even though a five-year-old Chevy would not be an obvious target.

My first stop was thirteen-year-old Jorge Martinez and his mother, Juanita Suarez. According to the case file, his father was an illegal immigrant who was deported when Jorge was two. Since then, Juanita has had a series of boyfriends, each lasting one to three years. Jorge came to the court's attention with his third runaway report, at age eleven. It seems that he was fleeing from the current boyfriend, who got violent when he was drunk. Juanita had been told that if she continued to let this man live with her, she would be evicted and her son would be taken from her. She chose to keep Jorge, who was placed on probation. The probation officer had gotten Jorge connected with the Big Brothers organization and dropped by once a month to check that there was no resident boyfriend. Juanita had a job as a cleaning lady.

I found the right door and knocked. I could hear a television cartoon show and a fan through the open window. A young voice answered, "Who is it?"

"I'm Mr. Gilbertson. I made an appointment with your mother."

"She's not here."

"Well, Jorge, I'm your new Probation Officer. May I come in and talk with you?"

"Mama told me not to let anyone come in when she's not here, and you're a stranger."

"Good point. I'll show you my badge through the window so you'll know that I'm official. Then you can come outside and we'll sit on the steps and talk."

"OK." Jorge emerged. He was smaller than I expected: skinny with short black hair and wary brown eyes. He accepted my outstretched hand for a limp handshake before we sat down. I started the interview.

"How are things going?"

"OK"

"How are you doing in school?"

"OK"

"What's your favorite subject?" My questions sounded awfully shallow to me. I would have to work on that.

"P.E."

"What did you do this summer?"

"Parks and Recreation." His awkwardness was matched by my own.

"Did you do anything with your Big Brother?"

"He took me fishing and I caught a bass that big!" Jorge held up his hands about two feet apart – a typical fisherman's exaggeration, but at least there was a sign of enthusiasm about something.

"Wow! That's a big fish."

"Carlos showed me how to clean it and we cooked it for dinner. He caught more fish than I did, but mine was the biggest."

"Did your mom cook them for you?"

"No. Carlos showed me how to cook them. He is a chef at an Italian restaurant. He knows how to cook everything. We made tamales for Christmas. They were even better than the ones my nana makes. It was really fun. I'm going to be a chef when I finish school."

"That's cool. How often do you see Carlos?"

"He takes me somewhere nearly every Sunday. Yesterday we shot hoops and washed his Mustang. This week we are going to a movie. It would be boring without him."

At this point an Hispanic woman with a shopping bag approached, "You must be the probation officer."

"That's right. I'm Don Gilbertson. Here's my card."

"The bus was late. Come in and sit down. I need to get off my sore feet. Jorge, put the groceries away and bring me a glass of cold water."

I followed her inside and we sat on a sagging couch. She kicked off her shoes as Jorge brought us both jelly jars filled with water and disappeared back into the kitchen.

"What can I do for you sir?"

"It's more a question of what I can do to help Jorge. He's seems to be doing OK."

"He's a good boy. He hasn't been any trouble since he got his Big Brother. He is even doing better in school."

"That's good news. I'll be checking in with you every month, but if anything comes up between times just give me a call at the number on the card and we'll see what we can do."

"Thank you. Do you mind if I soak my feet? They get awfully sore."

"Go ahead. I'm ready to leave now. It's been nice to meet you." I stood up and hollered to the kitchen, "Bye, Jorge. I enjoyed talking with you. Keep up the good work in school."

He poked his head out of the kitchen and called back, "I will. *Adios*."

"*Hasta la vista*." My first official visit was done. Despite my rocky start with the questions, I was feeling relieved. This job didn't seem so hard.

I re-read the file for my next stop. Danny Donovan was another repeat runaway. Now fourteen, Danny's record went back three years. The first three times he ran away, the police found him within two days and returned him to his parents. The fourth time he was picked up on a curfew violation with bruises on his back and legs. The court investigation concluded that he had been beaten by his drunken father. Danny had a poor record at school but had a tested IQ of 130. He was put on probation and placed into Rainbow Pastures. Originally an orphanage founded by a Baptist missionary couple, it had grown to a collection of eight cottages at the edge of the affluent town of Gilbert. Each cottage housed ten children and a married set of house parents. The children's ages ranged from eight to sixteen. The kids went to the local public schools.

Danny was there for a year-and-a-half, through the completion of eighth grade. There had been some problems during the first few months when he was caught smoking cigarettes he had gotten from a schoolmate, but the reports got better as time went on. His grades came up to a B average and his mother participated in all the scheduled family counseling sessions, with his father quietly in attendance. Mr. Donovan was now on a disability pension from his union and claimed to have his drinking under control. So Danny was returned home in June, shortly before his last probation officer quit. There had been no contact during July or August. I crossed my fingers, hoping that he had gotten off to a good start in high school.

I walked around the compound until I found unit 44. When I knocked on the door, I heard muffled voices inside. After what felt like an eternity, the freckled face of a red-haired boy appeared at the door.

"You must be Danny."

"You must be the P.O." He grinned.

"That's right. I'm Mr. Gilbertson." I stuck out my right hand. Danny opened the door wider and stepped back. "Are your parents home?"

"Ma's in the kitchen and Pa's hiding in the broom closet."

"What??" My mouth dropped open.

"He thinks that Dick Tracy has come to arrest him. Go in and see for yourself."

I stepped through the front room and back into the kitchen. The sink was filled with a pile of unwashed dishes. A gin bottle sat on top of a paper bag full of trash. Cards were spread over the dining table in an unfinished game of solitaire. I tried not to let my discomfort show.

A haggard woman in a housecoat apologized. "He still gets the DTs sometimes. When you knocked, he thought it was Dick Tracy. He thinks Dick Tracy is after him for something he did a long time ago." She turned to the closet and opened the door. "It's OK dear, the man is not going to hurt you."

The gaunt man, with a couple of days of gray stubble, was huddled in the corner of the closet. He held out both quivering arms in front of him. "You finally caught me. Put the cuffs on, I'll go quietly."

"I'm not Dick Tracy. I'm Danny's new probation officer. I just came to see him."

"Are you going to take him away?"

"No."

"Too bad." He mumbled, while shaking all over.

"He doesn't mean that," his wife said. "He needs a rest. I can take care of him. You go talk to Danny."

I was nonplussed and glad to escape from that scene. Danny was in the front room, slouched down on one end of the couch. I sat down at the other end.

"That was embarrassing." I admitted.

"That's why I never have friends over. You get used to it."

Wanting to change the subject, I asked, "What's Rainbow Pastures like? I've never been there."

"Mostly boring."

"Did you like the people who run the place?"

"They are nice but uptight. They hassle you about little things, like table manners and how you made your bed. They like it out there in the sticks, but they wouldn't last long in the projects. That 'Love thy neighbor' and 'Turn the other cheek' stuff might work with little kids, but here it would just get you beat up and robbed. You have to act tough and have friends to protect you. If you don't stick together, the Spics and Blacks will beat the shit out of you."

"Do you like it better here?"

"Not really, but Ma needs me. When Pa gets drunk, he gets mean and picks on her. I'm strong enough now to stop him from beating her. I don't know why she stays with him."

Having no answer, I waited until he continued. "She says you get married for better or worse. She goes to Mass nearly every day and prays for him. That doesn't do any good either."

"Maybe it gives her a peaceful break in her day and gives her hope."

"Maybe, but it doesn't give me any hope."

"What is your hope?"

"I want to get a lot of money and get out of here. Maybe I'll win the lottery."

"That's a mighty long shot. With your brains, you have a much better chance of getting rich by going to college and on into business. Education is really your best hope. How are you doing in high school?"

"The classes are too easy and boring. The teachers don't really care what you do as long as you don't give them trouble. I don't think I can stand eight more years of sitting in school. I need some money sooner than that."

"There aren't many jobs for kids under fifteen, but if you keep clean until your birthday, I'll be able to get you a part-time job at Safeway. I know the manager."

"Oh, goody, goody." His sarcasm was strong. "A chance to bag groceries for five dollars an hour."

"It's a start, and better than nothing."

"So I'm just stuck here."

"For now. Hang in there and things will get better. Here's my card. You can call any time you want to talk. Otherwise, I'll be back to see you in two weeks."

"Yeah, right."

I went back to the kitchen and called Mrs. Donovan out of the back bedroom to give her a card and bid them farewell.

I sat in my car for a few minutes, breathing deeply to let some of the tension leave my body. I liked the kid and wanted to give him encouragement. But inside my mind, I agreed with his feeling that his situation was hopeless. I didn't have anything concrete to offer him. Maybe I was hopeless too. I couldn't understand why they had sent him home from Rainbow Pastures. He seemed to have been doing so well there.

When I discussed the case with my supervisor the next day, I got a lesson in the reality of placements. For starters, there are not nearly enough beds in effective residential facilities to meet the need. Secondly, residential treatment is expensive – at least four times as costly as foster placements. The best use of the department's limited resources was to try to return children to their families after a year in a treatment facility. A year is usually enough to establish better habits. Danny's good grades in school were evidence that the placement had done its job. Al made it clear that I was the only resource that the court had for Danny. It was my job to keep him on the straight and narrow. I seriously doubted that I capable of succeeding in that task. The good feeling I had gotten from the meeting with Jorge was destroyed by concern over the mess I was in with Danny and his family.

I made a short phone call the next week. Danny sounded cheerful and claimed everything was going well. Relieved, I thought I must have over-reacted to the first visit.

I was sitting in church that Sunday when the pager started vibrating. My reaction was distinctly not pious, but at least it was close enough to the end of the service that I could delay the call back until coffee hour. The dispatcher informed me that Danny Donovan had been brought in by the Phoenix Police on charges of burglary and possession of drugs. He was being processed into detention. Oh shit! There was nothing I needed do, or could do, until Monday morning. I spent the afternoon watching football on TV with my wife and a few friends. The games and company were good enough to keep me from worrying about Danny until after dinner.

Once our company left, my mind was stuck on Danny. I called Mrs. Donovan to confirm the time of the arraignment. She would catch a bus in the morning, but her husband was too ill to come. 'Yeah,' I thought, 'He's drunk as a skunk.' She didn't know what she would do if her only boy get sent away. "He's really not a bad boy. He just got mixed up with the wrong crowd. He went out to play with his friends after supper last night. That was the last time I saw him. The police called this morning before the bus was running. I only got to talk to him on the phone. He said he was all right. Will he be able to come home tomorrow?"

"I doubt it. The charges are pretty serious. I expect that he will have to stay in detention until the disposition hearing." I didn't tell her that there was no way in hell that I would recommend that he be returned that home.

"I'll be praying for him." She sounded so pitiful that I guess I should have felt sorry for her, but all I really felt was disgust. Praying wouldn't help him. At this point I don't know what would.

"I'll see you in the morning. Good-bye."

A copy of the police report was waiting for me in the morning. A neighbor had called to report a strange car outside of his home in the Palmcroft district around 4:00 am. As the patrol car arrived, the officers saw a person with a backpack climbing out of a window down the street. One officer pursued him on foot while the other drove to the other side of the block to cut him off. The suspect jumped over a fence into a backyard where he was attacked by a German shepherd, allowing the officers to capture him. The backpack contained a wallet, a small purse, two watches, a jewelry box and an opened pack of cigarettes. The only things in the boy's pockets were some pills in a plastic baggie and a high school ID card for Daniel Donovan. The pills were later verified to be amphetamines. The officers cuffed the suspect, placed him in the back of the squad car and drove around to the front of the house. The car, an older model Ford, was gone. The suspect claimed he didn't know anything about a car; he had walked there. An African-American man answered the door bell; he had been awakened by the barking dog. He was an emergency room physician whose shift ended at midnight. He identified all the objects in the bags as belongings from his bedroom. There was no forced entry. He liked fresh air and slept with the window open.

The suspect had been bitten by the German shepherd, so they needed to go back to that house to confirm that the dog had a current rabies shot. The officers had escorted the suspect to County Hospital for treatment, which had put them into overtime. Throughout their questioning, Danny had insisted that he was alone. He was just wandering around and saw the open window and took a chance.

When I met with Danny, he was surprisingly nonchalant. "Are you going to send me back to Rainbow Pastures?"

I wished I could, but I doubted they would take him back. I didn't know what the options were. "I'm not sure what the judge will decide. These are serious charges."

"Like I told the cops, I was just walking around when I saw the open window and went in. I needed some money."

"Are you sure your friends didn't give you a ride? That house is more than five miles from your place."

"No. I didn't even see the car that the cops talked about."

Shakespeare came to mind: 'I think the lady doth protest too much.' I pushed the issue. "Your mom said you went out with your friends after dinner and never came home. What did you do all that time?"

"We sat around and played cards until about one then we split up. I didn't feel like going home, so I started walking around."

"Had you used any drugs?"

"No. Never." Danny was looking down at the table, avoiding my eyes.

"What about the pills that were in your pocket?"

"I took them from the house."

I wasn't buyinh his story. "So I'm supposed to believe that a doctor, who can legally get prescriptions for any pills he wants, leaves a baggie of speed sitting out in his bedroom. And while you stuffed everything else you took into your backpack, you put the pills in your pocket."

"That's right. Look, I didn't hurt anybody. Insurance will pay for everything." Danny was getting agitated.

"You think when they woke up and discovered that their valuables had been stolen that they wouldn't feel hurt?" A definite tone of sarcasm had slipped into my voice.

"I figured they would be upset. That's why I left them three cigarettes. If my stuff were stolen, I'd need a cigarette to calm down."

"I believe that part. What did you plan to do with the stuff you took?"

"I'd leave the ID in the alley and sell the rest in the projects."

"Who were you going to sell it to?"

"I'm not a narc. There are plenty of people who will buy stuff without asking any questions. I'm not going to rat on anybody."

"I can't help you if you're not honest with me and tell me the whole truth."

"You couldn't help me if you wanted to."

That line hit me like a punch to the gut. Given his attitude, he was right. It also slammed the door on trying to get him to open up. We had only met a couple of weeks before; that wasn't enough time to build trust regardless of my ability or lack of ability.

The conversation continued with an explanation of the court procedures. Mrs. Donovan arrived in time for the hearing and sat quietly while Danny pleaded guilty to the charges. The hearing officer ordered Danny held in detention until his disposition hearing, which he scheduled for the following Friday morning.

At the end of the hearing, Danny turned to his mother and spoke softly "I'm sorry Ma."

"I'm praying for you," she replied and slowly walked away.

The possession of drugs eliminated any possibility of a return to Rainbow Pastures. With a felony so soon after release from a residential treatment facility, the only viable disposition was commitment to the State Department of Corrections. The paperwork would be easy; breaking the news to Danny wasn't. When I explained the situation, Danny protested, "I never took drugs!" His anger masked the start of tears.

"You were in possession of amphetamines when you were picked up. Having that on your record is enough to prevent Rainbow Pastures from taking you back."

"That's not fair! I was just holding them for a friend."

"That's not what you told the police or me earlier."

"I'm not a narc."

"Try to make the best of the situation. If you stay out of trouble in the youth center, you will probably be out in a halfway house in six or seven months. If you focus on your education, you can still turn things around."

Danny regained his swagger. "Don't worry about me. I can handle it."

Friday's disposition hearing went as expected. That afternoon, Danny was on the bus to the secure Arizona Youth Center. I spent the afternoon trying not to feel like a failure. I had only known Danny for two weeks, nowhere near enough time to form a meaningful relationship. Apparently neither I nor the system had the resources needed to straighten his life out. The burglary clearly marked him as seriously delinquent, but I didn't see how time in a reform school would help anything. There has to be a better way, but the system left me no choice. What a waste.

In late December, an obituary appeared in the newspaper for a Daniel Donovan, aged 15. He died in a fall. Survived by his parents. It had to be Danny. I did not take time off work to attend the funeral. I didn't know if I'd be welcome. I had another follow-up visit with Jorge the following week. As always, it was a pleasant break from the office. Jorge was still enjoying success and the guidance of his Big Brother. Afterwards, I walked over to pay my respects to Mrs. Donovan. The visit was prompted more by curiosity than sympathy.

Mrs. Donovan answered the door.

"Hello, I'm Don Gilbertson."

"Yes. I remember you. You tried to help my Danny. He liked you."

"I was so sorry to hear about his death."

"His friends got him killed."

"Do you mind telling what happened?"

"Come in and sit down." I did. She slumped down beside me and continued. "Danny was behaving well in that school. They let him come home on a weekend visit for Christmas. He went out after dinner with his friends. He said he had to go because they were holding a welcome-home party for him. He couldn't say no. The police came around midnight and told us that they had found his body lying in an alley. They didn't know how it happened. There were no witnesses. He told me he loved me before he left. That's the last thing he ever said to me."

"That's an important memory."

"A bunch of those skinhead friends of his came to the funeral. They stayed together in the back. Only one of them talked to me. He said he was Danny's best friend, he showed me a tattoo on his arm with 'D.D.' in a cross. He said that Danny was a straight-up loyal guy. He had taken the fall without telling on any of his gang. That's why they threw him a party. The party was held on the roof of a warehouse, where nobody would bother them. Things got out of hand when some of the guys got high. Danny went crazy when someone gave him angel dust. He claimed he was Superman and bet that he could jump to the roof across the alley. The boy said he tried to stop Danny, but Danny was too strong. Danny's last words were 'I can do anything. I can fly!' Then he jumped and hit the pavement. All the boys just ran away. No one stayed with my Danny." She was crying.

I tried to be comforting without being dishonest. "It was a terrible accident. Danny never wanted to hurt anyone."

"He was a good to me," she replied.

Over the last three months I had experienced enough successes to build up my self-confidence. Yet, I didn't get much sleep that night. I kept seeing Danny's face in one of his rare smiles and thinking that if I had only gotten to spend more time with him, I could have changed his attitude, maybe even enough to change the end of his story.

Jimmy

I was a bundle of nerves on the morning of my first solo intake duty. Was I going to be able to project enough authority while at the same time being perceived as helpful and caring? Would the parents accept advice and instruction from a young person who had no children of his own?

Coming in early that Tuesday, I pored over the thin files of the two teens scheduled for interviews. Both were runaways. The first was a sixteen-year-old boy who took off after a family argument over his school work. He argued with the police officer who picked him up after curfew. When his parents were contacted, his father declined to pick him up at the substation, stating that "a night in jail would teach him a lesson."
I'm afraid that's a common misconception shared by many parents and police officers. The training materials we got included research showing that detention did not reduce recidivism, but added an additional layer of resentment that had to be worked through. The second case involved a fifteen-year-old girl with a history of three prior runaway incidents lasting a day or two. Each time, she had returned home on her own. This was the first time the parents followed up with a request for help.

The actual interviews went by in a blur. I honestly don't know what I said after reading the Miranda Rights. At least I got through them without making any embarrassing blunders. Both kids expressed contrition, which helped. Both sets of parents accepted referrals to family counseling. According to the book, I succeeded that morning. A great feeling of relief settled over me when I completed the paperwork and sat down with my sack lunch.

I had a "walk-in" scheduled for three o'clock the same afternoon. Mr. Butler had called in for help controlling his eleven-year-old grandson. He had requested the latest possible appointment so the boy wouldn't miss school. He and his wife had taken Jimmy in six weeks ago, when his mother had died in a car accident – hit by a drunken driver on her way home from work. Now, they were being evicted from their trailer park because Jimmy had created too many disturbances.

Mr. Butler was wearing worn jeans, a khaki shirt and work boots. His face was deeply tanned and weathered. His black hair had flecks of gray showing. I guessed he was around fifty. His wife was a plump, light-skinned brunette wearing a plain cotton dress. Jimmy was notable for his small stature, barely four feet tall and skinny. His face bore a strong resemblance to his grandfather's. Mrs. Butler spoke first, apologizing for her husband's appearance. He had just gotten off work and didn't have time to clean up. This raised a doubt in my mind. Was the request for a late appointment really based on concern for the boy's school attendance, or the grandfather's work schedule?

I introduced myself. "Hi. I'm Don Gilbertson. I want to understand your problem and help you explore your options. Jimmy, wait here while I talk to your folks. Then I'll talk with you and we'll all get together at the end to decide on the next steps."

"Are you going to put me in jail?" Jimmy's response was a mixture of curiosity and fear.

"That's the last resort. We want to keep that from happening."

As soon as we were seated in the interview room, Mr. Butler started in. "We don't want to lose Jimmy, but we need help. He is running wild and we can't control him. He's not mean or anything, just too rambunctious. He created so much commotion in the trailer park that we have to move." There was no anger in his voice, only sadness.

"He's been through a lot. Maybe he just needs more time to get used to us." His wife chimed in.

"Can you back up a minute and fill me in on Jimmy's history? I need a better understanding of the situation before I can offer any meaningful suggestions."

Mr. Butler let out a long sigh before answering. "Jimmy has never seen his father. My daughter Jenny fell in love with a boy in community college. We met him once when they announced their engagement. He seemed nice, but when he found out that he had gotten Jenny pregnant, he insisted that she get an abortion. When she refused, he disappeared. Jenny had to drop out of school. She was already working as a waitress at Denny's. She lived with us until Jimmy was ready for kindergarten, so Nana could look after him while she was at work. She saved a lot of money and found a nice apartment in Mesa so Jimmy could go to a good school. She got a better job there, at Bill Johnson's Big Apple. We were living in Maryvale back then. It had been a nice neighborhood when we bought the house, but it's not safe anymore. The gangs and illegal immigrants have taken over. I was worried about my wife getting attacked while I was at work, so we sold the place and bought a trailer where we could be near Jenny.

"Jenny was a very devoted mother. Jimmy always came first in her life. She didn't date until this year. She only worked lunch shifts, so she could be home after school. Dinner shifts produce a lot more in tips. That's why she started working Friday nights. If she had kept to the lunch shift, she'd still be alive."

His wife reached over to put a hand on his shoulder. "Now, John, don't go blaming her for that. She was doing what she thought was best for Jimmy. Nobody would expect that she would get killed by a drunk driver. It could happen to anyone anytime."

"I know. Jenny liked her independence. She never asked us for help. We mostly saw them on holidays and at Sunday dinners – Nana cooked a big meal every week. Those were good times."

A faint smile appeared on both their faces. The following silence lasted so long that I almost broke in. His face darkened before he continued.

"When the police notified us of the accident, they said that Jenny had died instantly. The other driver was going over seventy when he crossed the center line and hit her head on. There was nothing she could have done. We rushed over to the apartment to be with Jimmy. Some lady from the Welfare Department was there. She had Jimmy packing a bag to take to a foster home with him. I put a quick end to that! She had the nerve to ask if we had a copy of the will or a power of attorney. She said she had to do her duty. I told her that I was doing my duty by taking care of my grandson. Family comes first."

"Are you Jimmy's legal guardians now?"

"Yes. All my spare time has been tied up in red tape. We had to hire a lawyer to get custody. We needed to get a court document and a death certificate to get Jenny's bank account changed to Jimmy's name. That's the only money he's got. The drunk wasn't insured. We even had to pay for having her car towed to the junk yard. We turned the spare room in the trailer into Jimmy's bedroom and cleaned out the apartment. We sold some of Jenny's stuff at a yard sale and gave the rest to the Salvation Army. Then there was another hassle getting Jimmy covered by my health insurance. Then we had to find a new place we could put our trailer."

"You've been through quite an ordeal."

"It has been worse for Jimmy. Naturally he was sad and mad at the world. He lost his mother and he had to change to a new school. There aren't any other kids in the trailer park. We figured he would get better with time, but he has gotten worse."

His wife told more of the tale. "At first, he mostly stayed in his room watching television with the door closed. When I asked what was bothering him, he said 'Nothing.' So I was glad when a friend from school started coming over. But then this Charlie started getting Jimmy into trouble. The neighbors started complaining that they were making too much noise and were riding their bicycles through their lots. They got the manager to evict us at the end of the month. There is a clause in lease that limits children to two-week visits. I thought they would make an exception under the circumstances, but the manager insisted that once he got complaints, he had to enforce the rules. He did help us get into another park out in Apache Junction. The new place has a playground for the kids."

"The move and the deposits cost us almost fifteen hundred dollars. It wiped out our savings account, but we'll manage somehow. That's not why we're here. It was after we were told we had to move that Jimmy really started misbehaving. He rode his bike right through Mrs. Crawford's flower garden and smashed her plastic flamingo. When we tried to get him to apologize, he called her names then locked himself in his room. His teacher called last week to tell us that Jimmy hadn't turned in any homework for a week. When we asked him about it, he said he didn't have to because we would have moved to another school before any report cards came out. Then on Thursday, he didn't come home from school until 7:30. We were worried to death that something had happened to him. He said he was over at Charlie's and forgot what time it was. We always have dinner at 6:00, so it was cold and dried out. He said he didn't care. We told him he needed to come straight home from school before he went to a friend's house." I was thinking, if it were my child, I would have done something harsher than just talk to him.

"He didn't come home from school on until after dinner time on Friday either. That's when I called the police and they told me to call the Juvenile Court. So here we are. What should we do?"

He was looking to me, fresh out of college, for expert advice in child rearing. I could provide some hope, but no answers. "You are working through a difficult situation. I don't have any instant solution and I definitely need to get to know Jimmy before I give any specific advice. At this point, the best I can do is to point out a few possibilities for you to think about. Jimmy's relationship to you has had to change. As grandparents, he got to be with you mostly for the fun times and he was probably the center of your attention during those visits." Nana started nodding in agreement. "It's not the same now that he is with you full time, especially since you have had to spend so much time dealing with all the details of Jenny's death and the move. So Jimmy may be feeling that he isn't getting as much positive attention as he wants. It's not anybody's fault, but it could contribute to his acting out. Another thing that has changed is that now you have the job of parenting, including rules and disciplining. I'm sure that your routines and rules aren't exactly the same as his mother's. Boys his age need limits that are consistently enforced. They tend to push their limits and seek more freedom. They may protest and try to avoid disciple, that's part of growing up, but firm limits provide them with security. Jimmy may be confused by the changes and not be sure of exactly where he stands, and it would be natural at this stage for him to idolize his mother and miss her ways of doing things."

Nana asked hopefully, "Are you saying that this is just a stage and he'll grow out of it?"

"I'm afraid it's not that simple. It could happen, but he might need some help. Counseling might help."

"You think he needs to go to a psychiatrist? Doesn't that cost a lot of money?"

"Not a psychiatrist, but a family counselor. We have a list of several experienced counseling agencies that charge on sliding scales that make sure the services are affordable. It might help Jimmy if he talked through the things that are bothering him."

"I don't think that would do any good. We've tried to get him to talk, but every time I ask him what's wrong, he just says 'Nothing'." The Butlers were taking turns responding to my comments.

"He might be afraid of saying something that will upset you or make you be disappointed in him. That can make it too scary to share his worries with a parent. It can be easier for a kid to talk about some things with an outsider he's not emotionally attached to. It is not a sure thing, but I think it might be worth a try. I'll let you think it over in the waiting room while I talk with Jimmy."

I opened the door for them to leave and beckoned Jimmy over. He sat down and looked at the floor. "Are you going to put me in jail?"

"That is not part of the plan, and it is definitely something that your folks don't want to happen. They tell me that you've been getting into a lot of trouble lately and they asked for me to help you change that." He nodded without looking up. "I want to understand what's been going on. Tell me about Mrs. Crawford and her flamingo."

"She's an old witch. She'd yell at me every time I went by. I wasn't doing nothing wrong, I was just riding my bike down the road. She called me and Charlie names. When Grandpa told me we were being kicked out of the park, I knew she was the one who complained. She made me mad, so when I went by her trailer I swerved over and kicked her stupid flamingo. If they don't allow children, they shouldn't allow ugly plastic flamingos either."

I couldn't keep from chuckling. "I don't like those plastic flamingos either. But neither of us has the right to destroy other people's property, even if we think it is ugly. That's vandalism and it could get you thrown in jail. Mrs. Crawford isn't all bad; she didn't file a criminal complaint against you. It sounds to me that you blamed her for a lot of anger that you had built-up inside."

"OK, so I screwed up. I couldn't help it. I had good reasons to be angry."

"True. Still, being angry doesn't help your life get better. We are going to have to work on expressing your anger in ways that don't hurt anyone." This time, Jimmy did not make a defensive response. I wrote down a note on my pad, mostly to buy a little time before changing the subject. "The other thing that really upset your grandparents was when you didn't come home after school in time for dinner."

"I don't know what's the big deal. I got home before dark. That's all Mom cares about. I can fix my own dinner in the microwave."

"Every house has its own rules. Your grandparents do things a little differently than your mother did. Your Nana puts a lot of work into fixing dinner and having it ready for the whole family to eat at six o'clock."

"Mom's way was better. Besides, I didn't know what time it was. I don't have a watch." The defensive anger was back, full bore.

"When I talked with your grandparents, they described how you used to have dinner together every Sunday. Having the whole family together and talking over dinner were their happiest times. They really want dinner time with you to be special."

"They were just saying that. They don't really care. They don't even want me to live with them." Tears were starting to well up in his eyes.

"Whoa! What makes you say that?"

"It's true. I heard Grandpa talking to that welfare lady. He said he said he had to take me because it was his duty."

"What does the word 'duty' mean to you?"

"Duty is something you have to do even though you don't want to. It's like a giant chore."

"That's one meaning. There's another meaning that may be a little more old-fashioned. To your grandpa, doing your duty means taking care of what's most important, no matter what. His family, including you, is the most important thing in his life. Your folks told me about that night. The lady was trying to put you in a foster home. Your grandparents have been going through a whole bunch of work fighting to keep you. They really do love you and care for you, and I'm not just saying that."

The tears were now streaming down Jimmy's face. I offered him a Kleenex.

"I don't know why I'm crying. I didn't even cry at Mom's funeral. Mom always called me her brave young man."

"Many of us have been told that men aren't supposed to cry. But that is not really true. I remember watching the playoff game that the Suns lost to the Lakers. After the game, several of the stars were sitting in front of their lockers, crying. That shows that tears aren't a sign of weakness, they show that you really care." That brought a silent nod. "When you are hurting inside, crying can let some of the hurt get out and heal. I know you've been through a lot and I suspect that you've kept a lot of the hurt hidden inside yourself." Another nod. Jimmy's eyes were focused intensely on mine. "From what I've seen and heard today, I really believe that you're going to be able to make things better. I'm going to suggest that you go to a counselor, someone you can talk to and help you better understand what's been going on. What you say to the counselor will be private. He won't tell me or your folks what you say. If you go, I don't want you to keep anything hidden from him, even if it feels scary. Are you willing to give that a try."

"Okay, I'll try."

"It's time for me to bring your folks back in so we can plan the next steps."

As his grandparents came back into the room, Jimmy blurted out, "I messed up. It's all my fault. I'm so sorry."

Nana went over and put her arms around Jimmy. "Now, now, dear. It's okay. Don't cry. It's going to be alright."

Grandpa stopped dead in his tracks at the sight of the tears in Jimmy's eyes. He spoke quietly before he sat down. "It is not all your fault. We've all made mistakes these past few weeks."

I took back the lead. "It is clear to me that each one of you has good intentions. But even with the best intentions, misunderstandings can lead to big problems. I think that a lot of Jimmy's attitude and misbehavior stemmed from a misunderstanding. Jimmy, can you tell your grandparents why you thought they took you in?"

"You tell them."

"OK. Jimmy told me that he thought the word duty meant something that you didn't want to do but you had to do anyways. So, when he heard you tell the social worker that it was your duty to take care of him, he thought that meant that you didn't really want him."

"Oh, no!" Nana broke in. "Jimmy we want you more than anything. You have to believe that."

"I do, now. I'm sorry. I'll really try to be good."

Both Nana and Jimmy took Kleenexes from the box and wiped their eyes.

Grandpa spoke, "That's a huge load off my mind. It explains a lot. Everything is going to work out now."

It was a touching moment, but I was scared that it was too good to last. "This is a good start, but I wouldn't count on the difficulties disappearing by themselves. I know that Jimmy wants to be good, but changing habits takes time. I want you to be ready to deal with some cases of backsliding. Also, after all that Jimmy has been through, I really think that counseling would help him sort things out in his own mind. I suggest that you start by calling Prehab for an appointment. They are based in Mesa and have an excellent reputation."

"We'll call them tomorrow."

"Normally I would set up a follow-up visit at your home within a week, but I know you are going to be very busy with the move, so I'll call you next week to set up a convenient time. Here's one of my cards for each of you. If anything comes up, feel free to give me a call."

I walked them out. All of us were smiling. I felt that I had finally nailed the interviews. This was what the unit was created for. I got a troubled family headed toward a loving solution without getting them entangled with the court.

I was drained. It is amazing how exhausting it is to really listen and connect with strangers. I forced myself to write up the case notes before I left for the day. The objective prose mandated by the department's protocol recorded the facts, but did not capture the essence of the encounter.

I decompressed on the drive home, so I was ready for the evening. We met some friends at the local sports bar for the Monday Night Football between the Bears and Judy's hometown Eagles. I stuffed myself from the hot dog based buffet. Our small group was heavily outnumbered by Chicago fans. That made the 28-24 Eagles victory all the sweeter. I had reached my three beer limit by the start of the fourth quarter, so I finished the game on coffee. At home after the game, Judy and I enjoyed the perfect ending to a good day.

That Friday at 11:00 am, I got a call from Mr. Butler.

"I'm afraid that Danny has run away. He has been real good all week, so when he asked if he could go and say good-bye to his friend Charlie, we let him go. He's been gone for three hours. He as supposed to be back no later than 9:30 when the truck was arriving. Now they have the trailer hooked up and are starting the move and we have to be at the new place when they set it in. The phone is disconnected until Monday morning, so I don't know what to do."

"Where are you calling from?"

"I'm at the manager's office."

"OK. There is no use in calling the police until he has been gone for more than twenty-four hours. Why don't you give the manager my card and have him call me if he spots Jimmy? If we don't hear from him by 3:00, I'll come look around for him. If I find him, I'll bring him to the new trailer park. I'm writing a note to myself – please remind me of the addresses of both places and give me a description of his bicycle."

After providing me the requested information and a general idea of where Charlie lived, he thanked me profusely and we hung up.

The call disturbed me. I doubted that Jimmy had really run away, but I didn't have any other explanation for his being gone that long, barring a serious accident. If he had run away, the odds of my spotting him, much less catching him, by driving around the neighborhood were miniscule. My whole weekend would probably be ruined by fretting about Jimmy. I certainly wasn't ready to give the paperwork in front of me the attention it deserved, so I got another coffee and sat down to an early lunch at my desk.

About 11:30, the phone rang again. This time it was Jimmy, sounding confused and scared. "They left without me. I can't believe they'd do that."

"Whoa! Slow down a minute. You were supposed to be home two hours ago. Your folks called me before they left. They are very worried about you. Where were you?"

"I just went over to Charlie's. Yesterday was his birthday and he got two new R.C. cars, so we had to play with them. I didn't know what time it was." He still wasn't taking responsibility for his actions.

"You didn't HAVE TO play with the cars. That was a choice you made. Your grandpa told me that they had to go with the trailer when it was moved, so I agreed to pick you up. Are you at the manager's office?"

"No. I didn't want to get in more trouble with him. I'm at the Circle K across the street."

"Stay right there and I'll come and take you home. It will take me at least a half-hour to get there, so you need to wait for a while."

I spent the drive time rehearsing different things I might say to him. I never did come up with words that sounded right. It took forty-five minutes in traffic to get to the Circle K. Jimmy was sitting on his bike next to the pay phone.

Jimmy spoke first. "Where have you been? I've been waiting forever!"

"I got here as soon as I could. Put your bike in the back seat."

He shoved his bike into the back, climbed in beside me and slammed the door and whined, "You said you would be in thirty minutes."

"What I actually said was that it would take AT LEAST that long. Did you really think that I wouldn't come?"

"No. I believed you."

"But you still got worried while you were waiting."

"Yeah."

"That's a normal reaction. I know that feeling. Put on your seat belt so we can get going."

When he was buckled up, I started driving east and continued the conversation. "I want you to really think about how bad it felt when I was later than you expected. When that happens to me, I get a real knot in my gut and my mind can't help but worry that they will never come and that I'm going to be deserted. Is that what you felt like?"

"Kind of." He whispered.

"I want you to remember that feeling. Do you think that Nana gets that same feeling when you come home late, even though she trusts you and you know that nothing is wrong?"

"I guess so."

"I know you don't mean to hurt your Nana. That's why I want you to remember that feeling. If you think about what she feels like, you'd do something differently." The message was delivered. I paused to let it sink in.

When we approached the Apache Junction mobile home park, I asked, "What do you think you punishment will be?"

"Grandpa will probably ground me for a month."

They were outside when we pulled up to their space. Grandpa was fastening an aluminum skirt around the bottom of the trailer. Jimmy ran to Nana while I got the bike out of the back.

Nana was hugging Jimmy and babbling with relief. "You had us so worried. We were afraid that you had run away. Don't ever do that again. It's after lunch time. You must be hungry. Let me fix you something to eat."

"I didn't run away. I just lost track of the time when I was with Charlie. I got really scared when I came home and you were gone. I'm sorry."

Grandpa spoke next. "I believe you are sorry, but this is too serious to go unpunished. You are grounded until we see the counselor on Wednesday. You will stay in the house except when you are helping me with chores or you are at school. There will be no television."

"So I'll have to stay in my room when you and Nana are watching TV?"

"No. The television will be unplugged when you are home. We'll find something else to do."

I was pleasantly surprised by Mr. Butler's delivery. He had obviously thought this out. I told him, "You are handling the situation very well. I'm glad you have set up an appointment with a counselor. You should know that

Jimmy called me on his own initiative; there was no contact with the manager."

"Thank you for bringing Jimmy home. I'll let the old manager know that he is OK."

"I know you are really busy now, so I'll plan on coming back to visit next Thursday afternoon, unless you call me sooner."

"That'll be fine."

I then went home feeling greatly relieved. I was getting the hang of the job. More importantly, I had really made a difference with this family.

I wanted to share my success at work. Alan was in the break room when I arrived on Monday morning, glaring at the empty coffee pot. I started a fresh pot and described the incident while it brewed. Alan's only response was a sarcastic, "How sweet."

This lack of camaraderie was my biggest disappointment about the job. I had expected more of a team atmosphere with lots of sharing of ideas and hints, especially from the experienced officers. Instead, we pretty much worked alone. We were out in the field meeting clients for almost half the week. Most of the time in the office was spent either on paperwork or in confidential client interviews. I actually had more conversations with the supervisor of the steno pool than with any of my colleagues. Even my supervisor, Bert, spent most of his time isolated in his office or off at meetings. About the only time I saw him was at the weekly staff meeting.

That week the staff meeting focused on the coffee pot. Alan complained about it being left empty several mornings that week.

Linda immediately jumped in. "Don't look at me. Why are the women always expected to make the coffee? I refuse to support that stereotype."

"It's not a matter of sexism. When I come in early, I make the first pot." Bert pontificated. "Whoever takes the last cup, should make a new pot. It's that simple."

"I never leave the pot empty." Linda rejoined.

"So, you're the one that leaves just a few drops in the bottom?" Alan smirked.

"That's not funny." Bert tried to control the discussion. "Look. Free coffee is one of the few perks of this job. The County isn't obliged to provide it. They could replace it with a vending machine is it causes problems."

"Speaking of perks," Heather opined, "Why doesn't the County provide herbal tea instead of just coffee. It is much healthier and has a calming effect. If everybody drank tea instead of coffee, they wouldn't be so edgy."

She was greeted by groans from the rest of us. So much for team spirit.

When I arrived at the Butler's the following Thursday afternoon, Jimmy and his grandpa were in the driveway working on Jimmy's bike.

"How's it going?" I greeted them.

"Fine. Jimmy has been helping me with all of my chores, so now we're fixing up his bike. We're almost done, then we'll wash up and come in."

"No hurry."

Nana appeared and invited me in for a glass of iced tea. Once inside, she commented, "Jimmy's attitude has really changed. I don't know what you said to him, but he's a whole new boy. He adores John now. They spent almost the whole weekend fixing things together."

"I'm glad to hear it, but the time your husband is spending with Jimmy has a lot more to do with the improvement than anything that I've done."

"John is really enjoying showing him how to use tools. He's been poking around everywhere looking for things to fix up."

We exchanged a few pleasantries until Jimmy came in.

"You wanna see my room." It wasn't a question, so I followed him a few feet to the tiny side room. The surprise was that the bed was made and everything was neatly put away.

"I can see why you're proud of it. It looks really good. By the way, I see you are wearing a watch."

"It's a new Timex. Grandpa gave it to me on Monday for being such a good helper. Now I always know what time it is." Jimmy was beaming.

"No more excuses for being late."

"I start home fifteen minutes early to make sure I'm on time."

"That's a good plan. Sit down. I want to ask you a few things."

Jimmy sat cross-legged on the bed, leaving the single chair for me.

"What did you think of your counselor visit yesterday?"

"It was OK. He's a cool guy. Do I have to tell you what we talked about?"

"No. Your conversations with him are confidential. You can keep them just as private as you want. I just want to know if you think they are helpful."

"He told me a way to avoid nightmares. I often think about how much I miss my Mom and then I have a dream about driving a car with her and crashing into a tree. He told me that when I get in bed, I should try thinking about a happy time that I had with my Mom. Last night I thought about a time we went to the zoo and I had a different dream. The elephant escaped and let us climb on his back, then we rode him through the zoo and all the way home. Everybody got out of our way. It was funny."

"That's a great dream. I seldom remember my dreams." I went on, "You seemed to have survived your week without television."

"It was only six days. It wasn't so bad. I spent a lot of time helping grandpa and he showed me how to fix things. Then, after I finished my homework, we played cards. Nana taught me how to play Hearts. She usually wins, but I won once yesterday. Do you want to play?"

"I like Hearts, but not today. I have to head for home."

"We'll play next week. Come earlier so you'll have time."

I realized that I had set myself up for that one, so I said, "Fine by me, if it's OK with your folks."

We went back to the living room and wrapped things up, including scheduling a visit and card game for 3:00 the next Thursday.

When my supervisor asked about the status of the James Butler case, I happily told him what had transpired. He pointed out that the thirty-day clock was running and wanted to know if I was ready to close the case.

I replied "I want to spend more time and stabilize the situation. I've established a good rapport with Jimmy."

He cut in, "Would you describe the family's situation as a crisis?"

"No, not at this time."

"Then you need to close the case before thirty days pass. Our performance is being evaluated based on the number of cases that we keep out of court by resolving the family crisis during the pre-trial period. Think of our unit as an hospital's emergency room. We can't afford to provide everyone with long term care. We have to just treat the crisis and send them back into the community. You did a good job with the Butler case. Now release him."

"I understand. I'll close the case in time." I didn't like the rule, but now I understood it.

Nana greeted me at the door the following Thursday. "Jimmy's teacher called us yesterday." I reacted with a grimace, thinking 'What else has gone wrong?'

"She told us how pleased she was to have him in her class. He wrote the best Thanksgiving paper in his grade." She thrust the paper at me. "Here, you read it."

The essay was a two-page paean to his grandparents. The handwriting was a little sloppy, but the grammar and spelling were good. The content was excellent. It particularly noted how they helped him whenever he got in trouble. This news brought a smile to my face. "This is great. How have things been at home?"

"Great. Jimmy couldn't be better. He's waiting for you to get here and play cards. Sit down at the table. Would you like something to drink?"

"A glass of cold water would be good."

The four of us spent the next hour playing a friendly game of hearts. I saw a different side of gentle Nana as she gleefully stuck her husband or me with the Queen of Spades. She won by a large margin. I edged out Grandpa for third place. It was a relaxed, comfortable atmosphere. When we finished, Jimmy asked, "Can you play again next week?"

"Actually, based on everything I've seen and heard today, I recommend that we close this case. I think that you have all done extremely well and don't need to be involved with the court anymore."

"I agree." said Grandpa. Nana nodded. Jimmy chimed in, "Does that mean you're not coming back?"

"That's right."

"But I thought you were my friend!" Jimmy had a knack for putting me on the spot.

"I do like you a lot, Jimmy. I wish your family were my next door neighbors, then I could see you around often. However, my mission is to try to help kids who are getting into trouble find a way to improve their situations. Thanks to your grandparents and your attitude, your situation is now really good." Jimmy nodded, so I continued, "Unfortunately, there are still too many kids who are in trouble, so I have to move on."

"Don't forget me."

"Don't worry about that. I'll remember you for the rest of my life."

We shook hands all around before I left. I drove home in a strange mood. I should have been elated by the success. I had really achieved the goals of our unit in this case, at least in the short run. I wished I could have kept in touch with the Butlers and seen Jimmy grow up. The problem with doing crisis intervention is that you never really know your long-term impact.

Ronny - Part I

Ronald Griffith was the only client on my inherited caseload who was officially classified as a juvenile delinquent (instead of an incorrigible child). Initially, he had been referred to the court for repeatedly shoplifting when he was nine years old. The first two times he was apprehended for pocketing candy and potato chips from convenience stores, the police released him into the custody of his mother with a warning. The 'third strike' got him placed on probation.

The pre-court investigation reported that Ronny lived with his mother in a run-down shack on the west side of South Phoenix. The place was filthy and infested with cockroaches. His mother worked irregular hours as a barmaid in a biker bar. Ronny was born to a seventeen year old unwed mother. They had never established which one of three boys was the father. Ronny had performed well in school until third grade when he his performance plummeted. His fourth grade teacher described him as a day-dreamer, often staring out of the window instead of paying attention or doing his class work. He was quickly placed in a temporary foster home.

Ronny's grandparents, Randy and Liz Griffith, stepped in and requested custody. Mr. Griffith had broken his back in a workplace accident and was on permanent disability, so he would be home during the day to supervise Ronny. Mrs. Griffith held steady employment as a bookkeeper for JC Penny's. They lived in a two bedroom apartment off Northern Avenue and the Black Canyon Freeway. (At least that was directly on my way home, so it would be a convenient late afternoon visit.) After a social worker determined that the grandparents and their home met the requirements for a foster home and his mother waived her parental rights in court, they were granted permanent custody as Ronny's legal guardians. That process took three months.

Almost five years later, he was still on probation. The file was thick with monthly reports that revealed very little about Ronny or his family. There were no additional police reports. The grandfather consistently reported that everything was fine except that they needed more money. School attendance and performance were "marginal." The early reports said he was restless and often inattentive. He had been diagnosed as ADHD in fifth grade and put on Ritalin. That had "solved the problem." After that, the contacts seemed to have been perfunctory. Three years with a clean record would normally merit an early release from probation. I wondered if my predecessor was sandbagging his workload by keeping an easy case.

I was greeted by the yapping of a small dog as I approached their door. I pressed the doorbell. A male voice answered, "Come in, it's not locked. Shut up Daisy!"

A daschund kept sniffing my shoes as I entered a living room furnished with two large recliner chairs, a worn couch, four wooden TV tray tables and a large television set, currently showing a dinosaur chasing a good looking blond woman. The place reeked of cigarette smoke. There was a bric-a-brac cabinet in the corner with a folded American flag in a triangular case on top. I wondered who had died in combat. A middle-aged man with a beer belly was slouched in one of the chairs with a cigarette in his hand.

"Hello, Mr. Griffith. I'm Don Gilbertson from the Probation Department."

"Call me Randy. Everybody does."

"Okay, Randy. Is Ronny home?"

"He's in his room. Go on back." Randy turned his attention to the TV and his smoke.

All the doors into the hall were open. A tidy kitchen with a Formica-topped table and four chairs was on the right. The bathroom was between the two bedrooms on the left. The back bedroom had an unmade bed with cowboy sheets and a stuffed bear, a book case with one shelf of books and three shelves holding toys. The décor looked like it belonged to a young child, instead of a fourteen-year old. A slightly chubby, freckle-faced boy occupied the chair at a cluttered desk, drawing with a pencil. A group of drawings were taped to the wall above the desk, mostly dragons and robots, but one realistic horse.

"Hello Ronny. I'm Mr. Gilbertson."

"I'm Ron, not Ronny." He snapped.

"Sorry. I guess the records are out of date, Ron. Did you do all of those drawings?"

"Yes."

"I particularly like the horse. It's very life-like. Did you copy it from a book?"

"I drew it from memory. It's supposed to be the one they show at the beginning of so many movies."

"Ah! I thought it looked familiar. You have quite an eye for detail."

"Thank you, but I like dragons better. I'm working on a new design." He showed me the picture he was working on. It was a frontal view of a flying dragon with its head raised.

"That's cool. I suppose you know that I'm your new probation officer. I want to get to know you and see what I can do to help."

"I don't need any help."

"Okay. So tell me what you like most about living here?"

"No cockroaches. I hate cockroaches."

"Yeah, they are dirty creatures, especially when they crawl up out of a drain." I was glad the file had given me a context, so I didn't look startled.

"It's worse when they get in your food."

"Yuck. So what do you least like about living here?"

"Nagging. Granny yells at me all the time. Sometimes it makes me really mad."

"Is that how your closet door got dented?"

He looked chagrinned. "That was a long time ago. I don't hit things any more."

"What do you do now when you feel really mad?"

"Most of the time I just slam the door and turn out the lights. If I'm too mad to lie down, I go into the alley and throw rocks at the telephone poles. Yeah, I know I shouldn't do that, but it calms me down."

"That's one way to burn off the adrenaline that your body builds up when you get angry, but it would be better to bounce a tennis ball off a wall."

"I guess so."

"What does she nag you about?"

"Mostly chores. I know what my chores are and I always do them during the day. I don't need to be reminded over and over."

"What are your chores?"

"I feed the dog, clean up her messes, take out the garbage, vacuum the floors and do all the dishes."

"It sounds like you do a lot to help out."

"I have to. Randy can't do much because of his back and Granny works all day. Aren't you going to ask me about school?"

We'd been hitting on some sensitive areas and Ron was visibly tense. I took his hint and moved to safer ground. "Okay. How is school going?"

"It's boring. Eighth grade is easy. It's all stuff I already know."

"It's only September. The first month of school is usually spent reviewing things. It's supposed to make up for the stuff you forgot over summer vacation."

"I didn't get a vacation! I had to go to summer school for math."

"That's tough." I wasn't going to probe too hard at the first meeting. "Do you like to read?"

"Yes."

"What kind of books do you prefer?"

"Ones with dragons." Ron smirked.

"I should have guessed that one. So, what else do you do for fun?"

"I hang out with my friend."

"Doing anything in particular?"

"Nope. We just hang out. There's nothing to do around here. Sometimes we go up to the mall. Don't tell Granny that; she thinks I would get in trouble and steal something there, but we just look at stuff and talk to friends."

"That's normal for teenagers."

We heard Randy's voice from the front of the apartment. "Hi Honey. Ronnie's new case worker is here."

I turned back to Ron. "It sounds like your grandmother is home. I ought to go meet her."

"See ya later." He turned back to his dragon drawing.

I returned to the living room and met a heavyset woman in a plain blue dress. "Hello Mrs. Griffith. I'm Don Gilbertson."

"We're simple people. Just call me Liz. I hope you do more than the last two case workers did to straighten out Ronnie."

"I'll do my best. The department has reorganized in a way that will let me spend more time with Ron than his last probation officer could."

"He needs a firm hand." She was adamant. "He's starting to get sassy with back talk. He's already taller than I am and it won't be long before he outweighs me, the way he eats."

I aimed for a soothing tone. "That's pretty typical for boys his age."

"If he doesn't knuckle down and control his mouth, he'll never amount to anything. I was too easy on his mother and she got into all kinds of trouble."

Her tone of voice indicated that she wouldn't accept any contrary opinion, so I didn't try. "I'll be back next Thursday and talk to him some more."

Randy tried to be encouraging. "Maybe he'll listen to you because you're young. He certainly doesn't pay much attention to what his old grandfather says."

Grandmother headed for the kitchen. "I've got to start fixing dinner."

I said my good-byes and left.

The visit unsettled me. My thoughts about pushing for a quick termination of probation had dissolved. The Griffiths lived with a harsh view of the world. I viewed Ron's anger and boredom as a dangerous combination. His grandmother's expectations of growing trouble could easily become a self-fulfilling prophecy. On the plus side, Ron had been surprisingly open with me. He had cautiously revealed a lot about his feeling. I felt I had done a good job of establishing rapport. Some how that made me feel responsible for making Ron happier and more hopeful. The problem was that I had no idea of how to do that.

When I arrived the next week, the TV was quiet; the dog was not. Randy was ensconced in his recliner smoking a cigarette.

"Hi, Don. Do you want a beer?"

"No thanks. I'm on duty"

"Ronny is in his room. Mother says that he has to finish his homework before any television or playing. He's mostly a good kid. He plays cards with me a lot. I was wilder than him when I was a kid, and I turned out alright. He does have a hot temper – he gets that from Mother's side." Referring to his wife as 'Mother' struck me as odd, but I perceived to describe their relationship.

"We were high school sweethearts. That was in Kearney. All our families worked in the copper mines. She'd get mad a lot even then. She broke up with me three times, but we got back together for the Prom. We had some beers afterwards and that's when I got her pregnant with Clara. We graduated before anybody knew. Her family stayed really mad at us, so we moved to Phoenix and got married. I got a job with the pipe fitters union as an apprentice. It takes five years to become a journeyman, so we were short of money at first, so Mother had to get a job and leave Clara with a neighbor all day. That wasn't good for her, but we had to do it. Clara was a little cutie. She was always boy-crazy and that's what got her in trouble."

"Once I became a journeyman, I was doing good. We went out for dinner every week and went to Las Vegas for vacation. Then I fell from a scaffold and broke my back. They said I'm lucky that I'm not paralyzed, but the pain never goes away and I'm stuck here with nothing to do. Ronny is my only company."

"You're lucky to have him." I figure Randy isn't going to be much help since he just wants someone to be his buddy. "I'm going back to talk to him."

"OK. The John Wayne movie starts in ten minutes."

As I entered his room, Ron was tucking some papers into his backpack; his math book was out on his desk.

"Do you want me to check your math homework?" I asked.

"No! I'm done."

"Then we've got a few minutes to talk before your John Wayne movie starts. I'm curious; what do you want to do after you finish high school?"

"Get a job and my own apartment, and a car – a Corvette."

"'Vette's are expensive. What kind of a job would you do?"

"Anything that makes a lot of money."

"Okay. If you could do anything you wanted to in the world, what would it be?"

"Does it have to be in the world?"

"Anything in the universe."

"I want be the first person to live on Mars."

"That would be quite a trip. I don't think I could stand being cooped up in a little spacecraft for all those months."

"I don't get claustrophobia. I like small, dark places. I used to sleep in the closet all the time. It's peaceful and cozy."

"You know all the astronauts have college degrees. Have you thought about going to college?"

"College costs too much money."

"There are ways to get it paid for, G.I. benefits, for example. You might enlist in the military."

"I'm not joining the army. They killed Uncle Pat."

"What happened?"

"He was riding in a helicopter that crashed and burned him to pieces."

"Ouch. That's really sad. That kind of accident is pretty rare." Now I knew who the folded flag was for.

"He was my favorite relative. He used to take me fishing and now he is dead. There's no way I'd be in the army."

I was tempted to try to convince him that it was a freak accident and shouldn't deter him, but it wasn't a time for rational arguments. He was grieving. "I'm sorry about Pat."

"I wish he were here and you could meet him. He was funny."

"That would have been nice." The conversation had reached a dead end. "I'm afraid it's time for me to go. Your movie is starting. I'll be back next week."

We went to the front room together and I said good-bye to Randy.

He replied, "Good-bye, Don."

Ron added, "See you next week, Don."

Ron's last comment left me in a quandary. Our training included warnings about maintaining a proper professional demeanor and distance. Should I have allowed Ron to call me by my first name? Teachers would never permit it in school and it would definitely not be proper in court; yet, at summer camps, the staff always went by first names and that didn't cause any problems. His grandmother would have probably said he was being sassy, but his tone was more wistful, certainly not disrespectful. Uncle Pat was probably close to my age; maybe that had something to do with it. I wished the boundary was clearer. It was probably no big deal, just worry stemming from my rookie insecurity.

Ron had revealed glimpses of his inner concerns. He had a number of seriously unresolved issues. That was what I should be worrying about. I was seeing just the tip of the iceberg.

I made another attempt to paint a positive future during the third weekly visit. I discussed using his drawing talent to become a commercial artist or film animator. Instead of enthusiasm, Ron responded with a flat, "Yeah. Maybe." I still hadn't found a key that would open him up.

Catch and Release

My morning intake cases on the last Monday in October had been a pair of "catch and release" teenage boys. They had been picked up in a park after midnight with the remains of a six-pack of beer in their possession. The Scottsdale police delivered them to the detention center only after determining that none of their parents were at home. Both sets of parents had been at a party and called in about two am in response to the messages the police had left. Neither boy had any priors, so it was preordained that they would be released to their parents after a warning.

The first case went smoothly. The parents started by expressing their disappointment in their son, who seemed to be genuinely remorseful. They settled on a two-week grounding and were on their way to school and work by 8:15. My role had been strictly bureaucratic, seeing that the process was followed and documented for releasing a detainee to the custody of his parents.

The other family presented a stark contrast. The mother announced, "I'm here to pick up my son, Henry Roberts. Where do I sign?"

The receptionist replied, "You'll have to wait for a Probation Officer to talk with you first."

"Well! I never had to wait when I picked him up at the police station."

I invited her into the interview room while they brought Henry from the detention area. My first question was, "Did your husband come with you?"

"He's at work. You know what people would think if he was late to work on the morning after a party, besides that, a curfew violation is not really a crime -- It's more like a parking ticket. The police should have just dropped my son off at home. He had a key."

Despite her belligerence, I explained calmly, "Under Arizona law, once a police officer has taken a juvenile into custody, he is required by law to either release him to a parent or legal guardian or to bring him to the juvenile detention facility. Since the Scottsdale police were unsuccessful in their attempts to contact you and your husband, they brought him here."

"That's a stupid rule!"

Henry came in at this point. "If you had given me the phone number where you were, they could've called you and I wouldn't have been stuck in this place."

"So I was supposed to tell your dad's boss that we had to leave his birthday party to pick up our son at the police station and kill his chance at a promotion. It's your own fault. You were supposed to stay at home and not go out with that trouble-maker John."

I ploughed into the formal interview, "The curfew violation by itself is a minor issue. I am much more concerned about the beer. John told the police that Henry brought it from home."

"He was lying to protect himself." Henry broke in.

"Henry would never take his father's beer. Bob keeps careful tabs on his supply."

"John bought the beer. Honestly, Mom."

The mother maintained her glare and tapped her fingers impatiently on the table while her son looked at his knees. My warning speech about the seriousness and potential consequences of underage drinking fell on two pairs of deaf ears.

As soon as I finished and had her sign the release form, the mother walked away telling her son, "We have to hurry or I'll be late for my hairdresser."

'We'll be seeing you again and I hope someone else is on duty that day.' I kept the words inside my head and tackled the paperwork. I had a hard time describing the mother without using words that were inappropriate for an official court document.

I was beginning to understand Alan's cynicism. I wondered if he had been more idealistic when started out two years ago. I wondered if this job would turn me into a cynic as well.

Dorothy

The next case was a referral called in by a parent, not much information to go on. The form stated Mr. Isaac Groeder said he could no longer control his fifteen year old daughter, Dorothy. She was blatantly disobedient, snuck out of the house through her bedroom window and lied to him. He needed someone to straighten her out before she got into serious trouble.

When I went to meet them in the waiting room, I was struck by their appearance. He was dressed in a long-sleeved white shirt buttoned to the collar and a pair of black trousers held up by black suspenders. His face was weather-beaten and tanned, topped by black hair with hints of gray. She wore a blue calico dress, also with long sleeves, high collar and a hem low enough that no flesh showed above her white socks and black shoes.

I explained the procedure. "My goal for this meeting is to understand your problem well enough to explore possible solutions with you. We have thirty days to try to work out a solution before a court hearing will be scheduled. In the meantime, I'll be working with you to see if there is some way to resolve the problems without formal court action."

"That would be good." Mr. Groeder replied.

I asked Mr. Groeder to follow me into the interview room while Dorothy waited in the lobby.

"How long has the problem been going on?"

"Not long. Dorothy was always a good child while her mother was alive. My wife got the cancer two years ago and we had to move to the city so she could get treatment."

"Where did you live before?"

"In Fredonia. We had a place with a big garden, and I ran my own garage. It is a good place to live except that the closest hospital that could treat my wife was more than six hours away. I am a good mechanic, so I was able to get a job in Phoenix while she got treatment. The doctors did the best they could, but the cancer was too big. This summer she was too sick and weak to get out of bed. Dorothy took good care of her while I was a work. Still she died in August." He was holding back tears. "Now we are all alone. When I am at work, I cannot watch over Dorothy. The city is full of sinful things; and she is falling into them. I am afraid for her."

Fredonia is an isolated village north of the Grand Canyon known as a haven for religious fundamentalists; that explained a lot. "Are you planning to move back to Fredonia?" I'm thinking that would be the easiest way out for all of us.

"The doctors and hospitals took all of our money. And, without my Martha, we could not grow enough food in the garden, and the garage would not make enough money. I cannot go back. I need to keep my job here to take care of us and pay back the doctors."

"I understand. Please tell me exactly what Dorothy does that causes you to worry so much."

"On Friday, when I got to work I discovered I had left a toolbox at home so I had to go back to get it. As I drove up, I saw my daughter climbing out through the window of the neighbor's house. She was wearing indecent clothes for a girl, short pants and a T-shirt. We had a big argument when I made her put those clothes back and drove her to school in her proper clothes."

"Did she steal the clothes?"

"Oh no, nothing like that. Her friend Jessica let her borrow them. I checked. This had been going on for a couple of weeks. Every day after I left for work and Jessica left for school, Dorothy had been sneaking into her room and changing into these sinful clothes for school. She would change back before I got home."

"Did she tell you why she did it?"

"She said that was what all the girls wear at school. They laughed at her dresses. The school shouldn't allow that, but they do. The school doesn't even keep the children in their classes. They telephoned me to say that Dorothy was absent that day even though I saw her go in the door. Martha could have straightened it out, but I didn't know what to say to them."

"Did you ask Dorothy about the reported absence?"

"She said she just skipped her classes and walked back home so they wouldn't make fun of her. That's not right. She needs to obey her parents and go to school. The judge needs to make her understand that. I can't watch her all day. I have to earn a living."

"Maybe she would go to school if you got her some school clothes."

"Her mother bought her plenty of good clothes. The clothes she wants are indecent. They go against the Bible. I read the newspapers. Many teenagers in the city wear indecent clothes and they drink alcohol and smoke the drugs. That is the way girls get pregnant before they are married. I cannot have my daughter wearing sinful clothes."

"Pants and T-shirts are not related to drinking or drugs." I tried to explain the reality of modern life, but he cut me off.

"The law says the children have to obey their parents. The judge will make her do as I say and follow the Bible!"

I tried to hide my exasperation. "The Constitution requires a separation of church and state, so the court will not enforce the Bible. The court requires only adherence to the minimum standards of our society. I'm afraid the judge would not be able to make Dorothy live up to your higher expectation."

"But you must honor your father and mother. The law says a child must obey her parents!"

"The actual wording of the law is that the child has a duty to obey any reasonable order from his parents. In our society, the judge would rule that the school's dress code is reasonable."

He shook his head and muttered, "That is not right."

"If you go to court, your daughter would probably be placed on probation. Dorothy would become a ward of the state and have to follow the rules set by the court or be placed in a foster home or institution. Here is a copy of the standard conditions of probation that the judge issues." I handed him the one-page form that specified that the probationer must report regularly to his/her probation officer, not break any laws, avoid alcohol and illegal drugs, be home by midnight every day and either attend school regularly or be employed in a job approved by the probation officer.

"This is all?" He was still shaking his head. "My daughter needs more. Maybe I am not a good parent. Maybe she needs a woman's hand to guide her."

"Do you have any good friends in Phoenix?"

"Only Mr. and Mrs. Silverstein. They live next door. Mrs. Silverstein did a lot to help us while my Martha was sick. First she brought us meals, then she started looking after Dorothy while I was at the hospital. She's a good woman. She's already done so much. I don't want to impose on her any more. We don't take charity. We've always stood on our own two feet. This is not good. I just don't know what I can do."

"What about your church?"

"They are good people, but Dorothy is the only teenager there. They are mostly young families and grandparents. They don't socialize with us. The pastor agrees that teenagers need a firm hand to keep them away from trouble. He is the one who told me to call the court to get her straightened out."

Another dead end. "I can't tell you what to do. There is no perfect answer. If you go to court, then the judge will decide what happens with Dorothy. You would not have any choice. It would be better to try to work something out without filing a formal charge with the court. I can refer to you to a family counselor to help you make a plan."

"No! No psychologists. They are godless."

I felt like everything I had said had fallen on deaf ears. "Those are the only options that I can think of. You are going to have to decide what you are going to do. I need to talk to Dorothy now, you have some time to think about the options, then we will all sit down together to talk about the next step."

I braced myself for the interview with a rebellious and sneaky Dorothy. The required opening speech does not help establish rapport with the client. "Since this matter could end up in court, I am required to read you your rights. You have the right to remain silent. If you give up that right, anything you say can be used against you in a court of law. You have a right to an attorney. If you cannot afford an attorney, the court will appoint one to represent you. Do you understand these rights?"

"Yes." Dorothy looked intimidated.

"If your case goes to trial, you would probably be placed on supervised probation or placed in a foster home."

"That's not fair. I didn't do anything wrong." Her tone had changed from fear to anger. "Papa doesn't listen to me. He just doesn't understand. I need friends, someone to talk to. When Momma was alive, I could talk to her. Even when she was sick in the hospital, she would listen to me and encourage me. Papa doesn't care how I feel. He just tells me what to do. I miss Momma so much." Dorothy dissolved into tears.

"I talked with your father, and I can agree that he doesn't understand a lot about modern teenagers in the city. But, I think you are wrong about his not caring. As I watched his eyes and listened, I could tell that he really does love you."

"Then why doesn't he tell me."

I thought about my own father's tough exterior. "Men are taught to be strong, and I am afraid that many men think that being strong means not showing their emotions and not showing any doubt. He tries to solve your problems by giving you answers and telling you what to do. He wants to do what is best for you."

Her sobbing eased. "His answers don't work. He doesn't know what is best for me. He should trust me."

"It is hard to trust someone when you see them climbing through a neighbor's window. If you had Jessica's permission, why didn't you use the door?"

"Her parents left for work before I changed, so I had to leave their doors locked and I didn't have a key."

"So her parents didn't know what was going on?"

"Jessica told her mom that she was lending me some clothes for school and her mom told me that I could come over anytime I wanted."

"Do you really think that her parents approved of your sneaking into their house?"

"Well, when Papa told them about it, they said I shouldn't have done it, but they didn't get mad. If the other kids saw me going to school in the clothes Papa gets me, they would shun me. Last year, I always had to eat alone; nobody would sit near me in the cafeteria. I got teased every day. I hated it, but at least I could be with Momma in the afternoon. I was afraid to change at home because Papa doesn't give me any privacy. He would have found the clothes and thrown them away. Sometimes I just want to run away ... but I promised Momma that I would look after Papa and finish school. I try to make Papa happy, but he won't let me be happy. He doesn't have any friends. I cannot live like that!"

"He told me that one of the neighbors is a good friend, Mrs. Silverstein. What do you think of her?"

"She's great. She's Jessica's mother. If the judge sends me to a foster home, she could be my foster mother and I could stay with Jessica." I was taken aback by both the connection and the animation in Dorothy's voice.

"That won't happen. The judge will only give custody to a relative or a licensed foster home. You can't choose the foster home. The foster home might be anywhere in the county. You would go to a different school. If you want to be with Jessica, you'll have to work something out with your father."

"Papa will never change."

"Then you'll have to be the one that changes. I'll try to help you, but your father is the boss."

"It's not fair."

"No it's not, but that is your situation. I am going to bring your father back in so we can decide on the next step."

I figured that we would be setting a court date and I would be hunting for an acceptable foster placement. In the meantime, I would try to prevent a yelling match that would end with Dorothy running away or getting put in detention. As we started the joint session, both of them were looking down at their feet.

"I've listened to each of you, and one thing is clear. You both are trying to do your best and you care deeply for each other."

Mr. Groeder interrupted. "I have been thinking about the things you said and I have something to tell Dorothy. Dorothy, I thought I was doing the right thing when I moved us to the city and put you in that school because I thought the doctors here could cure your Momma. I was mistaken and now we can't go back. I have made things hard for you. I don't understand the city ways and I don't know how to raise a daughter without your Momma. You need to have a woman look after you. I think it would be better if you stayed with Mrs. Silverstein during the school week. I am thinking about asking her and her husband if they will take you as a boarder. I will pay her for it, of course. If she agrees, you must obey her and do things her ways."

"Ooh, Papa!" There was a big smile on Dorothy's face. "I can share Jessica's bedroom; it has two beds." She looked at her father's pained expression and the smile faded. "But I would come home every day to fix your supper, I promise."

"You don't have to. That is a big promise."

"But I want to. And I already promised Momma that I would take care of you."

Mr. Groeder turned to me. "Will the judge permit me to do this?"

"As long as you don't go to court, you don't have to ask the judge. You are the parent and can arrange the living arrangements for your daughter that you think is best. If you wish, I can come to visit and see how it is going around 6:00 next Tuesday." I handed each of them a business card. "If I can help you in the meantime, call the number on this card and they will get a hold of me."

"Thank you, Mr. Gilbertson. We will see you on Tuesday."

Dorothy walked behind him as they left the building.

The following Tuesday I drove up to their small tract house in south Scottsdale. Mr. Groeder greeted me at the door. He looked tired.

"I think we might be all right. Mrs. Silverstein agreed to let Dorothy stay with her as long as she wants to. She wouldn't take any money for rent, only for food."

"How are you and Dorothy getting along?"

"She is behaving better and not talking back. During supper she tells me about what she is doing. It sounds good ... if it is true. She is in the kitchen fixing supper now."

Dorothy was as bubbly as her father was dour.

"I'm sharing a bedroom with Jessica, she has twin beds. It's great. I always wanted to have a sister and now I have one. I even have my own school clothes. Judith, I mean Mrs. Silverstein, took me shopping at Marshalls with the money Papa gave her for me."

"I see that you aren't wearing them today."

"I wore them here the first day to show Papa, but just muttered that he can't stand seeing me like that and turned away. When I came back in a dress, he said I looked like my mother. I come in through the back door, so nobody from school can see me. The kids at school think I am normal. I am happy for the first time since Momma got sick."

"That sounds good. I'll check in with you again next week."

I gave a similar encouraging message to her father on my way out, but I was not feeling encouraged. The distance between them was still too great. I wondered which would end first, her "honeymoon" with the Silverstein's or her father's acceptance of playing second fiddle to the neighbors in his daughter's life.

Something was definitely different when I came back the next week. Mr. Groeder immediately led me into the kitchen. "There is something I want you to see. Dorothy got her report card this week. She got a C in the geometry and B's in everything else except that she got an A in Home Economics. These are very good grades, no?"

Dorothy looked up from the vegetables she was chopping and smiled.

"Yes those are good grades," I replied.

"Dorothy is a very good cook. You should stay for supper. We have plenty of food."

"Thank you very much, but my wife is already fixing our dinner."

"Aah, yes. A man should eat dinner with his family."

I turned to Dorothy. "It must be hard, keeping up with all your school work, splitting your time between two houses and fixing dinner every night."

She replied, "It is not so hard. Papa sacrificed everything to try to help Momma. This is not so hard. Now I am the only family Papa has, and like he said, a man should eat dinner with his family."

It was Mr. Groeder's turn to smile quietly.

I concluded, "I would like to officially close your case. You have worked things out very well by yourselves. I don't think you need any help from the court."

"That would be good," Mr. Groeder responded. "You have been most helpful but now we can handle everything ourselves."

I went home with a great sense of relief. I was glad that I would not have to see them again. The case was a success, but I wasn't happy about the result. I was uncomfortable around him and his values, and while I admired Dorothy's strength and determination, I never grew to actually like her. Still, it was their life to lead (not mine) and they were satisfied with it. I had done my job.

Ronny – Part II

The first time I went to check on Ron in November, his grandfather was waiting with a piece of paper from the school. "Ronny is failing math again. Mother says he has to do all his homework at the kitchen table now so we can watch him." He spoke in the cheerful tone of an office gossip sharing a juicy tidbit. "I can't help him. I never learned that Algebra stuff. I never was any good at math myself. Maybe you can help him." To me, this sounded like he was giving Ron an excuse for failing.

"I'll give it a go. Math was my best subject."

I went straight back into the kitchen. Ron was sitting at the table, clearly in a bad mood. "I guess you heard that."

"Yeah. I'm no good at math. Granny nags me to buckle down and try harder. It doesn't work. Even when I try my hardest, I still mess up. I must be stupid."

"I don't believe you are stupid. There are lots of other reasons people have trouble with math. Let me see you do the next problem."

The assignment in front of him was division of fractions. He promptly wrote down the next item, inverting the divisor and started multiplying the revised numerators. I observed his fingers moving as he calculated the result and resumed while he calculated the denominator. After another pause, he divided both the top and bottom by 2 leaving 12/27 as the answer. "There."

"That's good as far as it went, but you might be able to do more. Are both 12 and 27 multiples of 3?"

The fingers started moving again before he said, "Yes. See I messed up again. I'm stupid."

"I'm pretty sure I know what the problem is and it is definitely not stupidity. You know all of the steps to solve the problems, you just get hung up with the multiplication." I went into a spiel that had worked with some of my reform school students. "In other subjects, if you miss out on a topic, you can skip over it and go on to the next topic. But math keeps building on the early pieces. If you miss out on memorizing the multiplication tables, it leaves a hole that blocks you from doing well later. I bet that something disrupted your learning back in third grade, maybe an illness, or moving to different schools or "

Ron muttered, "I hate her."

"You hate your third grade teacher?" I was taken by surprise.

"My mother! She ruined everything."

"Please explain."

"I got the chicken pox in third grade. She just left me home with nothing to do for a long time." I leaned forward and listened intensely.

"Then she moved in with Harvey."

Ron paused and took a deep breath between each disclosure.

"I had to go to a new school where I didn't have any friends."

"Harvey is the meanest man in the world."

"They got drunk and fought a lot."

"Sometimes there was nothing in the house for me to eat."

"I was always hungry."

"When Harvey was drunk, he called me 'a useless little bastard' just because I don't know who my father is." His voice broke, on the verge of tears. My stomach as in a knot. I struggled not to interrupt with pity but let him continue.

"Sometimes he grabbed me for no reason. He would pull down my pants and beat me with his belt. Mom just stood there and watched.

She just stood there!" He stopped and looked down.

"Nobody deserves to be treated like that." My response was louder than I intended. "It must have felt terrible."

Rom looked back up into my eyes. "That's when I started staying hidden in the closet. He never looked for me there."

"I think that was a smart move. There's no way you could have stopped them from drinking and fighting. Did you tell anyone about it?" There was no hint of this in the file.

"No. He said he'd kill me if I told anyone and one of his buddies would kill me if I got him locked up."

"I know this is scary, but I'm going to have to report this to Child Protective Services. I won't use your name, but someone who would do that to you will probably hurt other kids and the report might help them stop him. What is Harvey's last name?"

"Please don't tell."

"I have to. It's the law. I told you because I'm not going to do anything behind your back. I'll be very careful to write the report in a way that you won't be identified and the report is confidential. They won't even disclose that I'm the one who reported him."

"Alright, already. Cartwright. Harvey Cartwright."

"Thank you. It was brave of you to tell me. Obviously you had a lot bigger concerns going on during third grade than worrying about multiplication tables."

"Yeaaaaaah." He let out a long sigh.

We sat face-to-face in silence. I had no words for the empathy I felt. The tension melted away in the quiet.

After a couple of minutes, I sensed that it was time to move on. "Are you ready to get back to math?"

"Okay."

"Got a blank piece of paper?" He tore a page out of his notebook and handed it to me. I marked off a grid with my pen and filled it in with the multiplication table from one to nine. "I want you to spend a few minutes each day filling in what you missed in third grade. If you memorize these combinations so that they become as automatic as recognizing simple words, math will go a lot faster. I want you to stop counting up on your fingers. For the time being, you can look at this table while you are doing homework. But every night before you go to bed, I want you to practice writing out a multiplication table."

"Are you going to tell Granny that I'm supposed to write them every day?"

"This is just between you and me. I'm not going to nag you about it. I want you to try it because it will make your homework easier. Don't to too much at once. This week, just work on getting the 2's through 5's faster."

"I'll try."

"Great! See you next week."

"Good-bye, Don." His offhanded farewell knocked me off balance. Students are never permitted to call teachers by their first name and it would certainly be considered disrespectful in court. Yet, there was no disrespect in his tone of voice; it sounded more like a sign that I had earned his confidence. Was it a positive thing or had I just lost the 'professional distance' we are supposed to maintain? This job feels like walking a series of tight ropes without an adequate net. We are not supposed to get emotionally involved, but to be effective, the clients must know that we care for them. There's a fine line in there somewhere.

The drive home wasn't long enough to decompress. I had wanted Ron to open up to me. Now that he had, the story of his boyhood was horrible beyond my comprehension. The multiplication table tactic had worked, as far as getting his mind on a manageable task, but I didn't expect he would follow through. I stopped off at the high school fields and practiced racquetball; It felt good to work up a sweat smashing something against a wall for fifteen minutes.

I submitted a report on Harvey Cartwright's "alleged" action the next morning. I doubted it would result in any action. The exercise in futility rekindled my anger at the S.O.B. Since I was not in the mood for doing good casework, I whiled away the time before lunch constructing a neat version of the multiplication table and a pair of fill-in-the-blank grids on another blank sheet. I Xeroxed a bunch of the blank girds, hoping that wasn't another futile activity. At least I had the weekend with Judy to look forward to. Friday night, my parents would take us out to dinner, usually Newton's Prime Rib or Neptune's Table, for a meal that was beyond our budget. I devote Saturday morning to the yard. I take over two hours and a couple of beers with my manual push mower. (A rotary mower would be faster, but they don't do a good a job. Our lawn is the best on the block.) In the afternoon, we go visit model homes that we can't afford. It's a form of free entertainment that mixes daydreaming with a chance to criticize the decorators. Sunday mornings are devoted to church. Attending mass is important to Judy; I relish the chance to interact with normal families. Both activities help us maintain our perspective on life.

The next visit started on a positive note. Daisy greeted me with a wagging tail instead of annoyed yapping. That turned out to be only the first pleasant surprise. Ron immediately announced that he had done a multiplication every night and showed me a stack of scrawled papers.

"That's great. I made you a nicer copy and some practice sheets to save a little time. Let's see how many you can get right in four minutes."

"Okay." He started filling in one of the practice grids. There were some pauses, but no finger counting. In just over the four minutes, he had completed the rows for 2 through 6 with only one mistake. He wrote 44 for 6 times 7.

"Time's up. You got farther than I expected. I had only asked you to get through the fives. Only one mistake." I change the 44 to 42 on his paper. "I'm proud of you."

He flashed me a big grin. I had done something right after all.

"Next week, concentrate on the 7's. That's the hardest one because they don't follow any pattern."

"I'll learn 'em."

His math assignments had moved on to algebraic expression. No multiplying was involved. I sat and watched as he completed the homework with no errors. When he was finished, I asked, "Are you doing anything fun this weekend?"

"No. Weekends are boring."

"Would you like to go to the zoo some Saturday?"

"That would be cool."

"I make you a deal. If your folks approve, once you can complete the multiplication table with no errors in under four minutes, I'll take you to the zoo."

"It's a deal." Ron stuck out his arm and we shook on it.

The next week, Ron showed me an 80 he got on a math test. Two weeks after that, he finished his multiplication table in four-and-a-half minutes. When I announced the time, he asked, "So are we going to the zoo on Saturday?"

"No. The deal was under four minutes."

"Aren't you going to cut me some slack? Just this once?"

"You don't need any slack. You are smart enough to meet the challenge. I bet you make it next week."

"I will."

He did. Ron took the lead in getting Randy's permission. "I aced my math. Can I go to the zoo with Don on Saturday?"

"How much does it cost?"

"Nothing," I replied. "I have a pass that gets us both in for free."

"Then you can go after you finish your chores."

"I'll be ready by 10:00."

Ron came out the door as I approached it. Liz called out after him, "You'd better behave for Mr. Gilbertson. Don't get into any trouble."

We started with the orangutans; they always put on a good show. Then we worked our way around to the tiger exhibit. I didn't do much talking. Most of the conversation came from Ron pointing out details about the animals. I bought corn dogs and fries, the cheapest lunch on the menu. Ron thanked me as we sat down and cleaned up after both of us. After lunch, we dawdled over the 'dangerous' animals, local rattlesnakes and Gila monsters followed by a darkened enclosure with more exotic species. Ron was fascinated by the piranhas, twelve-foot long boa constrictor, small sand sharks, and vampire bats lapping up a bowl of blood. Suddenly, he froze in front of me and started shaking. I looked around for the cause of his fear. A couple of kindergarten-sized boys were admiring the last terrarium; it was filled with Madagascar cockroaches.

I tried to calm Ron. "Those bugs are leaf eaters from Africa. They can't hurt you. They are actually kind of pretty."

"They give me the creeps." He gripped my arm tightly.

"I can see that. You're safe here. Go ahead and look."

"No!"

The other people in the exhibit were looking at us. I felt embarrassed; Ron didn't seem to notice. I tried to get him out of there quietly. "Let's move on to the porcupines and coyotes." Ron kept his head turned to the back wall as we sidled outside. Looking at the other animals quickly calmed him down. On the drive home, we talked about animals we had seen in the wild, with no mention of bugs.

Doing math homework together had become a Thursday ritual. When he finished, Ron asked, "When are we going to the zoo again?"

"That was pretty much a one-time deal. I had fun, but the weekends are the only time I have to do things with my family and to do the yard work."

"I could mow your lawn."

"Thanks, but I need the exercise." There was no way I was going to let that kid chop up my lawn. I am also determined to keep my home life a sanctuary where I can escape from the pressures of this job.

We did visit the zoo again during his school's spring break. This time, he took a deep breath and braved up to watch the Madagascar cockroaches. I viewed that as a significant step. It came only after a couple of other breakthroughs.

The first came just before Christmas. I arrived later than usual that Thursday. Liz was already home from work, sitting in the living room smoking with Randy.

"Did Ronnie tell you how he broke my favorite glass?" She asked.

"No. When did that happen?"

"On Monday, but I didn't find out until yesterday."

"We haven't spoken since last Thursday."

She yelled, "Ronnie, get your ass in here."

I wondered why this was a big deal as I sat on the sofa to hear the details. Ron came in and sat at the opposite end of the sofa.

"Tell Don how you broke my favorite glass."

"It was an accident. I was doing the vacuuming. Rick had left the glass on the edge of a TV table and it fell when I bumped the table." He started out calmly.

"Don't go blaming your grandfather. You should have been paying more attention to what you were doing. You were probably daydreaming again."

"I was paying attention, but Daisy started barking."

"So now you're blaming the dog. You have to start taking responsibility for yourself. And, why did you hide it?"

Ron spoke angrily, "I didn't hide it. I cleaned it up. Did you want me to leave pieces of broken glass all over the floor?"

"Don't give me any of your sass." Ron glared then looked down at the floor. Liz turned to me. "See what we have to put up with. You deal with lots of boys. What do you notice about Ronnie?"

I thought that she was the one who was out of line, but getting into an argument would only make things worse. Still, I determined to start with a positive approach. "The first thing that comes to mind is how observant he is. He has a great eye for details. It is almost like he has eagle-eyes."

Liz was caught off guard, but she confirmed my observation. "Yes, he does. When we go places, he always spots the sign before me and Randy."

Ron looked up. This wasn't what he expected either. I moved forward into more sensitive areas. "The other thing that I've noticed is how much he cares about being good. He has more chores than most boys his age, but he has never complained to me about them. Ron appreciates having a clean home and he wants to do his part. He tries hard and gets upset with himself over little mistakes. I think that is a big part of his short temper."

I laid it on awfully thick, but their faces told me that it was sinking in.

Liz responded. "I suppose that's so. He usually does a good job. I just worry about the teenage years." I had misjudged her; what she actually wanted from me was hope.

"I think he'll be one the ones who gets better with age."

"I sure hope so. He doesn't lose his temper as much as he used to." Her mood had lightened to as close to cheerful as I had ever seen. She then switched to asking about my plans for Christmas. After a short chat about family dinners, I left after exchanging happy holiday wishes.

At the year end caseload review, my supervisor questioned the amount of time I was spending on this mild case. I took umbrage when he pressed me, stating that tutoring math is not part of our job; the school should be providing that service. Maybe so, but the math help is what had opened the door for his major change in attitude. I stood my ground. But afterward, I had to admit that at least part of the reason I was seeing Ron every week was that it provided me with evidence that I really was doing some good. That kind of reassurance was all too rare.

Frankie - Part 1

A police officer patrolling his beat in northwest Phoenix at three on a Saturday morning spotted a body under a bush in Solano Park. It turned out to be a sleeping twelve-year old boy, name: Frank Duncan. He told the officer that he ran away from home that afternoon to avoid being whipped. The officer took the boy home and released him into the custody of his mother, Mrs. Janet Duncan. She was both angry and relieved. She claimed that it was the first time that he had run away but that he had been causing a lot of trouble at home recently. She wanted the law to make him spend the night in jail "to teach him a lesson." Instead, the officer referred her to the Juvenile Probation Department. She called immediately and got an appointment for Tuesday morning.

There were only two people in the waiting room when I came out to meet the Duncans. From the rear, I saw a muscular six-foot-two frame with square shoulders and fairly short hair, dressed in dark trousers and a long-sleeved blue work shirt standing at the counter with a pale, skinny boy in a striped T-shirt and baggy jeans. I guessed he was ten years old. There must have been a mix-up with the paperwork.

"Good morning. May I help you?"

They turned in response to my greeting. The adult face was definitely that of a woman, round and smooth except for a few wrinkles. The cowering boy's freckled face was narrow with sharp features. I saw no family resemblance.

"Yes. I'm Janet Duncan. This is Frankie."

From her abrupt tone, I expected she would be demanding that her son be held in detention. This was going to be awkward. My first impression left me expecting the worst. Still, I had to go through the full procedure maintaining a positive front. I made the standard introductory comments and then led Mrs. Duncan into the interview room.

"Please start by telling me your concerns about Frankie's behavior."

"The real problem is his attitude. He thinks he doesn't have to do anything unless he feels like it. He won't obey Nora any more. Nora is my housemate; she stays at home all day. He lies to her all the time and he won't talk to me."

Yikes, a real red flag. I thought she might be one of those butch lesbians. That put me in a mine field. 'Open and notorious cohabitation' is a criminal offense. I definitely wasn't prepared to explicitly probe that area. Possibly they were just splitting the rent. I stuck to her son's behavior.

"How long has this been a problem?"

"Only the last couple of months, since his brother Tony moved out. Frankie never liked Nora, but he didn't used to cause her trouble."

I wondered if Tony had taken the heat, then fled in anger. "When did Tony move out?"

"The first of July. He joined the Air Force as soon as he graduated from high school. They gave him a month leave before he reported to boot camp."

I had guessed wrong again. "How did Frankie get along with Tony? That's a pretty big age gap."

"Frankie really looks up to Tony. Tony looked after him and protected him. Frankie really misses him."

"Even though Frankie may understand in his head that Tony's leaving is a natural step forward, at a gut level the loss can create anger."

"I know. Frankie really needs a man to talk to."

Boy, had I been off-base. She wanted support for him, not punishment. "Does he have any contact with his father?"

"No. Larry is a long-haul truck driver. Frankie was only two when he found out about me and Nora. He took it as an insult to his manhood. He just took off with the truck, leaving the house and boys to me." She replied in a matter-of-fact tone, with no rancor. "His lawyer sent us the notice for the divorce. He has never contacted us since. He doesn't pay child support or anything. My job with Courtesy Chevrolet pays more than he makes anyways."

The apparent reference to a homosexual relationship confirmed by suspicions. No appropriate follow-up question came to mind, so I picked up on the job. "What is your position there?"

"I'm a lead mechanic."

"You must be a good one."

"Why do you say that?" Her tense question indicated that she suspected prejudice in my compliment.

I tried to show a sympathetic understanding. "Garages tend to be pretty male-oriented places and dealerships put lots of pressure on their mechanics to beat the book rate times for repairs. So I figure that any woman who makes it as a lead mechanic at a dealership must be extra good."

She relaxed a little and explained, "I was always a Tomboy. My father taught me how to fix cars in our backyard when I was a little girl. I was the only girl taking Auto Shop in high school. Larry was the only boy in the class who thought that it was cool. When I started working, I got razzed a lot and had to really prove myself, but I've been doing it long enough that the other mechanics have accepted me as one of the guys."

My effort at active listening was paying off as she continued.

"Nora was my best friend in high school. She got teased worse than I did. I was on the track team for shot put and discus. I was strong enough that the other kids didn't dare bother me. I didn't get asked for many dates. That was OK because Nora and I had already discovered that we weren't attracted to boys. Still we tried to do what you're supposed to do and got married about a year after graduation. Larry was a good friend and I don't regret having his sons. Nora got stuck with a violent drunk. She came to me for comfort. I'm the only real friend she's got. She never had any kids. When she finally left her husband, I took her in. Larry was on the road at the time. When he got back, he left and Nora stayed and helped me raise the boys. She doesn't have any kids of her own." Her candor surprised me and made me glad that I hadn't jumped on her first reference to Nora.

"I don't know why I'm telling you all of this." She pulled up short, worried that she had disclosed too much.

"It's good. The more I know about your background, the less likely I am to misinterpret something that Frankie says to me." Probing a twelve-year-old boy's feelings about having gay parents would be a delicate task. I'm not a psychologist; my task was to look for a legitimate way to divert the family out of the court system. "I'd like to back up a little and explore ideas for getting Frankie connected with a man he can talk to. Have you heard of the Big Brothers program?"

"Yes. I called them about Frankie and got him on their waiting list. But they said the list is so long that it will probably be at least eighteen months before they will be able to get him matched. That is too long."

"That's too bad. The other resource in your area that comes to mind is the Boys and Girls Club. Has Frankie ever joined?"

"No he hasn't. He comes straight home from school to do his homework before dinner."

"I know most of the staff there. The librarian, John, is a college student. He could supervise Frankie's homework."

"That might work."

"Speaking of homework, how is he doing in school?"

"He has to work hard to get average grades. We make sure he does all the assignments, otherwise he would skip a lot of his homework."

"Does he like school?"

"I wouldn't say that. At least he doesn't hate it any more. He is naturally shy. He cried when we dropped him off at kindergarten and part of first grade."

"I think I have enough information to get started. I want to talk with Frankie now. After that, we'll all get together and plan the next steps."

After advising Frankie of his Miranda rights, I asked him, "Why did your mom bring you here?"

He kept looking down at his hands and replied in a whisper, "I was bad. I ran away."

"Was this the first time you ran away from home?"

"Sort of."

"What do you mean by 'sort of'?"

"I ran away from Nora a couple of other times, but I came back as soon as Mom got home."

"Did you get punished those times?"

"They sent me straight to bed without any supper." He looked so pitiful, I felt sorry for him.

"Why did you stay away this time?"

"Nora told me to bring my mother's belt. She said I was going to get a beating with the buckle that I would never forget. I climbed out the window instead of bringing the belt. I was too scared to go back home."

"Has she beaten you with a belt before?"

"No."

"Has your mother ever beaten you with her belt?"

"No!" He looked up, glared at me for a moment, and then looked back at the floor.

At least I didn't have to instigate a child abuse investigation. "What made Nora so mad at you?"

"She said I stole money from her purse, but I didn't do it."

"Have you taken money from her purse before?"

"Only once, when she wouldn't give me my allowance. I had done all my chores so I just took it. I got caught because she counts her money. I know not to try that again." Frankie finally established eye contact.

"How much is your allowance?"

"Two dollars a week."

"What are your chores?"

"Whatever Nora tells me to do."

"Like what?"

"Mow the yard! Pull all the weeds! Do the laundry! Wash the dishes! Vacuum the house! Take out the trash!"

"I get the idea." She sure put him to work. I tried to shift to a positive note. "Tell me about your best friend."

"Tony, my big brother is my best friend, but he's gone away."

"What about school friends?"

"I'm not allowed to have friends over to play. That doesn't bother me, because if they met Nora, they wouldn't be friends anymore."

"Do you teased or bullied at school?"

"No. Just a little, like everybody else."

"Let's think about what we could change to make your life better. You've figured out that taking things from someone's purse and running away from home only make things worse. So, what changes might help?"

"I wish Nora would go away and Tony would come back."

He was tugging at my heart strings. Wishing wouldn't work; we had to deal with his reality. "I wouldn't plan on either of those things happening. Tony's enlistment will keep him in the Air Force for at least four years and Nora has been living with you and your mother for more than eight years. There is nothing you and I could do to change that. I was thinking more of having something to do afterschool so you didn't come home until after your mother got off work."

"I want to get a job, but I'm not old enough."

"Have you ever tried the Boys and Girls Club near your school?"

"No. I don't like playing sports that much."

"They don't only have a gym. There's a library, wood shop, games room and even a swimming pool."

"No. I can't swim."

Since he was saying no to everything, I changed my phrasing. "Would you mind doing your homework in the library, where there's a guy Tony's age to help you?"

"No."

"Good, then I'll introduce to Larry at the Club I think you'll like the shop leader as well."

Frankie reacted with a start, confirming my hunch. "Mom won't let me join."

"We'll see about that. When I talked to her, I felt she really wants to help you become happier, but you'll have to do your part by not complaining so much at home and by not running away again."

"Why can't I complain? Nora gets to complain all the time."

"I'll tell you what: when you are talking just to me, you can complain all you want. But complaining to Nora and your mother just gets you into to more trouble."

"I know that."

"Then it's time to bring your mother in with us to make a plan."

In this case, I was especially glad I had thirty days to sort things out. Frankie came across as a helpless victim, but that could be a manipulative act. His mother appeared to be creditable and appropriately concerned. Nora was the key bone of contention and she was still at home. I needed to stay tentative and attempt to be neutrally supportive until I got to know her. Mrs. Duncan promptly agreed that going to the Boys and Girls Club after school was a good idea as a first step, but she was also adamant that Frankie had to be threatened with punishment to make him behave. I resisted the urge to comment that threats hadn't kept him out of trouble so far. Instead, I ended with overview of the options.

"I will schedule a tentative court date in thirty days. During that time, I will meet with Frankie every week, and either of you may call me at anytime if you have a concern." I paused to pass out my calling cards. "If things have improved sufficiently over the next month, you can drop the runaway charge. If the case goes to court, the judge will have the final say as to what happens. It is possible that he would send Frankie to a foster home or a treatment facility or even to the State Department of Corrections. The most likely result is that Frankie would be placed on probation and I, or another probation officer, would be assigned to provide periodic supervision. Frankie, you need to understand that if you get picked up by the police while under the court's jurisdiction for running away or any other reason, they will probably deliver you to the detention center where you would be locked up at least overnight. Do you understand?"

He nodded. He hadn't said a word while his mother was in the room.

I got up and turned to Frankie. "I'll come by your house tomorrow afternoon and take you to the Boys and Girls Club." I held out my arm for a handshake and received a limp hand in return. Mrs. Duncan gave me a firm handshake on her way out.

I pulled up to the Duncan house at 3:45 the next afternoon. It was a small brick cottage, painted white. The lawn was well-kept, not a weed in sight. Frankie answered the doorbell and let me in. A short, plump middle-aged woman with stringy black hair was knitting in a rocking chair in the corner of the room.

I introduced myself. "Good afternoon. I'm Don Gilbertson."

"I know who you are." She snapped, "You're the boy's probation officer. Did he tell you that he steals money from my purse?"

So this is what Frankie puts with. I hesitated. She jumped back in, "I bet he denied everything. He lies all the time. You should have locked him up to teach him a lesson."

I was not prepared for such a malevolent greeting. My reply was more defensive than helpful. "The court has strict criteria for pre-trial detention and Frankie's case doesn't come close to meeting them. Besides, locking kids up usually only makes their problems worse."

"Harrumph."

Frankie was cowering in the corner of the room, with his eyes on me.

I announced, "I'm taking Frankie over to the Boys and Girls Club to introduce him around and get his membership application. We'll be back in about an hour."

"Keep him as long as you want."

Frankie followed me out to my car. Once we were buckled in, I commented, "She seems to be in a bad mood this afternoon."

"She's always like that. She yells at me and blames me for things I didn't do every day."

"I'm glad that you didn't argue or complain while we were in the house; that would have only made things worse."

"I know, but sometimes she makes me so mad that I have to say something."

"I know the feeling. So when it's just you and I, you can complain and vent your feelings all you want."

He exhaled audibly as the tension left his body. The drive to the Club took only a couple of minutes. I picked up a membership application and a guest card for Frankie at the front desk then led him into the library. Four boys were playing chess at one table. Three girls were studying together and Larry was sitting in at the back table helping two boys with their Math homework. Frankie stood quietly by my side while I introduced him to Larry, barely looking up in response to Larry's cheerful welcome. At least he cracked a smile when one of the boys said, "Hi, Frankie."

To move things along, I asked, "Will you shoot a game of pool with me?"

"I don't know how."

"Then I'll teach you. Come on." He reluctantly followed me to an open table in the game room and stood by while I racked up the balls for a round of eight-ball. Frankie was almost rigidly tense as I showed him how to form a bridge with his left hand to stabilize the cue and positioned him to aim down the length of the stick. He scooped his first shot and the ball only moved a few inches.

"See. I'm no good at this." He dropped the cue on the table.

Damn it! He had accepted the idea that he was a failure and I would make it worse if I let my irritation show. "It takes practice to get good. Very few people succeed on their first try. Don't worry about winning. I'm going to win because I've had lots of practice. I just want you to relax and get used to the way you hold the stick. Take a few more practice shots."

On his next attempt, he hit the front ball with just enough force to move a couple of balls. He smiled. My irritation dissolved. I broke up the pack with my first shot, sinking nothing. By the time we finished the game, Frankie had sunk three of his balls and wanted to play again.

"It's time for me to go home now. But you can come here any time."

"I want to play with you."

"We can do that next week."

"OK."

When I dropped him off, his mother was still at work. Nora accepted the application and replied to my attempted conversation in monosyllables.

I made a follow-up phone call to Frankie's mother the next day. I was surprised by how pleasant and encouraging she was. She had signed the application and Frankie had completed all of his homework at the Boys and Girls Club before coming home for supper. She ended by saying, "It's good he has a probation officer. He'll listen to you because you're a man." I thanked her, but thought that the reason he listened to me was not because I was a man, but because I listened without yelling at him.

The next week I arrived for our visit later in the afternoon, but still before Janet got home. The meeting started with the same sour mood. Frankie stood quietly fuming while Nora went through a litany of his sins and the harshness of her own life. When she finished her rant, I asked Frankie to show me his room. It was small and sparsely furnished with bunk beds and two chests of drawers, both painted white. Both beds were made with white sheets and army surplus blankets tucked in with neat hospital corners. I thought Tony was finding Air Force life to be relatively plush and relaxed.

"Boy, your room looks neat."

"Mom inspects it every morning before I get breakfast."

"I see." There appears to be no place for fun in this house. "So, tell me about the Boys and Girls Club."

"I like the shop. I'm making a model boat out of wood. You should see it. Charles says it the best one he's seen anyone make there."

"Can you show it to me?"

"I'm keeping it at the Club."

"Then I'll come to the Club next week so I can see it."

"Are you getting all your homework done at the club?"

"Most of it. I have to do a report for history that isn't finished yet. I got all of the notes and pictures ready. I'll do the writing after dinner."

"Sounds like you're on top of it. How are things at home?"

"OK, I guess. You heard her."

"Yeah. I didn't hear anything that sounded like you were being bad."

"She thinks I'm a bad boy."

"I don't."

We heard Janet's voice as she greeted her partner. We returned to the living room. I sat on the sofa and asked Janet, "I wanted to get your view on how things are going now with Frankie."

"He's doing better. He's still sassy, but not as much."

"And, how does he like the Boys and Girls Club?"

"He likes it just fine. They are mighty loose over there. He needs a firmer hand. But, at least he's getting most of his homework done there."

"Maybe we should try scheduling counseling for him." I made the pro forma suggestion, expecting a refusal, so that the offer would be in the record.

"He doesn't need counseling. He knows what's right and wrong. He needs to know that he can't get away with lying and stealing. He's been better because he knows you are checking on him. That's why I took him to the detention center."

I conceded defeat as far as clearing the case in thirty days. "In that case, I'll go ahead and schedule a disposition hearing. I'll be recommending formal probation. The judge will probably follow that recommendation, but you need to know that once we are in court the judge has the final say and he can order something that you don't like."

"I understand. Frankie needs to face the judge and accept the consequences."

I spent the rest of our interview gathering the background information that belonged in the standard pre-disposition report.

This job had become so frustrating that I couldn't leave it at the office. Concern over Frankie made it hard to fall asleep at night. I didn't see probation as the solution to Frankie's problems. Taking him into court was distasteful because it struck me as blaming the victim. I viewed Nora as the real problem, but since I hadn't observed anything that would stand up in court as child abuse, I had no power over her. I felt I had made some progress with Frankie and that the Boys and Girls Club connection was a definite plus. With time on probation, maybe Janet would slowly come around.

As I described the home situation for the court report, I had to confront my own prejudices. Prior to meeting Janet, the word 'lesbian' evoked a picture of ultra-liberal, highly demonstrative young women – dressed like the Hippies you would encounter in an artist colony. That was nowhere close to this reality. If Janet fit a mold, it was that of a hard-working blue collar man with a Victorian sense of values and child-rearing.

The disposition hearing should have been routine, and for the most part was. However, after confirming my recommendation for probation and reading the standard conditions, the hearing officer launched into a protracted stern speech. He admonished Frankie with the threat of incarceration if he did not respect and obey the authority of his parents and parole officer. Janet nodded at the confirmation of her belief in the punitive approach. I cringed. He had just made my job of creating a more supportive and positive environment more difficult, if not impossible.

I determined to avoid the embarrassment of a weekly tirade from Nora, so I scheduled my weekly visit for Tuesday afternoons at the Boys and Girls Club. These contacts quickly fell into a routine pattern. He'd be sitting in the library with a book open.

"Hi, Frankie. How's the homework coming?"

"Okay. I'm almost done."

"What's going on at home?"

He responded with a litany of his peccadilloes and punishments followed by venting his grievances against Nora. His offenses were mainly not doing some chore soon enough and making a mess. I encouraged him to hang in there. He still needed to work on controlling his temper, but nothing he had done sounded too serious.

When he finished his litany, he said "Do want to see what I'm making in the shop?"

"Sure."

We'd head over to the shop. It was easy to compliment his handicraft. His projects stood out as neat and tasteful examples in the midst of a mostly slap-dash collection. Depending on which tables were open, we played a game of ping pong or shot some pool before I left.

The case continued this way for four months. Janet expressed her satisfaction with the state of affairs in biweekly phone calls, though she remained concerned that the backtalk hadn't completely stopped. Frankie was happy to see me each week. The conditions of probation were being consistently upheld. I was the only one who wasn't satisfied. I felt that I was only keeping a lid on the situation, mitigating the impact of the lousy home environment, but not doing anything to change it for the better.

Carl

The chubby little black boy in the waiting room looked so small and innocent. Surely he didn't belong here. He cuddled against an overweight woman in a loose brightly colored dress and was flanked by a thin man with a weathered face dressed in khaki work clothes. How can an eight-year-old be considered to be incorrigible? I was thinking that there must be something terribly wrong with parents who'd give up on controlling such a young child. I would have a hard time maintaining the appearance of an open mind during the interview.

The report said a neighbor had called the police when she heard an intruder in her house. When the intruder turned out to be a little boy, she didn't want to press charges. The boy denied stealing anything. He said he saw his mother in the house and went inside to see her. He told the police his address and they took him home and turned him over to his grandmother. She said he couldn't have seen his mother because she had been dead for two months. She said she tried to watch him but he would sneak away and she didn't know what to do. The officer referred her to the Juvenile Court and called to set up the appointment.

The kid's name was Carl Green. Parent/Guardians were listed as Bob and Violet LaRue. I greeted them by name and asked the adults to come with me.

Mr. LaRue demurred. "One of us has to stay with Carl. He'll get scared and wander off if we leave him alone. Violet can tell you all about our problem." He spoke with a Caribbean accent and a raspy voice. I glanced down at his hands and noted yellow stains on his right index and middle fingers, confirming that he has a heavy cigarette smoker, which explained the rasp.

I accepted his proposition and led Violet to the interview room. She didn't wait for a question before unburdening herself.

"De po' boy ain't been right since his Mamma got killed. Some drunk driver done hit her right in front of her house. She jus' comin' home from work. Ain't no sidewalks aroun' dere. Me and Carl was waitin' for her. We seen it happen; saw dat ambulance come and take her away. He misses his Mamma somet'in' terrible. He don't understand that she never comin' back."

"That's really rough, especially at his age." Violet's sing-song voice put me off. My sympathy was all with the boy.

"He always been a mama's boy. Real quiet. Don't play much with the other chillum. Since he mamma die, he gets de nightmares and dream about her even when he awake."

His reaction to the trauma sounded normal, especially if the boy was moved into new surroundings. "How long has he been living with you?"

"All he life. De father got sent back to Haiti befo' he born. So me daughter and de baby stay live wid us. I take care of him while Clara worked at the hospital. I get him at the school bus ever'day to make shore he safe."

"So what do you usually do in the afternoon?"

"We watch the television an' he help with cookin'. We used t' go places, but can't afford extras now. My husban' work hard every day 'cept Sunday only he still don't make as much money as Clara did. We have a hard time since she die. De man what hit her don't have no insurance, so we got no money. De people from de

- 84 -

hospital helped pay for de burial, but that was all. We don't want no charity. We scrapin' to get by." She sounded resigned, no sign of anger, no expectation of a better life.

I did not know what to say. It was a rotten environment for raising a kid, but I was in no position to solve their economic problems. There address in South Phoenix wasn't near any Boys and Girls Club, or Y.

"Tell me, how is Carl doing in school."

"Not so good. De teacher say he not payin' attention and not doin' he work. He Mamma was de smart one; she help him with de homework. I cannot help like dat. I only went to school three years in Haiti. I'm doin' the bes' I can but its not enough. I'm afraid. Please help us." She sounded more pathetic than sympathetic. The school district was underfunded and had recently been the subject of a newspaper series detailing mismanagement. About the only resource that was left to explore would be a counseling referral.

"There are some counseling services that can help. Do you have medical insurance for Carl?"

"Jus' de Medicaid. Bob's boss don' give no insurance. So we have no money for doctors."

"I understand." What else could I say? "Does Carl take any drugs?" Seeing the look on her face, I quickly rephrased the question. "I mean, do you give Carl any medication?"

"No. We don't have no medicines."

"OK." I was feeling depressed and struggled to sound hopeful. "I'll do the best I can to get him help. Until I talk to him, I don't know what kind of help will be best. We'll try to refer you to a good program, so you don't have to go to court."

Her tone changed to fearful desperation. "Please, don't take my baby from me. He's all the family I got left."

I didn't want a big scene. Stay calm, I thought, or she may panic and bolt. While I had strong doubts about her competence, she meant well. "There are no official charges against Carl, so what happens to him is up to you. After I talk with him, we will all meet together and I will make a recommendation. The final decision will be up to you and your husband."

"Thank you, sir."

Back in the lobby, Carl was leaning against his grandfather. He continued to stare blankly into space as we approached."

"Hi, Carl. It's your turn to come and talk to me."

No reaction.

Violet spoke, "You gotta go with the nice man, honey."

Carl stood and reached for my hand. His grip was limp. He kept his head looking up toward me as we ambled into the interview room. He remained standing by his chair until I sat down in the chair next to his and told him to sit down. I eschewed my normal seat on the opposite side of the table in an attempt to create a less formal setting.

"I'm sorry about your mother's death. That was really sad."

"She's not really dead." Carl's voice was soft and flat; his face expressionless. His eyes glazed over into a blank stare as he continued. "She comes back and talks to me."

"Do you mean you see her in your dreams?"

"No. She talks to me while I'm awake."

I was getting spooked. I expected an emotional scene with either tears or anger. Instead, Carl spoke slowly in a soft monotone and no eye contact. Maybe he was visualizing his vivid dreams. "When you are lying in bed?"

"Sometimes, and sometimes when I'm walking or eating."

"Do your grandparents hear her too?"

"No. I'm the only one who can hear her."

His matter-of-fact answer confirmed that I was in way over my head. Maybe there was some cultural influence here. I think of Haiti as the home of voodoo and Carl's demeanor was reminding me of a movie zombie. Turning from that disturbing image, I shifted to the incident that brought him here.

"Did your mother's voice tell you to go into that house where the policeman found you?"

"He didn't find me. The lady called him."

"What did the voice say just before you went inside the house?"

"She knew I was hungry so she tol' me to go in the back door an' wait in the kitchen. She said she woul' make me a peanut butter an' jelly san'wich."

"Did the lady inside the house look like your mother?"

"No. She an ol' lady."

"So, your mother wasn't in the house."

"She was there alright. I jus' couldn't see her 'cause she an angel."

"Doesn't she have to be dead before she can be an angel?"

"She died but she come back to take care of me."

"You know you're not supposed to go into other people's houses."

"But Mamma tol' me to go in. She said, ' Come in, Carl. It's nice in here.' "

"When you got off the school bus, did you go home with your grandmother?"

"Yes."

"Why did you go back outside?"

"He tol' me to."

"Your mother's voice told you to go outside?"

"Not she, He."

"Who's he?" The emergence of a second voice gave me a sinking feeling. I had read about schizophrenics in my psychology classes and Carl fit the description. Our usual family counseling referrals wouldn't be appropriate. We were in uncharted territory.

"I don't know his name, but he talks to me."

"So you've heard him before?"

"Lots of times."

"Did he ever talk to you before your Mamma was hit by the car."

"Yes."

Carl still seemed devoid of emotion. I could feel my heart pounding. Still I maintained a calm façade throughout the session, or at least I thought I did. "Tell me about your dreams."

"They scary. Bad guys chase me in cars. When they catch me, I yell and then I wake up and Grandma comes and sits with me. I don't like to go to sleep, but Grandma makes me go to bed a eight o'clock every night."

"Your grandma takes good care of you?"

"Yes, She cooks for us and gives me clean clothes. Grandma loves me."

"I know." I wondered if his problems had started before his mother's death. "What grade are you in at school?"

"Second grade."

Either he had a late birthday or had been held back a year. "When is your birthday?"

"March 3."

OK, so he was already behind in school, more evidence that his problems preceded his mother's death. "Do you like school?"

"No." Carl was adamant, raising his voice for the first time. "Why you ask so many questions?"

I guess I had pushed as far as I dared. "I'm trying to get to know enough about you so I can help you stop having so many nightmares."

"How you do that?"

"I don't know how to do it myself, but I can get you an appointment with a doctor who knows about these things. I think it's time for you folks to come in and join us. So just sit here a minute."

"OK."

I stepped out just long enough to take a deep breath and ask Mr. and Mrs. LaRue to follow me back in. I would have to choose my words carefully to prepare the family for an intensive treatment program, yet I was neither qualified nor authorized to make a psychiatric diagnosis and Carl was not yet under the official jurisdiction of the court. I sat down across the table from the family.

"I'm glad you came to get help. Carl is in a difficult situation and should get longer term help than I can provide."

"I don't know if we can do dat. He's not a bad boy an' besides we have no money."

"I agree that he's a sweet boy, but he has been through a lot. You were very lucky that he wandered into a house where the owner did not hurt him or press charges. He might have gotten attacked by a dog."

Carl whispered, "I wouldn't get hurt; Mamma tol' me."

"I'm afraid that if you don't do something now, he will wander off again and get hurt."

"I can't keep watchin' him all de day and night." Violet sounded more worried than defensive.

"Exactly. You are doing the best you can. I am going to make an appointment for Carl with someone who can help him without costing you much money. It may take a while to make the arrangements, so please wait here until I get back."

Mr. LaRue nodded at his wife. She replied, "OK."

I paused outside of the interview room to blow out some of the tension. Then I swung by my supervisor's office to get his recommendations for mental health referrals. I got as far as mentioning Carl's age, the hallucinations and lack of insurance when Bert broke in.

"There are really only two options. County Mental Health and the State Hospital."

The words State Hospital conjured up images from the movie "The Snake Pit." My face must have reflected my thoughts because Bert added, "Surprisingly, the State Hospital has the best pediatric psychiatry program in the state. Dr. Channing has built a national reputation with his results. Unfortunately, it has only twenty beds and a long waiting list, so start with County."

I dutifully thanked him and called the County Mental Health Clinic. I told the receptionist that I wanted to make an appointment for a client.

"I can scheduled him for 2:00 on January 29."

"But that's almost two months away. The client is a nine-year-old boy who is having hallucinations. He needs to be seen soon." I sputtered.

"I'm sorry, but our appointments are first come, first served. Usually the wait is only a month, but many of our staff take their vacations at this time of year and things get backed up. Do you want the appointment or not?"

"I'd better take it. I'll call to cancel if I can find something sooner."

While the receptionist took down the information, I wondered what I could for Carl in the meantime. With our thirty-day limit on informal supervision, I could not maintain support until the appointment or make sue that they got there. As she started to hang up, I muttered to myself, "This is crazy."

"Sir, you shouldn't use that word to refer to our patients!" She was still on the line.

"I wasn't referring to the patients. Good-bye."

I thought I might as well try the State Hospital. I was desperate and had nothing to lose. The reception couldn't be any worse and I needed to calm down before returning to Carl's family. I introduced myself to the hospital's receptionist as Don Gilbertson from the

Maricopa County Juvenile Court and asked to speak with Dr. Channing.

"Dr. Channing is on another line. May I take your message and have him call you back?"

"I'd rather hold. I need information for a case."

The wait was only two minutes. "This is Dr. Channing. How may I help you?"

I gave him a quick description of my interaction with Carl, added that he was a Medicaid patient and asked if he could accept Carl as a patient or refer me to an appropriate program.

"Normally we only accept children from psychiatrists after out-patient treatment has been determined to be inadequate. Has he seen a psychiatrist?"

"I'm afraid not. His school teacher just sees him as one of several inattentive students in her class and we can't get an appointment for him at County for another two months. I'm worried that he will into more serious trouble in the meantime."

"I would like to help, but we have a long waiting list. The only other in-patient programs suitable for a child his age would require an out-of-state placement with a substantial fee."

"So, it sounds like my best option would be to request a court ordered commitment."

"You realize that a court order would only result in a seventy-two hour evaluation."

"I'm afraid I do. And what's worse, is that we would have to hold him in detention until a hearing next Tuesday. The Detention Center is no place for a quiet nine-year-old. I was hoping to avoid that. Still, with as severe as his symptoms are, I have to start something soon." I was a bluffing; I was sure that Violet wouldn't sign a complaint.

"I appreciate your concern, but you may be overreacting. Do you have any background in psychology?"

"Only as my minor at Cornell and a little reinforcement while teaching in a reform school. I started out expecting to refer the case to family counseling, until I talked with Carl enough to determine that his problems went beyond the trauma of his mother's death." "You may be right, especially about not putting him in the Detention Center. I just had a patient check out. So, I have an empty bed I could use for a seventy-two hour evaluation if he checks in by 1:00 this afternoon. I know that doesn't give you time for a court order, so his guardians would have to sign for a voluntary commitment."

"Thank you very much. I'm pretty sure that can be arranged. I send them over with my card so you'll have my contact information."

Dr. Channing gave me directions to his office and hung up. I was still uncomfortable with the whole situation. I was full of doubt; maybe I was overreacting, but at least now I had a plan – if I could sell it to the LaRues.

Returning to the interview room, I apologized for keeping them waiting and sat down on my side of the table. "I have some very good news for you. Dr. Channing, who is the best known expert in the state for dealing with problems like Carl's, has agreed to see him today. He will likely ask you to admit Carl to his hospital for a couple of days so he can run enough tests to find out exactly what Carl needs."

"I don't know about leavin' Carl in no hospital. Can I stay wid him?" Violet was agitated.

"I'm afraid not. I expect that they will want to watch him at night so they can find out more about his nightmares." I was stretching the truth without actually lying.

"I don't know..."

"We better do whut de mon says, Honey." Mr. LaRue spoke firmly.

"I guess so." Violet was resigned.

She cuddled Carl while I gave directions and my card to Mr. LaRue. When we were finished, I walked them outside to the bus stop. As I shook hands in parting, Carl startled me by hugging my waist and looking up with a smile. I responded with a pat on his back. Until that moment, I felt I had utterly failed to connect with him, yet at some level I had reached him. I was deeply touched and at the same time worried that I hadn't done him justice.

"Don't worry, Carl. The doctor is going to take good care of you." I was worried enough for both of us.

Violet gently pulled him off of me and I turned to go back inside. Luckily, Carl was my last intake case of the day. I wasn't ready to face another problem. I made a return call to cancel the appointment at County Mental Health. When I told my supervisor that Dr. Channing had agreed to see Carl for an evaluation, he expressed surprise: "You were very lucky to get that."

Fortunately, he did not ask how I had managed to talk him into it. I did vent some of my frustration. "I was surprised at how hard it was to get a mental health appointment, even being backed by the authority of the court. The County offered an appointment seven weeks away. How do working families get help with mental problems?"

"Many of them don't. They just try self-medication with alcohol and end up on the street."

His response did not alleviate my frustration. I fretted away the afternoon. I was full of doubts and second-guessed my handling of the situation. Had I overreacted in pressing for hospitalization? I resented having Carl dumped on me without more knowledgeable support. I resented the lack of options available to help Carl. As the afternoon wore on, my feelings of pity for his family morphed into anger at "the system." Officially, it was a successful case; I had diverted Carl from the court to a referral. I just couldn't shake my doubts about finding appropriate help from him.

Susan added to my sense of frustration. She stopped in to inform Jack and me that she had just submitted her resignation. "This job is hopeless. We're like Sisyphus, struggling to push his heavy load up a hill only to have it roll over him so he has to do it again the next day. I feel sorry for the kids, but that only makes it worse. We can't give them good homes. They are stuck and we are stuck with them. It's ruining my life, my attitude about everything. The pressure is too much. I've got to get out of here."

"Do you have another job lined up?" I asked.

"Not yet. I'll find something."

"Good luck."

Jack commented, "You may be right about the pressure, but we do some good. Somebody has to try to help these kids."

"I did try." Susan was close to tears. "I just couldn't do enough."

Friday afternoon around three o'clock, I was trying to catch up on all my paperwork before the weekend when the phone rang."

"Good afternoon. I'm Dr. Channing. I thought you should know Carl is severely psychotic. We admitted Carl for long term treatment this afternoon."

"Oooh." He had caught me completely off guard. He sounded cheerful as though this were good news.

"That's actually good news." Was he reading my mind? "With modern medications, his prognosis is quite good. Since you caught it before he developed any secondary disabilities or addictions, he should be able to live a normal life after treatment."

"Thank you. That really takes a load off my mind." The expert had vindicated my judgment.

"You're welcome. I'll let you get back to work."

My concerns about our mental health system were still there. I am repulsed by the idea of keeping a child on mind altering drugs, but I didn't have a say in the form of treatment, so I shoved my concerns to the back of my mind. I made ready to enjoy the weekend.

Carl refused to stay buried in my memory. My sleep that night was interrupted by a vivid dream that echoed his nightmares. Even now, every time I read an article about mental illness, I see Carl's smiling face looking up at me.

Christmas

For the first time in my life, Christmas Eve wasn't part of a vacation. New employees could not use any vacation days during their first six months on the job. I had to go in to work. Even worse, I was assigned to intake, so I was stuck in the office all day.

The office was nearly empty, just the eight recent hires plus an older supervisor who had volunteered for the duty because he's Jewish. Only the detention area was fully staffed.

The Christmas spirit must have reached the police departments because there were no new detainees. For the first time, there were no intake interviews scheduled for the day. The hours passed slowly as I puttered through paperwork and chatted with the other officers over coffee. Telephone calls to Frankie and Ronnie wishing them a Merry Christmas were as close as I got to performing any casework. I ended the boring day a little early, slipping out of the office at 4:45.

I stopped by my house just long enough to shave and change into my Sunday suit before Judy and I headed out for my family's traditional Christmas Eve dinner. Light traffic made the trip east on Camelback quicker than usual. Still, by the time we reached my Dad's place in the Biltmore Estates, three Cadillacs and a BMW were already in the driveway, signaling that we were the last to arrive. I had to park in the street. Before

I reached the door with our shopping bag full of gifts, Dad's latest wife, Suzanne, came out to greet us.

"Merry, Merry Christmas! I'm so glad you finally made it. We were getting worried." Her effusiveness was at least partially fueled by alcohol.

"And a Merry Christmas to you. We're actually five minutes early."

"Well come on in and let me introduce you to your brothers lady friend."

We followed Suzanne into the family room, where most of the clan were gathered. Grandpa got up from the card table where he was playing gin rummy with Uncle Rob. After giving Judy a quick kiss on the cheek, he handed each of us a cup of his infamous eggnog (a half-gallon of dairy eggnog, one pint of heavy cream, a bottle of rum and another of Jack Daniel's, liberally sprinkled with nutmeg). After exchanging quick "Cheers" with me, Grampa returned to his cards. I downed my eggnog in two rapid gulps, minimizing its contact with my taste buds. Judy took a small sip, made a sour-apple face and traded cups with me.

We sat on the sofa next to where my brother Steve was chatting with Dad over their Scotch and Sodas. "I've had a good year. I got to try four significant cases. That let me log the most billable hours of all of the associates in the firm, so I'll have a mega bonus."

"Then you ought to buy a car instead of leasing. Do you realize how much more profit I make on leasing and financing than on cash sales?"

"Leasing through the firm gets me a much better tax break. The government really socks it to single men living in apartments. I'm thinking about buying a home with a big mortgage that I can deduct. Do you realize that my income tax is enough to pay for my own personal policeman?"

I chimed in, "And do you realize that the average policeman is making fifty-percent more than I am?"

Steve looked chagrined, but Dad saw my comment as an opening. "You could change that by coming to work at the dealership."

"Dad, I spent the last five years preparing for a career as a teacher. I like working with kids. That is still my plan."

"I can teach you the business. You know I've put my life into building the dealership. I want to keep it in the family."

"I'm not a salesman. I'd never run the business as well as you do. Linda has always been the one with the gift of persuasion."

"That she has. She even persuaded me to pay for a European ski trip instead of coming home for Christmas." Dad chuckled. "At least you should let me get you into a better car than that old Chevy."

"That's awfully generous, but I'm better off with the Chevy at the places I go for work. If I pulled up in a Caddy, I'd be flagged as a pimp or a drug dealer."

"Aren't you afraid of getting mugged in some of those neighborhoods?"

"If I drove a shiny Cadillac, I'd be a target. An old Chevy or Ford gets ignored."

Dad threw up his hands in mock surrender. "I concede."

Granny came out of the kitchen to announce that dinner was ready. She eyed Judy up and down then commented, "You look mighty skinny. Is there something wrong?"

"No." Judy responded, "I'm the same weight I was at the wedding."

"That's what I mean. You've been married for six months. You should be showing by now. I want to see my great-grandchildren."

Judy turned slightly red, so I jumped in. "There'll be plenty of time for that. You're going to be around for a long time. We just want to have a year of getting settled before we have a baby."

"That's ridiculous. None of us is getting any younger."

There was no point in arguing or trying to explain. She had been eighteen when Dad was born.

The candle-lit table was set with a surplus of silverware and filled wine and water glasses. The plates and food were piled on the long side board. Enough of the best heat-and-serve food for at least three meals: a pre-sliced Honey Baked ham, a party platter of shrimp with cocktail sauce, stuffed mushrooms, tamales from Garcia's, microwave twice-baked potatoes, corn and peas from the Jolly Green Giant, a variety of pickles, olives, chutney and mustards and, of course, Pillsbury crescent rolls – nothing that required more than heat to prepare.

During dinner, Dad regaled us with his oft-told stories of what it was like to be a child during the depression, pausing only for an occasional quick bite or to refill the wine glasses. I guess being reminded of the times when all he got for Christmas was an orange in his stocking and a single shirt wrapped in old newspapers under the tree was supposed to make us feel grateful for all the material goods around us. Yet, the obvious happiness with which Dad recalled their picnics of peanut butter sandwiches and playing in the creek made me think of his current life-style as a wasteful extravagance.

As required by tradition, everyone reloaded their plates with a smaller serving of each item, while praising the cook. Skipping something would be inferred as an insult. Upon completion of the second helping, we each declared that we were stuffed and couldn't eat another bite – until dessert was mentioned. Despite our already sated condition, it was impossible (and rude) to resist a slice of mince pie doused with Drambuie and topped with a scoop of vanilla ice cream.

Family rules prohibited opening any presents before sunrise on Christmas Day. So, the men sorted the packages and carted them to the appropriate cars while the women divvied up the leftovers and loaded the dishwasher. That left us with a little more than an hour to kill before heading off to church.

Granny got out the cards, whereupon Grandpa and Dad retired to the den with snifters of brandy and cigars. The rest of us sat down at the table for a game of Hearts. Game mode evoked the old spirit of sibling rivalry, as I focused on setting my brother rather than on winning. I successfully dumped the Queen of Spades of Steve three times. His girl friend got off to the early lead, but crowed about her skillful play, making her the prime target of the rest of the group. This allowed Judy to quietly slip to victory. The conversation at the table stuck to mostly friendly banter about the game.

The game ended when Dad announced that it was time to leave for church. We formed a five car caravan with the Cadillacs in the lead, resembling a funeral procession. Safely alone with Judy, I could speak my mind.

"Next year, I'll save some vacation time and we'll spend Christmas in San Diego with your folks."

"My parents aren't that much better."

"Maybe not, but your siblings are a lot of fun. We could stay in Susan's apartment."

"Yeah. Sleeping on her sofa bed would beat being suffocated in my parents' luxury house."

"That's settled."

There is something magical about singing carols in a crowded church on Christmas Eve. By the time we started "O Come All Ye Faithful", all the tensions from my extended family and work had melted away. I felt at peace with the world and with myself. That was the true gift of Christmas.

Christmas morning, we woke up around nine. Judy and I had the whole day to ourselves, starting with a substantial brunch we fixed together. I wished I could have matched Judy's relaxed, leisurely mood, but my mind kept jumping to the unopened presents under the tree. As far back as I can remember, Christmas morning began with the ripping open of all the packages. Those childhood memories left a residue of impatience that I couldn't shake. I ate quickly, dumped the dishes and sat in front of the tree until Judy joined me.

We started with our gifts to each other. Judy was delighted by the Mix-Master I bought after watching her struggle to make cookie dough with our little egg-beater. Judy got me a bunch of clothes. I complemented her on the choice of colors, but my enthusiasm was mainly fueled by the thought that I could go another year without stepping foot into a department store. Judy's parents sent us matching Scandinavian sweaters and a check for two hundred dollars to "Treat Yourselves to a Luxury" according to the card. We quickly decided on using it to replace the nearly bald tires on Judy's car. The largest package was from my Dad. It contained two boxes: a set of eight crystal wine glasses and a case of vintage Pinot Noir.

Judy examined one of the glasses. "These are really nice."

"And they came with a year's supply of wine for us." I sneered.

"Unless we invite your family over for your birthday." Judy got a chuckle out of me.

"The sad thing is that they would actually have more fun if we celebrated with a picnic of hot dogs and root beer."

"Then that's what we'll do."

We had time for a walk around the neighborhood before the Suns game started on television. It was quiet except for the kids riding around on the bicycles showing their friends what they got for Christmas. I looked forward to our kids being part of that scene in a few years.

Marta - Part I

The workload had eased up during the Christmas season. There were still plenty of runaways, but the parents were generally eager to take them home. Almost a month passed without adding anyone to my on-going caseload. The respite ended on the second Monday in January.

I was summoned to the court room without an explanation at 10:10. I grabbed the sports coat I kept in the office and clipped on the time I kept in its pocket for emergencies. It wasn't a classy look, but it satisfied the court's dress code.

Except for a woman in a business suit and the bailiff, the court was empty. The bailiff looked up and said, "The judge will be with us in a couple of minutes."

"Can you tell me why I'm here?"

"One of the truancy defendants from Harding School failed to appear this morning, so the hearing officer is getting the judge to issue a formal subpoena."

"So, what does that have to do with me?" It was an honest question; I wasn't scheduled for intake until Thursday.

"The case is rescheduled for Thursday, so you will have to serve the mother today."

"How do I do that?" Serving papers wasn't in my job description.

"You go to her house and hand the papers directly to the person who is named on the subpoena. Wait as long as you necessary to see her. Don't tell her what it is until she physically has it. If she doesn't show up, you will have to be able to testify that she physically received the document."

My stomach tensed up. This was not going to be a pleasant encounter. My mind was full of what-if's: What if she wasn't home? What if she wouldn't open the door? What if...

The judge quietly entered the room. "Mr. Gilbertson?""

"Yes, your honor."

"Deliver this subpoena to Rosa Suarez at 2751 West Taft Street. Make sure she understands that if she does not appear in this court at 8:30 Thursday morning with her daughter Marta, I will issue a bench warrant for her arrest for contempt of court and contributing to the delinquency of a minor and that she will go to jail."

"Yes, your honor." That's the only acceptable response to an order from the judge.

I took the unsealed envelop from the judge, who promptly left, followed by the bailiff. The woman in the business suit handed me a folder saying, "Here's Marta's file." And she turned and left. I was alone in the court room with an uncomfortable feeling.

I went back to my office and read the file, which contained surprisingly little information. From her birth date, I calculated that Marta would turn sixteen on April 15, after which she was not legally required to attend school. She was in eighth grade, already two years behind most of her peers. She had amassed forty-two unexcused absences this school year, just about half of the time that school had been in session. The school had responded by sending stern letters to her mother every month since October with no response. The attendance record was signed by Mrs. L. Quinoz, the principal of Harding School, as the basis for the truancy complaint.

That was it. I wondered why Marta was two years behind her classmates and why the school had waited so long before taking any action other than mailing letters. There was nothing in the file that told me anything about Marta's abilities or personality.

Since I was acting as an officer of the court, I figured that I should look official, so I kept the coat and tie on when I drove to West Taft Street.

To call the neighborhood run-down would be giving it a compliment. The block held a collection of wooden shacks that had once been painted white, sitting on concrete blocks in lieu of foundations. The small yards were nothing but dirt. The only parked cars were junkers, several of them up on blocks. I feared that if I let my old Chevy get out of my sight, that it would be quickly stripped. 2751 was identified only by small numbers painted on the mailbox.

Nearing the screen door, I heard a girl call out from within. "Mom's it's a customer." Boy, did that cause a gut reaction! I wanted to get out of there as soon as possible.

As soon as I knocked, the figure of a brown-eyed woman with long black hair and heavily rouged cheeks appeared in a shiny red robe that was open enough that I assumed she wore nothing else. I have never felt more uncomfortable and awkward in my life.

"I don't know you." She snapped, "What do you want?"

"This is for you." I slipped the envelope through a tear in the edge of the screen door. She took hold of it. That was sufficient; she was officially served.

"What the hell is this?" She must have noticed the Maricopa County Superior Court return address.

"It's a subpoena requiring you to appear in Juvenile Court with your daughter on Thursday."

"I can't do that, I have to work." She shoved the envelope back through the door. I didn't touch it.

"You have been legally served. The judge told me that if you did not appear on time that he would issue a bench warrant for Marta and have you arrested for contempt of court and contributing to the delinquency of a minor." I kept up a firm, hard demeanor, which undoubtedly confirmed her impression of me as one of the enemy.

"That's bullshit. Marta ain't no delinquent. She's never caused no trouble."

"The school officials filed a truancy complaint stating that Marta is not attending school as required by law."

"That school weren't teachin' her nothing. She been goin' there for nine years and she only reads like a third grader. That's not my fault. It's their fault for not teachin' her. It's better for her to take care of the baby while I'm working."

"The court will work make sure that Marta gets a decent education. Its job is to determine what's in the best interest of the child." As soon as those words came out of my mouth, I knew I had said the wrong thing.

"I don't need no welfare workers prying into our business and telling me what to do. I know what's best for my daughter. I'm her mother!"

"That's true, Mrs. Suarez. You are her mother and you are responsible for Marta. So you need to have her at the court hearing on Thursday morning."

"That's **Miss** Suarez. Now get off my property!" She shouted loud enough for neighbors to hear.

"Yes ma'am." I wasn't about to get into a physical confrontation. I turned and fled at a walking pace. In the background I heard **Miss** Suarez yelling at Marta in Spanish.

It had not been one of my better performances. In my own defense, I had walked into a giant can of worms. Instead of just truancy, there was obviously prostitution going on in the house and an infant of unknown parentage. None the complications were even hinted at in the file I had. Still, I had come on as some kind of a cop and totally failed at establishing any rapport. I dreaded facing Rosa Suarez again on Thursday. I almost hoped that she wouldn't show up, then she would get arrested and Child Protective Services would take the children. That would let me off the hook.

I returned to the office in time for lunch with Jack, my office mate. I described my visit over coffee and sandwiches. I expected him to be shocked. Instead, he topped my story.

"The first time I made an appointment at one of my probationer's home, nobody came to the door. The mother just yelled for me to come on in. When I came in, she called me from the back room. She was ling on the bed completely naked, stretched out like she was posing for Playboy." That evoked a clear and enticing vision in my mind. "Then she did a Mae West imitation. 'Come on in, Handsome.'"

"You got to be kidding."

"It's the God honest truth. She laid there with her legs spread apart."

"What did you do?"

"I sure didn't enter the room. I asked where Tom was and she said he wouldn't be back for at least an hour so we had plenty of time. He was with friends at the park. So I went to the park. I haven't been back to his house since. I just meet him at the park."

"Good choice. How did your wife react?"

He shook his head. "I'd never tell her about something like that. She wouldn't believe that I just walked away."

That was a sad thought. Most of what goes on at work is either confidential conversations that can't be shared or uninteresting routine procedures that would bore my wife. When I told Judy about my day, she jumped on the humor in how I was greeted. "Mom, it's a customer." became an inside joke between us.

Thursday morning found me waiting outside the court room to see if Rosa Suarez would show up with Marta. By 8:20, it was too late to interview with Marta before the hearing. It looked like the truancy case was going to escalate into the arrest of the mother and placement of two children in foster care. Finally, at 8:28 by my watch, the family came in dressed up for church. Miss Suarez wore a simple black dress, high heels and a black lace shawl. Marta was wearing a modest white dress and was carrying a toddler, who had on brown shorts and a Superman Tshirt.

The judge started the hearing by asking why she hadn't appeared on Monday in response to the letter from the court.

"Sir, I never saw no letter from the court. Sometimes the junkies steal the mail in our neighborhood." I was surprised by the submissive tone of voice. The judge clearly wasn't buying that excuse, so she continued. "Marta often gets the mail before I do. She might have thrown it away, like she done with those letters from the school."

The judge followed up with a stern lecture on parental responsibility. Ms. Suarez looked sufficiently cowed and responded with a simple "Yes sir."

Turning to Marta, the judge asked, "Did you throw away mail from the schools and the court?"

Marta looked at her mother and nodded. I think she was more afraid of her mother than of the judge.

"Speak up. I need to hear a verbal answer."

"Yes." Her reply was just a whisper."

The judge put on his sternest look. "Marta Perez, you have been summoned here on a complaint from the school that you are a truant because you have skipped school over forty times since August. If you disagree with this charge you may plead not guilty and be scheduled for a trial with the school official present. Because of your ignoring the letters that were sent to your house and failing to appear when your hearing was originally scheduled, you would be held in detention until the trial."

"I have to be home to take care of my brother when my mother is working."

Miss Suarez chimed in, "I clean house for some rich people and they won't let me bring Pablo with me." ('Yeah, right,' I thought.)

"You will have to make other child care arrangements. Your daughter needs her education." The judge snapped. "And you, young lady, need to enter a plea. Are you guilty of skipping school?"

"Yes," came the whispered reply.

"In accordance with the laws of Arizona, I find that you, Marta Perez, are an incorrigible child and are now a ward of the state until your eighteenth birthday unless discharged earlier by this court. I am placing you on probation as of this moment. Mr. Gilbertson will explain the standard terms of probation to you and develop a plan for your education. If either you or your mother fails to cooperate fully with Mr. Gilbertson, you will be removed from your home and placed in a secure facility. Do you understand?"

They both answered, "Yes sir."

That ended the hearing and put the next step entirely in my hands. I was frankly caught off guard. I had expected a direct order for Marta to return to Harding School instead of me being ordered to develop an educational plan for a girl I hadn't formally met.

As I led the family to an interview room to go over the terms of probation, I could feel hostility coming from both Marta and her mother. I asked Marta to read each item out loud, mainly so that my voice wasn't laying down the law, but it also let me get an idea of her reading ability. She read slowly and quietly, but accurately, pausing slightly to sound out the longer words. She seemed to comprehend the meanings just fine.

Ms. Suarez started to object to the provision that the probation officer could visit at any time. "I teach the children not to let anyone come into my house when I'm not there."

"That's a good rule. I don't plan to show up at random times. We'll either schedule visits ahead of time, or I'll call first." That calmed her down somewhat. Also, I had no desire to ever interrupt and confront a "customer" and put myself at risk of bodily harm.

When we reached the item that stated: "The probationer shall regularly attend school or a job approved by the probation officer." Marta perked up. "That says 'or', so I don't have to go to school if I get a job. I can be a babysitter."

"Not quite. First, you heard the judge say that we need a plan for your education, that might mean going to a different school, but it does mean that you will need to continue your education while on probation. Secondly, for a job to be approved, it has to be supervised and aimed toward a career."

"But who's going to take care of Pablo?"

"Like the judge said, that is your mother's responsibility. If you want to be able to stay at home with your mother and brother, you will have to obey the judge's orders."

"Course she wants to stay with me. I'm the only family she's got." Once again, Miss Suarez's anger bubbled over.

"If you both cooperate, we can make that happen." I spoke without conviction. I had serious doubts that keeping the family together would be in the children's best interest. Still, I was required to give them a chance to make it work. "I need to talk with Marta alone for a few minutes. Miss Suarez, will you please wait in the lobby with Pablo."

Miss Suarez glared for a moment before taking Pablo out of the room.

Once we were alone, I softened my posture and tone. "So, Marta, tell me about school."

"I hate it." She spoke softly, even when obviously angry.

"Please be more specific. What exactly is wrong with your school?"

"The teachers are always picking on me and the others kids laugh when I make a mistake. They call me stupid because I was held back."

"I paid close attention to you when you read the probation rules. You obviously are not stupid."

"Tell it to the teachers."

"I will."

"Really?"

"Really. I'm going to talk with Mrs. Quinoz this afternoon. What's your favorite subject?"

"I don't have one."

"What do you like to do?"

"Take care of my little brother."

"Anything else?"

"I like to cook. I fix dinner every night."

"Hablas español?" For the record, I wanted to establish that she was bilingual.

"Sí. Y Usted?" Martz brightened up a little.

"Solamente un poquito. That's something you know better than I do. Being bilingual will give you an advantage in many jobs, once you have a diploma. But it is almost impossible to get a good job without a diploma."

"I know that." Her face sagged to a look of resignation.

"You are going to have to work real hard in order to graduate from eighth grade, and that probably means summer school."

"They're mean to me at Harding. Can't I just take care of Pablo and go to night school? He really needs me."

"You have to graduate from eighth grade first. The only night school programs that I know about are for high school classes. Do you know of any specific school you want to attend instead of Harding?"

"No."

"Okay. I'm going to call the school this afternoon and try to find a program that you can attend that will let you graduate. I don't know if it will be at Harding or somewhere else. I will call you this afternoon when I find out. I realize that you are in a tough situation, but you put yourself there by missing so many days of school. You are going to have to work extra hard and not miss any more school if you want to be able to be with Pablo at home."

"But what if I get sick?"

I didn't know if that was an honest question or if she was just looking for an excuse to ditch school some more. I certainly wasn't going to give her any wiggle room. "If you are really too sick to go to school one day, you will need to call me first thing in the morning, before school is supposed to start and I will come by your house to see that you get to a doctor."

With that, I called her mother back into the room and reiterated all the stipulations that I had laid down. As they walked out, little Pablo glommed on to Marta, who returned his smile.

I returned to my office feeling discouraged. Marta seemed like a sweet passive girl, an innocent victim of her circumstances. The prognosis was miserable. The fact that she was a good looking girl with full breasts made it even more likely that she would be pregnant before she turned eighteen. I couldn't see her as doing better than repeating her mother's impoverished lifestyle. Still, I had to at least attempt to get Marta to complete at least eighth grade, and aim for a G.E.D.

My next step was a phone call to Harding School. The secretary left me on hold for a good five minutes before Mrs. Quinoz came on the line. "This is Principal Quinoz, Mr. Gilbertson. Whose parent are you?"

"I'm not a parent. I'm Marta Perez's probation officer."

"She's not here."

"I know. She was in court this morning and has been placed on probation."

"Good. Then you can make sure she comes to school next week, especially on Tuesday."

"What's special about Tuesday?"

"It's the one-hundredth day of instruction."

"Huh?"

"Half of the state aid to schools is based on the attendance on the hundredth day of instruction." Her tone indicated that she felt everyone should know that.

"I see. What I'm trying to do is work out a plan that will have her graduate this year."

"That can't happen. She has already missed far too many days."

"What if she does extra work and goes to summer school?"

"That won't work. Putting her back in her classroom would be too disruptive."

I couldn't quite picture Marta as being disruptive. "Is there a Special Education program that she could participate in?"

"She doesn't qualify for Special Ed. We tested her and her IQ is slightly above average. The problem is her attitude, not her ability."

'I could say the same thing about you,' I thought.

"We're in a poor district and have to deal with a lot of dysfunctional families and transients here. We can't afford to provide special services to everyone. Some people just can't be educated."

I was irritated by being lectured at, but I needed help in solving Marta's problem. I asked, "Then why do you want Marta back in school?"

"To set an example for the other children. I'm going to put her at a desk in the front office and give her worksheets to fill out all day. The other children will see what happens to a person who ditches school."

"I don't see how that is going to help Marta." My blood boiled at the idea of punishing a child to cower other children. I swallowed hard.

"The people around here need to learn that they have to obey the law. Marta's punishment will help do that."

"The judge assigned me to make a plan for Marta's education. Since you apparently aren't able to provide that, I'll have to find an alternative."

"Good luck with that," she snapped. "Meanwhile, make sure you bring her here on Tuesday."

I was fuming when I hung up. What was a person like that doing in charge of a school full of children? I thought people went into teaching because they liked helping children. Obviously that was no longer true for Mrs. Quinoz.

My first attempt at finding an alternative was a call to CETA, the teen job training program run by the Department of Economic Security. Yes, they had openings for the sessions that started in two weeks. Yes, there was a culinary arts program. The minimum age for enrollment was sixteen. Sorry, no exceptions, but there would be another class starting in June.

I spent the rest of the afternoon in a futile attempt to find an alternate school program for Marta. There were programs available for every special education diagnosis and for kids sixteen through twenty, but nothing for girls like her. Marta was falling through a crack in the system. Her mother seemed willing to accept that fate. I wasn't. The frustration made me more determined to fight for Marta.

I reluctantly called Mrs. Suarez to tell her that I was working on finding a better school for Marta, so she did not have to go to school until after the weekend.

When I got home, I tried to unwind with a beer and the newspaper. The front page was the usual collection of local tragedies and national politics. I read the comics and sports sections first. While scanning the rest of the paper, the letters G.E.D. caught my eye in a feature article about immigrants learning to be citizens at a settlement house. The director was quoted as saying, "In addition, we offer English and G.E.D. preparation classes to help our new citizens become more productive in the American economy." The settlement house was in the same area as Marta's house. It was a long shot, but what the heck. I wrote down the director's name, Carolina Ramirez, and looked up the exact address and phone number for use in the morning.

Friday morning I crossed my fingers and dialed the settlement house. A cheerful "Good Morning" greeted me after the second ring.

"Is Carolina Ramirez available?"

"Speaking."

I introduced myself as a Juvenile Probation Officer with a client who I felt would benefit from the programs at the settlement house. I briefly explained Marta's situation. When I described the response I had gotten from the principal at Harding School, Ms. Ramirez responded, "Ah, yes. I've encountered that woman."

I took that as encouragement, so I directly asked, "Can I enroll Marta in your G.E.D. preparation classes?"

"We are not an accredited school."

"At this point, that's not important. I'm just looking for a way to get her into a positive environment until summer when she becomes eligible for the CETA program. In the meantime, any combination of educational program and work experience will satisfy the terms of probation."

"We might be able to work something out, if she is willing. We could use a helper in the mornings for our preschool program. She would need a food handling permit from the Health Department. She would work twenty hours a week at minimum wage with no benefits. Then she could take classes for three hours in the afternoon."

At last, a glimmer of hope. "That would work nicely. Can I bring her to meet you on Monday?"

"No, you may not." Her blunt tone stunned me, but she went on. "The only way this can work is if I can rely on her to arrive on time every morning. If she is interested, tell her to see me promptly at nine o'clock on Monday morning. Then if she shows a good attitude, I'll give her a chance."

"Thank you very much. I'll meet with her this afternoon and call you back with her decision." Ms. Ramirez had put me in my place, and I had to admit she was probably right. I had gotten caught up in a vision of myself as Marta's rescuer.

When I called the Suarez house, I had to let the phone ring for a good two minutes before a sleepy voice answered. A glance at my watch showed that it was just after nine. I told Marta that I wanted to come over and talk to her about an opportunity to work in a day care program and take some classes.

"Can you come after noon? Mama is still asleep."

"Okay. Let your mother know that I'll be coming over at two this afternoon."

The conversation deflated the hopes that I had gained from Ms. Ramirez. If the whole family was asleep at nine in the morning, it seemed highly unlikely that Marta would make it to the settlement house on time every morning.

Miss Suarez greeted me civilly that afternoon, asking me to call her Rosa. The three of us sat on the sofa; that, along with a TV on a table, was the only furniture in the small front room. Pablo was taking his nap in the back. My proposal received a lukewarm response. Marta still wanted to stay home and take care of Pablo. It was Rosa who accepted the deal: "You need to do what the man says, Honey, or they will take you away from us." It was not an overwhelming endorsement, but as close to a commitment as I was going to get.

After finishing the afternoon with three routine visits to other probationers, I called the settlement house and left a message that Marta had agreed to the Monday morning appointment. The case left a cloud of doubt hanging over my weekend.

I waited until two pm on Monday to call Marta. She wasn't home. Rosa said that she was "still at that settlement place you sent her." So, I went on my afternoon rounds and tried again when I got home. This time Marta answered.

"Hello, Marta. How did things go at the settlement house today?"

"Good. Carolina is a really nice lady. She said Pablo could go to their pre-school. Mama is coming with me tomorrow to enroll him."

"That's great!"

"Yes. The pre-school is really nice. They have lots of toys to play with and even get a snack for free. I like helping with the little kids."

"I'm glad to hear that. Did you go to any classes in the afternoon?"

"Yes. I'm the youngest one there. The English class is easy. Most of the other students don't speak English good. That Math class is hard, but the teacher says I just need more practice."

"Just make sure you attend every day and I'm sure you will do well. I'll check on you every week."

"Okay."

I gave Ms. Ramirez a call on Friday afternoon and got a positive report on Marta's attendance and attitude.

Ronny – Part III

January brought another significant visit to Ron's trailer. Randy greeted me with, "You gotta see his report card."

Ron came out of the kitchen grinning like the Cheshire Cat. His report card showed B's in every academic subject and an A in Art. Only Phys. Ed. merited a C.

"Wow! I am really proud of you. Your hard work has paid off." I congratulated Ron. We went back to the privacy of the kitchen table. There I commented, "It's no big deal, but I'm a little curious about the C from P.E."

"Sometimes I forget to take my gym clothes to school. I don't like to dress out when anyone else is around."

I saw a red flag. Was I opening up another tale of abuse? Time to proceed with caution. "I doubt there is anything about your body that would attract attention from the other guys. Do you get teased in the locker room?"

"No, I just don't like it."

"Try to get used to it. Kids who don't shower in Freshman P.E. can get hassled pretty bad."

"I know. I'll handle it then." His voice remained calm and relaxed.

It had probably been a false alarm; no need to probe further. "I'm sure you will. How are things going at home?"

"Good. I don't get nagged too much any more." We turned our attention to the Math assignment.

Liz arrived home before I left. It was a good time to announce, "Ron is doing so well that I sure don't need to check on him every week. He's earned lighter supervision, with monthly visits. Any of you can still call me if there is a reason you want to see me more often." I didn't want to sound like I was giving in to the other time pressures of my case load.

They responded with quiet nods. The next couple of visits were routine.

Frankie – Part II

In the middle of March, Frankie finally altered our little ritual his confessing to little mistakes and whining about Nora. When I asked, "What's going on at home?"

He replied, "I went to my cousin's funeral yesterday."

"How did he die?" I braced myself for an emotional outpouring.

"He killed himself."

"That's awful."

"Not really. Everybody was saying nice things about him at the funeral. He was always in trouble and was doing drugs. He stole from his mother to pay for them. He took an overdose of pills. It was on purpose. He left a note that said nothing would hurt him any more. Everyone's better off now." He spoke calmly, in a soft matter-of-fact tone.

His lack of emotion scared me. An edge of panic entered my voice. "Are you planning to commit suicide?"

"No. I was just thinking about death. Nobody would miss me if I was gone."

"Whoa. That's not true! For starters, your Mom would really be upset."

"No she wouldn't. She says sometimes they'd be better off without me."

I couldn't let that idea pass unchallenged. "Sometimes she comes home tired and when people are tired they say things they don't really mean. I know your

Mom has a tough outside, but I also have talked with her enough to know that she cares about you deeply and wants you to do well. She would miss you terribly."

"She would still have Nora and Tony. They don't bother her like I do." Frankie was looking down at the floor. His voice had dropped to a whisper.

"Frankie, look into my eyes. I want you to see that I mean what I'm about to say." He looked up. I continued, "Since I've gotten to know you, I've come to like you. You're a good kid and I really care about you. I want to see you grow up to be a happy adult. I know that it can happen. As you get older, you will have more choices and can make your own life get better. There is nothing that you could do that would hurt me more than killing yourself. For the rest of my life, I would feel that I had failed, that I had let you down. I don't emm..." My voice trailed off; I felt that I had gone way out on a limb and I couldn't figure out what to say next.

Frankie was watching me intently. The silence was awkward. Frankie spoke next. "Are you going to play pool with me today?"

"You bet. Let's go."

I shot poorly. I was focusing more on Frankie's demeanor than on my shots. Frankie sank his last ball before I did, but he left the eight ball close to a corner pocket. I sunk my last ball leaving a straight-in shot at the eight ball. I sunk it easily, but hadn't put enough English on the cue ball to stop it.

"You scratched. I won." A smile flashed across Frankie's face, then quickly faded. "You lost on purpose, didn't you?"

"Sometimes I mess up a shot, but I never lose on purpose. You won for real. I want a rematch next week."

The smile was back.

It took forever to fall asleep that night. I replayed our conversation repeatedly in my mind. He was mighty young for a high risk of suicide, but he was clearly thinking seriously about it. He denied planning to kill himself, so I didn't have any verifiable cause for action. I couldn't decide whether I had said too much or too little. It even crossed my mind that he might have invented the story about his cousin. He had never mentioned a cousin or aunt before. I dismissed that thought after considering that Frankie had never been creative in his stories or descriptions of troubles at home. Should I have reported it immediately, if so, to whom? Certainly not his mother -- that would only make matters worse. He had been in a good mood during the pool game, so I didn't see an immediate danger. Reporting the incident could wait until I met with my supervisor in the morning.

My supervisor reassured me. If anything, he thought I was overreacting. I returned to dealing with the rest of my case load. Doubts and worry would continue to haunt my mind until our next visit.

I got a call the next Monday morning before nine o'clock. A brusque alto voice came on the line. "This is Mrs. Schwartz, the principal at Simpson School. I understand that you are Frank Duncan's probation officer."

"That's right." I knew that bad news was coming.

"I had to call the police because he brought a gun to school."

"WHAT?" My response was more like an explosion than a question.

"It's not as bad as it sounds. He came into the office and told me he had a gun in his backpack. He said he was going to shoot himself, but he changed his mind because of you. I checked his backpack and saw the gun so I had to call the police and he is automatically expelled from school. I am concerned about what will happen he is turned over to his mother. He's afraid to go home."

I forced myself to sound professional. "I appreciate that. I would suggest having the police officer bring him to the detention center as a probation violator. We'll keep him here until we get something worked out. You can tell his folks that they can see him here."

"Thank you. I'll do that. Frank really looks up to you. From what he says, you saved his life."

"I'm afraid that's an overstatement." I didn't feel like a hero. He almost died because I didn't act more forcibly when he talked about suicide on Tuesday. Mostly I was scared that I would fail Frankie the way I had failed Danny Donovan.

"Excuse me, the police have just arrived. I have to go."

"Good-bye." I was glad the call was over. My mind and emotions were in turmoil. What should I have done? At least, something I had said took hold and gave him second thoughts. The one thing I felt sure of was that I had to get him out of that house and away from Nora. I didn't have time to sort things out in my mind before a call came in from Frankie's mother.

"The school called me and said that Frankie is being taken to the detention center because he brought a gun to school. She told me he took the gun because he was planning to shoot himself."

"That's what she told me too. He hasn't gotten here yet. It will take some time for the police to complete their reports and for him to be processed into the detention center. It will probably take more than an hour before I get to talk to him."

"I don't know what to do with him. His cousin killed himself recently. I think that what gave him the idea. I know he has been unhappy since Tony left, but I didn't think it was that bad. I don't know what I can do to straighten him out."

My first thought was, 'Get rid of Nora.' However, I tried to be diplomatic. "He told me about his cousin last week, but I didn't expect that he would try to commit suicide. Obvious, this is very serious so we will have to keep him here for at least a few days and have him meet with the psychologist. I expect that the court will place him in a residential treatment program of some type."

"He needs something to straighten him out. I've tried my best to teach him to be a good boy. I don't know what else to do. Should I take off work and come down to your office this morning?"

"It is going to take some time to figure out what's going on. I don't know if he will be allowed a visitor today. I expect he is pretty rattled and will need some time to calm down and get some rest. The initial court appearance will be tomorrow morning. You should be here for that. If you come around 8:00, you'll be able to visit with him before the hearing. Meanwhile, I'll let him know that you called and want what is best for him."

"Thank you. I'll be there tomorrow."

"I need to ask you about the gun."

"I have a license for my pistol. With two women living together and drug problems in the neighborhood, we need it for protection. I have a permit for it. After the principal called, Nora checked and my pistol is missing. I kept it hidden; I didn't think Frankie knew where it was."

"The Phoenix police will have it now. You'll have to talk to them about getting it back. I'll phone you this afternoon with the police report number."

"That can wait until tomorrow. I appreciate what you've tried to do for Frankie."

"Thank you. We aren't through trying to help him. I think we'll be able to find a way to help him. Good-bye." I spoke with more optimism than I felt.

By 10:00, Frankie had been processed into the detention wing, showered, fitted with a yellow jump suit and cloth slippers. He was placed in a suicide watch cell. The cell had a large window facing the guard station and a microphone for monitoring. The furnishing was limited to a built-in cot with a bare mattress plus a stainless steel toilet and wash basin - cold water only. On entering, I asked the guard to turn off the microphone, loudly enough so that Frankie knew our talk was private. He was huddled against the wall on one end of the cot, head down, arms around his knees. I sat on the other end of the cot. I tried to shut everything else out of my mind by focusing on Frankie's head. Seeing his eyes would have made that easier.

"Hello, Frankie."

"I can't do anything right," he muttered, without looking up.

"You did something very right when you decided to turn the gun in without hurting anybody. Now we have a chance to get you some help and make things better for the long run."

He looked up at me with a tear-stained face, but didn't speak.

"I thought you were feeling OK the last time we talked."

"I was."

"So tell me what happened since then. I want to understand everything that went on."

"I got in trouble on Friday because I lost my vocabulary homework. She gave me a zero even though I had done it at home. I just couldn't find it in my backpack. My teacher didn't believe me. That made me mad and I messed up on the test. She said that was because I didn't do my homework."

"That's tough, but teachers really can't give credit for an assignment unless you turn it in."

"Don't you believe me?"

"I do believe you. Besides, losing a homework paper is a pretty common mistake."

"When other kids do it, they don't get in trouble like I do. Every time the teacher sends a note home I get a whipping. This time I got into even more trouble when I got home. I asked Nora if she had seen my homework and she said that she threw away some papers that were left on the dining room table. She laughed and said that should teach me not to leave a mess. My homework wasn't a mess. I got really mad and called her a bitch."

I stifled an urge to agree with that assessment of Nora.

Frankie continued in a flat voice, drained of emotion. "When my Mom got home, I got a whipping and sent to bed without any supper. Saturday morning I had to rake up all the leaves. It was windy and the leaves kept blowing back. It took a long time to finish. Nora accused me of dawdling. She didn't look outside until after she finished her lunch. The wind had blown more leaves down. She said I was useless and hadn't done my job right, so I had to do it again. At Sunday school they talked about Honor Thy Father and Thy Mother. Brian started teasing me about having no father and two mothers. That's not true. I lost my temper and hit him. That was my fault. He hit me back and gave me a bloody nose. My Mom saw the bloody nose and when we got home gave me another whipping for fighting at church. She wanted to know why I was always causing her trouble instead of being good like Tony. I told her that I don't know what's wrong with me. I'm sick of always being in trouble. The only way I could think of to make it stop was to do like my cousin did."

He paused. Instead of probing, I decided to wait him out. After a long minute of silence, Frankie went on: "When my mother went shopping, I sneaked into her bedroom and took the gun from the drawer in her cabinet and hid it in my backpack, so I could kill myself at school the next morning. When I got to school today, I sat under a tree at the corner of the playground and took the gun out of my backpack. When I looked at the gun, I thought about what you told me." He looked up, tears coming into his eyes, his voice got louder. "I don't want to hurt you or my Mom. I don't really want to die. I just can't stand being hurt anymore!"

I wished I could promise that I wouldn't let anyone hurt him ever again. "You've been hurt a lot more than you deserve. We're going to figure out a way to change things for the better. I think the main thing is that we should find another place for you to live for a while so Nora won't be nagging you. That seems to be the main thing that gets you into trouble."

"Are you going to send me to reform school?"

"What I'm thinking of is a foster home or a good group home where you would get encouragement and support."

"The judge said if I got in trouble again, I'd end up in reform school."

As an officer of the court, I couldn't come out and say that the hearing officer was a jerk. "That judge likes to scare people. He thinks it will make them behave better. I don't think being scared helps people do their best."

"But I keep getting in trouble. I'm not good for anything."

"I know that's not true. I've seen some of the things you made at the Boys and Girls Club. They aren't just good, they're excellent. You are really good at making things with your hands." That drew a small smile. "Also, I've never seen you try to hurt anybody. You make a good friend."

"Really?" At last, a sign of hope.

"Really. Here's what's going to happen. We're going to have to keep you here for a few days. There will be an arraignment hearing tomorrow morning. Your Mom will be there. She already called me and wanted to know that you were alright. She wants you to get help. Next, our psychologist will talk with you and give you some tests to better understand how to help you. He's a nice guy -- I think you'll like him. Meanwhile, I'll be checking around to try to find the best place for you to go next."

"OK."

"Your Mom called me as soon as she heard about what happened. She is very concerned and wants you to be happy."

"I guess so, but Nora doesn't give me a chance."

"I think you are right about that. That's a big reason why I think you should live somewhere else for a while. Your Mom will be here tomorrow morning, before your hearing."

"OK." He paused and looked down at the floor. "I'm scared."

"I know. It's a scary situation. Try to take it easy today and not worry too much. I know that's hard to do in here."

"OK."

I was exhausted, and it wasn't even time for lunch.

We drew the other hearing officer for the arraignment. That meant the case was handled efficiently. We were not subjected to a moralizing speech threatening Frankie with reform school. Janet told the judge that Frankie was beyond her control and needed more help than she could provide. The hearing officer ordered the standard psychological testing and scheduled a disposition hearing for that Friday. I was left with three days to identify the best available residential placement for Frankie.

I expected screening the placement options on such a short time line would be a daunting task. It turned out to be too easy. The Probation Department had a chronic shortage of foster parents for boys. There were currently zero foster homes available. Most of the available group home beds were in drug rehab programs. I was left with just two options: Rainbow Acres and Sunrise Ranch.

The Sunrise Ranch was highly structured, based on a military model and operant conditioning. Such behavior modification programs were the current vogue in corrections, but I harbored a distaste for point systems that rely on "bribes" to encourage good behavior. Frankie didn't need more discipline; he had received an overdose of it at home. I felt that Frankie needed the more nurturing environment. So, while I wasn't thrilled by the heavily religious atmosphere of Rainbow Acres, I got on the phone to the director of Rainbow Acres. I gave her a summary of Frankie's case, playing to her Christian bias by emphasizing his regular church attendance. She agreed to hold their single opening for him, at least through the weekend.

The psych report confirmed my observations. No mental illness beyond depression that was attributed to his home environment. Frankie's IQ tested at 93, within the normal range. He scored above average on spatial relations and mechanic aptitude. Everything in the report was consistent with the planned placement in Rainbow Acres.

I called Mrs. Schwartz at Simpson School to arrange for Frankie's records to be sent to his new school and to assure her that he was now in good hands. All my ducks were in a row when I dictated my report to the court.

My luck was holding out. We drew the good hearing officer again for the disposition hearing. My placement plan was quickly approved. Mrs. Duncan had brought a box full of Frankie's clothes with her, so I could take him directly to Rainbow Acres. A tender farewell would have been out of character for Janet. But at least she was positive at the departure, telling her son that she hoped those people will be able to straighten him out and help him become happy.

Frankie was nervous in a scared sort of way as we drove out to Gilbert and his new home. He was quiet for the first fifteen minutes, then asked, "What if they don't like me?"

"Once they get to know you, I'm sure they'll like you. I liked you the first day we talked and the more time I got to spend with you the more I grew to like you. I'm going to miss our weekly meetings at the Boys and Girls

Club." That thought cut a hole through my professional façade and softened my tone.

"Me too."

"The first few days will probably seem strange. The rules will be different than you are used to, but you can adjust to that. A few of the other kids may tease you or do something mean at first, just because you are the new kid. If you can keep your temper, that won't last long. I talked to another kid who stayed there and he said it was a good place and the people were really nice."

Rainbow Acres soon sprawled to our left. On the campus of single story buildings, a flag pole marked the front office. The eight cottages look like spacious suburban ranch homes, painted white with red-tiled roofs. A barn, corral and garden are off to one side. The buildings are scattered around the desert landscape, connected by concrete sidewalks.

Frankie clung close to me as we entered the office. An elderly woman with a weather-beaten face jumped up from behind the desk and greeted us with a cheerful "Welcome, I'm Mrs. Dalhart, but everyone calls me Aunt Bess. You must be Mr. Gilbertson and Frank." She punched a button on the phone and spoke into it, "Uncle John, Frank has arrived." Turning back to us, she said, "Uncle John and Aunt Sally are your house parents. Uncle John will show you to your room and the schedule. The other children will be getting back from school in a few minutes. You'll meet them during the afternoon activities."

"It's good to meet you in person." I shook her hand and turned to Frankie. "I have to leave now. You are in good hands."

"Will you come and see me?"

Aunt Bess chimed in. "There are no visitors during the first six weeks. That allows you time to settle in and get used to us. After that, your parents and Mr. Gilbertson can visit on Sunday afternoons."

"So, I'll see you in six weeks." I shook hands with Frankie and drove home.

I felt a great sense of relief. Still, some doubts remained. After a couple of years, he would be returned home.

Kate - Part I

Kate was only five years old when the policeman took her away from her home and put her in an emergency foster home. According to the file in front on me, her mother had been arrested for selling drugs to college students. Since there was no father named on Kate's birth certificate and no nearby relatives, she was placed in long term foster care for the duration of her mother's five-year mandatory sentence. Doing that time, the only contact with her mother were Christmas and Birthday presents. Also, there were two "routine" changes of foster parents. The idea of routinely bouncing little kids from place to place annoyed me.

Kate was ten when she was reunited with her mother. In six months, mom was back in prison and Kate was back in foster care. Despite attending six different schools in six years, Kate got good grades throughout the period. That struck me as an unusual accomplishment. Her new placement was with the Slovaks, a couple whose own daughter had gone off to college. All the reports were positive for three years. The calm times ended abruptly when the foster father's company transferred him to San Francisco. Kate resented not being allowed to move with them.

Her next foster parents were the Hopkins, who had three other teenage foster girls in a three bedroom house. After three months with them, she ran away and was picked up at the Greyhound station when she tried to buy a ticket to San Francisco. The following summer, she ran away again. That time, she stayed missing for over three weeks. No comment or speculation in the file concerning her whereabouts during this period. When picked up, Kate claimed that her foster father, Mr. Hopkins, had molested her. An investigation, including interviews with the other three current foster children in the house, found no supporting evidence for her claim. Kate was moved to yet another foster home and started her sophomore year in yet another new school.

The file was full of dates of contacts and report cards, but it told me nothing about Kate's personality or interests. I got the impression that the parade of case workers had diligently processed the paperwork without ever getting to know the person. Five months ago, her tale would have evoked a sense of pity and outrage; now it was just business as usual.

I got stuck with the case because she had run away again, after getting into a fight with her roommate, who had to be taken to the hospital for a few stitches. She was picked up almost immediately and brought to the detention center as an incorrigible child. It was her third runaway in less than two years. Child Protective Services had given up on her. Instead of trying to correct their failures, they were passing the buck to the probation department. By the luck of the draw, she was now my problem. Maybe that's backwards – likely she would see me as part of her problem.

During the arraignment, I was a mere spectator. That gave me a chance to observe Kate. She was about five-six, wearing jeans and a loose yellow blouse that did little to soften her square shoulders. Her curly light-brown hair was short enough to expose silver-loop earrings. She sat bolt upright throughout the proceedings, including the hearing officers stern lecture. Neither her dark eyes nor small mouth betrayed any emotion.

"Yes, sir" were her only words in response to the hearing officer's questions of "Do you understand the charge?", "Have your rights been explained to you?" and "Do you plead guilty to the charge of running away from your foster home?" The hearing ended with Kate being ordered held in the detention center until her disposition hearing, scheduled for the coming Friday.

My primary job was to get her placed in a foster home or group home. There was neither the time nor the need to develop a counseling relationship with Kate. I just needed to gather enough information during the initial interview to be able to screen placement options and complete the paperwork. Consequently, I gave the standard terms of probation a perfunctory review, and got a perfunctory "Yeah, I understand it" as a response.

Then it was time to probe, "What was wrong with your last foster home?"

"My roommate was a real bitch. She was always taking my stuff."

"Is that why you beat her up?"

"She started it."

"How?"

"She called me a Lesbo."

"That was wrong, but punching her wasn't going to make her better."

"It would teach her what would happen if she ever called me that again. If I broke her jaw, she wouldn't be saying nothing at school."

"Were you worried about your reputation?"

"Not really. I mostly hang out with boys at school. Nobody would believe I'm a lesbian."

"If nobody would believe her, why didn't you just ignore her?"

"Ignoring her wouldn't help. She was always in my face and in my stuff. I just finally had enough and punched her."

"I see. You had roommates at the foster home before that. Did you get along with them?"

"Not really. That's why I ran away from there."

"According to the file, you told the case worker you ran because you had been molested."

"I told her that so she would move me somewhere else. The first time I ran away, I told the truth and they sent me back to the same place."

"So you lied when you said you had been molested?" My tone reflected my irritation.

"I didn't say that!"

"What really went on between you and Mr. Hopkins?"

"I'm not going to talk about that -- not to you!"

Her twitching muscles and angry glare signaled that she was ready to explode. I backed off.

"Then tell me about Mrs. Hopkins."

"She was just in it for the money. They fed us lousy food, except when the case worker came to visit. She didn't care what we did, as long as we didn't bother them. The older girls made me do all their chores."

"Did you tell your case worker about the situation?"

"Which one? None of them stuck around for long."

"So the last place you liked was the Slovaks?"

"I used to like it there. They treated me nice and gave me lots of stuff. I thought they really liked me." Her voice cracked a little. "But they only acted like they loved me. As soon as they got a chance to make more money they dumped me."

"I thought they tried to get permission to take you with them to California." I tried to defuse her sense of betrayal.

"That's what's they said. But if they really wanted me, they would have stayed here."

"I doubt it was that easy for them."

"You just don't get it, do you?" Kate slammed her fist down on the table. "Everybody wants cute little girls. When you get big and start doing what you want instead of whatever they say, they don't want you any more."

"So, that's what you think happened with the Slovaks?" I couldn't think of a way to refute her bitter conclusion.

She slumped back in her chair and crossed her arms. "I know it."

"You know that attitude doesn't make it easy for people to like you." I'm not sure whether I was more irritated by her attitude or by the system that turned an innocent little girl into such an untrusting teen.

"I have lots of friends. You adults are the problem. I'm not going act sweet to suck up to them."

"I'm not asking you to suck up to anybody. I just don't want you to act like we are the enemy. I want to find a good place for you to live and go to school until you're eighteen, and there aren't a lot of options."

"Why don't you just rent me an apartment? I can take care of myself."

I managed to return to a professional tone. I felt duty-bound to try to move her toward accepting reality. "That won't work for a couple of reasons. One, the court requires minors to be under supervision, and two, the amount that the county pays for foster care wouldn't cover the rent on a decent apartment, much less your food and other expenses. You are intelligent and do well in school and that's the key to your future success. If you stay in a foster home you can go to public school and move on when you graduate. If you won't cooperate, the court will end up placing you in a secure facility with a bunch of roommates and limited schooling. At your age, I wouldn't expect you to think of the foster parents as Mom and Dad, but as people who want to give you a chance to succeed. I'm asking you to hang in there for another two years."

"I will if nobody's always bugging me. I deserve some privacy." That was as much of a commitment as I was going to get.

"Do you go to church?"

"I don't believe in God."

"The reason I asked is that many of our foster parents, especially the ones who don't take in four kids to get the maximum money, choose to do it because of their religious beliefs. I'm trying to find out if attending church would be a problem for you."

"I don't mind church. I just can't stand people who tell you that you are going to hell if you don't believe their way is right."

"I can appreciate that. I'm going to try to get you into a home where you'll have you own room. I can't make any promises, but I'll do the best I can. It might help if I knew more about your interests. What kind of things do you like to do?"

"Playing sports and hanging out with my friends."

"Anything else I should know?"

"Not really."

"OK, that's enough for me to get started. Meanwhile, you'll see the psychologist tomorrow for some routine tests."

"I'm not crazy."

"Nobody thinks you are. These tests will mostly measure your abilities and preferences. I've got to go now. I'll see you again in a couple of days."

Kate was a rarity. I usually liked the kids I met and that empathy had been a major asset in getting positive responses from them. My personal dislike for Kate made working with her an onerous duty.

Going through the files of available foster homes that afternoon turned up one promising candidate. The Hightowers were third generation cotton farmers in Tolleson who had just completed the training and screening for certification by the county. Mrs. Stefani Hightower was a thirty-four year-old stay-at-home Mom with a five year-old daughter, Amy. They lived in a spacious three-bedroom house with a barn, two horses and a cat. Their only listed community activity was membership in the local Lutheran church. A cheerful phone call assured me that they would be delighted to accept Kate into their home on Friday.

The only unusual note from the psychologist's report was that Kate's IQ tested at 124. She definitely had the brain power to figure out what was in her best interest. I thought that if she learned to control her anger, she could still succeed in life. At our next curt meeting, Kate agreed that the Hightowers sounded like a good place and promised to stay put and obey them.

After a quick, *pro forma* disposition hearing on Friday morning, Kate signed for the two black trash bags that held her worldly possessions. As I started driving west, Kate was quiet, but not still. Her fidgety hands were in constant motion. Despite her stoic exterior, the uncertainties surrounding moving in with a family of strangers had her worried.

Suddenly, Kate blurted out, "Stop at that Circle-K," pointing to a convenience store ahead on our left.

"No stops. I'm supposed to take you directly to your new home."

"But I need to buy some cigarettes. I've got money."

"I can't do that. You are underage."

"I've been smoking since sixth grade. Nobody has stopped me yet."

"Oddly enough, in Arizona is not against the law for you to smoke, but it is against the law for anyone to supply you with cigarettes."

"That's dumb."

"Agreed. Still, as an officer of the court, I have to set an good example by upholding the law."

"You can make an exception just this once, pleeeze. I won't tell anyone." Kate put on a pleading smile.

"No."

"I really need a cigarette. I haven't had one since Sunday. If you don't stop, I'll tell them that you tried to molest me." Her fake sweetness hadn't lasted long.

Her threat set off alarm bells in my head. That kind of accusation could be a career ender. I hadn't quite completed the six-month probationary period before civil service protections would set in, but giving in now would only encourage future attempts at blackmail. At least her credibility would be undermined by her prior accusation against Mr. Hopkins. That thought made me aware that I didn't really trust my supervisor's support. "That could cause me trouble, but won't get me to help you. I don't respond to threats."

"You could lose your job."

"I'll take that chance. I'd rather lose my job than lose my integrity." It was an honest and firmly delivered decision, though I had no idea of what my next job would be. "Look, I know it's hard to quit smoking once you've gotten hooked on cigarettes. We both know that cigarettes are bad for your health. I also know you want to be independent, so you don't want to be dependent on tobacco."

Kate had turned her face away from me. I should have known better than to preach at her, but old habits die hard. At least it shut her whining down for a while. Ten minutes of strained silence ensued.

Kate broke the silence as we neared a gas station. "I have to pee real bad. Please stop."

I figured this was just another ploy. "Hold it until we get to the Hightowers. You haven't given me a reason to trust you. I'm afraid that if I stopped, you might run away."

"If I was going to run away, I would have done it when you stopped at a stop sign. You'd be stuck in the car and I could easily get away. Look, I really do have to go. If you don't stop, I'll end up pissing in my pants and on your car seat. Do you want me to meet my foster parents looking like that?"

"No. That would be embarrassing for you." She had a point about running away; I was in no position to stop a determined attempt. I pulled into the gas station and drove around to the side so the passenger door was right next to the ladies bathroom. "I'm going to take a chance on you. Do your business quickly so we're not late." I hopped out, went around and opened her door."

"You're not going to try to follow me in, are you?"

"Never. I'll be waiting by the door."

Kate went in. I paced back a few feet to the corner of the building. During the eternally long wait, a variety of scenarios ran through my mind. All of them unpleasant, half of them involving the cops as well as returning Kate to detention. Finally, a flushing noise briefly eased my worries. After another pause, a creaking sound preceded the appearance of a head poking out the rear window.

"Don't tell me the door is stuck." I growled. "Come out of the door and get in the car, NOW!"

The head popped back in. In a moment, Kate sulked out of the bathroom and into the open car door. I closed the door, pulled the keys from my pocket, got in and started the car.

"Fasten your seat belt."

Kate glared at me and complied. "I was only going to buy cigarettes. I really need a smoke."

"If you are hooked that bad, you really need to quit."

My comment evoked another glare. For the rest of the drive we shared a common mood of wordless fuming.

Finally, we reached our destination, a red brick ranch house in a stand of cottonwood trees set well back from the road, behind a horse pasture. Other than a metal barn to the right of the house, we were surrounded by empty cotton fields. The nearest neighbor was about a half-mile away. The crunch of tires on the long gravel driveway announced our arrival. Kate's body language shifted from sulking to nervous fidgeting. By the time I came to a halt, a round-faced, tanned brunette woman and matching child had emerged. They were wearing jeans and denim shirts.

The woman went to the right side of the car and greeted Kate with an extended hand. "Hello. I'm Stefani Hightower – call me Stefani, and this is my daughter Amy."

"Call me Kate." She gave the hand a tentative shake.

Amy held up a stuffed dog. "This is Snoopy. He's my dog but you can sleep with him tonight."

Kate actually smiled. "Thank you, but you keep him."

"My husband, Jeff, is out plowing now. He'll join us for lunch." Stefani was speaking to Kate and ignoring me, which I took as a good sign. "Come on in and I'll show you your room."

"Let me get my stuff."

I introduced myself, handing Stefani the manila envelop containing the court order naming the Hightowers as Kate's legal custodians and her medical records, then popped the trunk open and lifted out one of Kate's bag. Kate grabbed the other, declining Stefani's offer to help. Following Amy, we entered the home whose décor was straight out of "Sunset" magazine: tasteful, tidy, informal Western. Kate's room was next to a bathroom at the end of the hall with bare white walls and a matching oak set of dresser, bookcase, desk and bed.

"Wow, this is nice." Kate was stunned.

"I left the walls blank, so you can hang whatever posters you like."

"Even hard rock?"

"It's your room. Why don't you unpack and settle in while I fix lunch. After lunch we need to go get you registered at the high school."

"Can I help Kate?" Amy chimed in.

"Don't ask me. Ask her."

"Sure, why not." Kate didn't wait for Amy to ask again.

After leaving business cards with both Kate and Stefani, I headed back to the office for my own sack lunch and paperwork. Mrs. Hightower impressed me as being strong and down to earth, the kind of person who could handle Kate. I was pretty sure that I had successfully weathered the storm, but I also decided to minimize my exposure to risk by handling the follow-up contacts by phone.

I had braced myself for that first call. Mrs. Hightower gushed before putting Kate on. "Everything is going better than I expected. Kate does her chores without complaining and Amy just loves having a big sister."

Kate was more guarded.

"How is everything going?"

"Okay."

"Tell me about school."

"It's easier than my last one."

"Is there anything else you don't like about it?"

After a brief chuckle, Kate answered, "The teachers play favorites. The jocks and cheerleaders get by with murder."

"I'm afraid that happens at a lot of schools."

"You don't have to tell me. But most of the kids are cool."

"So you're making some good friends."

"Yeah. Especially Janis. She gets me cigarettes."

"I'm sorry to hear about cigarettes."

"Are you going to report me?"

"Nope. I can let little things like that slide." After her pause, I continued, "How are you getting along with the Hightowers?"

"Okay."

"What do you like about them?"

"Stefani's a real good cook. They feed me well."

"I hear that Amy really likes you."

"She's fun most of the time."

"Any complaints?"

"Not really."

"Okay. I'll call you again next week. Bye."

"Bye."

Relieved that nothing bad had happened, I hung up. Maybe all the hassle on the drive from court was a one-time test. Maybe the Hightowers were giving Kate the kind of love she had gotten from the Slovaks, and that was all she needed. More likely, she and Stefani were in a honeymoon period, and one of these weeks I would get an earful of problems and demands.

Ben

Sometimes I felt like I was caught in a soap opera. A revolving cast of characters emoted over the same few plot lines. The parents asked me to force their child to change; the teenagers said they want to be good and would be happy if only their parents would change. The script called for me to actively listen and be sympathetic until they have calmed down and then refer them to family counseling so they can work out their issues without tying up the court's resources. At least half of the cases were nominal successes. The family departed after the intake interview with no further action needed by the probation department.

A few of these sessions ended with positive feelings on all sides. The families that are truly committed to working out their problems with the help of a counselor usually do. So when the clients left with hope, I was satisfied that I had accomplished something worthwhile.

All too often, a parent went away feeling disgruntled. He or she had to take time off from a job, and I did not supply the punitive result that was expected and desired. There was often a reluctant acceptance of a counseling referral for the child, but in most of these cases I didn't sense a desire to change. I suspected that our meeting wasted everyone's time and the family would continue to muddle through their conflicted lives by relying on their old habits. From this bleak realization I learned to encourage digressions into personal interests during the interviews in the hope of finding a positive connection the family can build on. Every once in a while a digression got out of hand.

Albert Schultz had made the appointment because he felt his sixteen year old son was out of control. He frequently stayed out late, didn't tell his parents where he was going, argued whenever they tried to correct him, and slept all morning when he didn't have to go to school. When I probed for specifics, staying out late meant not being home by ten o'clock on Friday and Saturday nights. He looked appalled when I informed him that his town's weekend curfew for teenagers was 1:00 am.

He explained, "That's no good. Early to bed, early to rise makes a man healthy, wealthy and wise."

"Ben Franklin." I wondered if his son was named for him.

"Yes. He knew what it takes to succeed." This launched Mr. Schultz's recounting of his life. I admit that my mind had wandered as Albert Schultz rambled on and on about his own life. I did pick up the gist of his fifteen minute monologue. He had an impoverished childhood, growing up in a Brooklyn tenement. During high school, he worked in a garage after school, mostly doing grunt clean up labor. As soon as he graduated, he joined the navy and became a machinist mate. He retired after twenty years, with the three stripes of a petty officer. By avoiding booze and gambling, he had saved enough that he was able to buy a house and equipment to open his own machine shop in Glendale. He met Freda at the German-American Club, got married and had Ben. They made sure that Ben had all the childhood opportunities that he had lacked. Now he was worried that he had spoiled his son.

I sensed that he was insecure and sought my approval. My periodic nodding encouraged him to continue. He segued into a lamentation about the changing world making it harder for the little guy. Computerized lathes were taking the skilled jobs away from master machinists. He couldn't compete for large orders. He needed to have a reputation for perfection in order to get enough one-of-a-kind orders to survive. There was no future in his business for his son. He'd have to sell everything when he retired. Great craftsmanship was no longer valued. I finally cut him off by asking directly about his son.

"He was a good little boy. But he fell into a bad group of friends when he got into high school. Now he does want ever they want. He doesn't want to obey his parents any longer."

This was an all too familiar a tune. I didn't bother to respond to it. "How are his grades in school?"

"Grades are not the problem. The school is too easy. They give him good grades even when he doesn't study. The teachers should make the students work harder."

"Is it fair to say that your real concern in his attitude at home?"

"Yes. That's it. He needs to show me and Freda more respect."

"That is an issue that can often be helped through family counseling. We have a list of experienced counselors that I will give you."

"Yes, we can try that. Freda can take Ben to a counselor, if you make him go."

"It would be best if all three of you attended."

"I have too much work. I don't have time for anything else. Freda can go with him." Freda was nodding while I got a sinking feeling in my stomach.

It was time to switch and see if I could make any headway with the son.

Ben Schultz was a tall, lanky, blond. His elongated face with narrow-set blue eyes bore a strong resemblance to his father's. He slouched down in his chair, legs stretched out in front and arms crossed loosely across his chest.

I sat down across the table. "I'd like to start by hearing your view of what the problem is."

"My Dad. He's the problem. He acts like I'm still five years old. He won't let me do anything. His ten o'clock curfew on weekends is ridiculous. No teenager goes to bed that early."

It was another all-too-familiar tune: 'It's the other ones' fault. I'm the victim here.' The tricky part was shifting the focus to his choices without getting into an argument.

"That is an unusually early curfew for boys your age, but under the law it falls within a parent's prerogative. There are still lots of people who believe in early-to-bed, early-to-rise."

"My dad is always saying that. I hate it."

"Have you tried showing him that you can handle late-to-bed, early-to-rise?"

"What?" Ben looked genuinely puzzled.

"I got the impression that what really bugs your father is when you stay in bed all morning, instead of joining him for breakfast and getting your chores done. To his mind, that looks like laziness and confirms that he is right about going to bed early."

"I'm not lazy! I have more chores than most of my friends and I do them every day. I do all my homework and get almost straight A's. I work plenty hard."

"You don't have to convince me. Your parents make the house rules. If you want anything to change, you have to consider how your actions look to them."

"My dad is too stubborn. He won't change."

"Maybe not, and if he does change, it won't be overnight. I don't have any magic, just ideas for you to consider."

"Yeah, right."

"Why do you think your father is so hard on you?"

"He doesn't think I'm good enough."

"That's not the impression that I got from listening to him. It's more like he sees the world as a hard, demanding place so you have to be strong enough to struggle through its hardships. He's actually proud of you, especially of your school work."

"If he's so proud of me, why doesn't he ever tell me?"

"I don't know. Maybe he thinks that bragging is a sin."

"That would be my dad." Ben's voice was softer. That seed had taken hold.

I shifted to exploring his hopes for the future. "What are your plans for after high school?"

"I'm going to be an architect."

"That's a tough college program and highly competitive."

"I know." He perked up. "It's going to take five years at the U. of A. I've started a portfolio of designs to help me get in. As long as I keep my grades in the top five percent of my class, I'll get a tuition waiver."

"I'm impressed. You have a good plan. I wouldn't want anything to derail it."

"So you're trying to tell me I have to put up with my dad's stupid rules."

"I guess that sounded like 'just grin and bear it.'"

"Yeah. I don't think I can keep grinning."

"That wouldn't work for either of you. If you walked around the house with a silly grin on your face, your dad might really go ballistic. I am suggesting that you try to de-escalate the conflicts with your father. You told me that you wished your father would tell you he was proud of you. I bet he wants to hear you express your appreciation of his hard work for the family. It might also be worth getting up earlier on the weekends to avoid getting hassled about it. I'm not agreeing with all your dad's rules. I'm just suggesting that you can do some things to make your home life less unpleasant."

"So, you think it's my fault."

"No. What I'm thinking is that you are the one with the most to lose and that you are capable of making things better."

"Maybe. I don't know. We both have hot tempers. I don't know if I can hold it in when he makes me mad."

"I might be able to help a little with that. Here's my card. When you feel your temper build up, I want you to call me and vent your anger at me instead of firing back at your dad."

He took the card. "I can try that."

"OK. Now it's time to have your parents join us and go over the plan for the next thirty days."

We went through the standard arrangements for pre-court cooling off period, including the suggestion that they try family counseling. Mr. Schultz remained skeptical. His wife seemed greatly relieved. I was cautiously optimistic that Ben would become more outwardly compliant.

The following Tuesday, I finished up my scheduled meetings by 4:00. The Schultz residence was in Glendale, off 53rd Avenue and Thunderbird, only about four miles from my house. So, I decided to stop by on my way home and check on Ben's mood. The neighborhood was well established with horse privileges. One acre lots featured barns that were almost as large as the houses. The landscaping was plain, not like the fancy horsey estates in Scottsdale. The address I was hunting was the only house on the street without a corral, though it had one of the larger white barns. The house itself was a Spanish colonial ranch, white with a red tile roof and a porch running the length of the south-facing front.

Mrs. Schultz answered the door wearing a white apron over a simple blue dress. She greeted me with a small smile. "Pardon my mess, I was in the middle of baking some pies."

"I hope I didn't interrupt. I was in the neighborhood and just wanted to drop by and see how things are going."

"Ben's not here right now. He stayed after school to work on a project. But he's doing better. He hasn't argued with his father since you talked to him."

"I'm glad to hear that. Did you make an appointment with a counselor?"

She frowned. "I took Ben to see the counselor yesterday. Alfred was too busy with work. It didn't go well. Ben doesn't like the counselor; he said he asks to many pushy questions. The counselor said we should schedule another appointment when the whole family can come. Ben doesn't want to go back. He said it would be a waste of time. Do we have to go back?"

"No. Ben is probably right. If he didn't get along with that counselor, going back for another session probably wouldn't help. A different counselor might help, but if Ben and his father are working things out for themselves, they may not need a counselor."

"Do you want to talk to Alfred?"

"If he's available."

"Alfred is out back in his shop. I'll take you there."

"Thank you, but I'll find it myself so you can get back to your cooking."

I approached the barn with trepidation. My first encounter with Mr. Schultz had been far from cordial. I figured that he would not take kindly to being interrupted at work, so I paused at the door and opened it slowly and quietly. I was looking at Mr. Schultz's back as he leaned over a large, humming lathe. I was impressed by the neat collection of equipment. A second large lathe occupied the space to the right of where his was working. A work bench ran the entire length of the wall to my left surmounted by a vast collection of tools mounted on pegboard. The end closest to me held a desktop computer and a much smaller lathe. I had three or four minutes to admire the layout before the humming of the lathe stopped. Mr. Schultz set his chisel on the workbench and picked up a micrometer before he spotted me and took off his safety goggles.

"What's the problem?" He asked.

"No problem. I just stopped by to see how you and Ben were doing. Your wife tells me things are going better."

"So far."

"This is quite a shop you've got here."

"You have to have quality tools to do quality work. Do you know much about tools?"

"I've done a fair amount of woodworking, but I don't know much about metalwork."

"Well come over here. This is a SouthBend lathe, the best, made in America, costs $30,000. It lets me mill parts to a tolerance of one-hundredth of a millimeter, that good enough to the tightest Air Force specifications." He continued with a half-hour tour of his shop, explaining more technical details than I could possibly absorb. What I do remember is his obvious pride in his craftsmanship and his appreciation of my interest in his work. My opinion of him had changed from a cranky old man to a caring, dedicated worker that I respected. I went home rooting for the whole family.

The following Thursday, I endured an unpleasant staff meeting before heading out to the field. None of our staff meetings were pleasant affairs. The bureaucratic announcements and reminders seemed unduly detailed. Typically Bert spent twenty minutes going over material that we could have gotten from spending three minutes reading a memo. That was just a boring ritual. What I detested was the second part of the meeting. Bert was convinced that team cohesion and morale would improve if we shared our feelings about our personal lives as well as about work. He would start with an emotional description of the current state of his current relationship, sometimes joyous, but more often fraught with worries about disagreements. I considered my home life to be a refuge from the tension at work and had no interest in subjecting it to the critiques of my coworkers. Some of the others had no such inhibitions. Susan would give a rambling account of some activity with her girl friends. We were freed from that digression when she resigned in December. Jack updated us with tales of his nagging wife, repeating complaints that he had vented in our office over morning coffee. Linda typically retaliated with feminist tirades about how society repressed women in general and her particular. Mark limited himself to commenting how the stress from this job made it hard to relax at the end of the day. Heather offered New Age spiritual solutions to everyone's woes, trying to recruit us into joining her for weekends of crystal gazing in Sedona. Alan would then respond with some sarcastic commentary.

When Darrel, out newest hire, got his turn, he either regaled us with the tale of his latest conquest of a hot chick he had met at a bar or boasted about his latest basketball performance. Darrel's qualifications were that he had grown up in the inner city and became a basketball star at the University of New Mexico before playing two seasons in the Continental League. According to Bert, this made him uniquely able to relate to the poor, minority boys who made up a significant portion of our case load. From what I had seen, Darrel was a lazy, spoiled egotist who related only to himself. The rules didn't apply to him, so I was not surprised that he was once again late for the start of that week's meeting.

The meeting started with "good news". Mark was promoted to be a shift supervisor for the detention officers, starting the next week. Good for Mark; he deserved the increased pay. I should have been happy for him, instead, my thoughts turned to the extra work it would mean for me until a replacement was hired and trained. My selfish worry became exasperated by the next, "bad news", announcement. Bert explained Darrel's absence. He had been fired for turning in false time reports. The investigation began when Darrel was seen playing basketball in a men's league at the Salvation Army at a time that he claimed to be visiting probationers. No surprise there. I didn't expect Bert to admit that he had made a mistake in hiring Darrel. I figured that we would get a pep talk expressing appreciation and sympathy for the extra work required while we were shorthanded. Instead, Bert delivered a Jeremiad about the seriousness of fudging our mileage, as though the rest of us were as untrustworthy as Darrel. I sat there quietly seething at the insult to my integrity. For once, I looked forward to the roundtable sharing session.

Jack started the ball rolling by announcing that his wife was divorcing him. He was moving into a studio apartment this weekend. While Linda was offering sympathy and describing how own experience with life getting better after her divorce, I was struck with the realization that, with Mark's departure, I was the only person with an intact marriage in the unit. What an incongruous situation for a profession that was formed to help other people straighten out their lives. I didn't really hear the rest of the conversation; I was pondering my future. Was I really more secure than my colleagues, or was it only a matter of time before this job messed up my personal life?

I fled the office as soon as the meeting ended. I had a scheduled meeting with Ben and his parents. Usually my drive time was spent thinking about the client and rehearsing how I would talk to him, but this time, my mind was stuck on how screwed up my unit was.

Mrs. Schultz answered the door. "Good afternoon, Mr. Gilbertson."

"Good afternoon. How are things going?"

"Much better. We haven't had an argument at dinner since the last time you were here. Right now, Ben is helping Albert in his shop. Go on back and see them."

"Thank you; I will."

The shop was silent except for the whirling of the lathes Ben and his father were working on. I waited by the door, not daring to disrupt their concentration. Mr. Schultz paused first. He walked over next to Ben and commented, "Just a little steeper angle ..." I was starting to savor the signs of success.

Ben looked up and spotted me. "Oh, Hi."

"Good afternoon. How are things going?"

"Good." Ben replied.

"Better," admitted Mr. Schultz, "but he didn't finish his chores before school."

"I just skipped one waste basket because it was almost empty."

"ALMOST doesn't cut it. A job isn't done until it is completely done. You didn't do your job this morning."

Ben look at me. "What difference does it make if I left a couple of pieces of paper in my trash can?"

"You see what his trouble is. He doesn't pay attention to details and then he tries to make excuses instead of fixing the problem and doing it right."

"I'm not making excuses. I'm just telling him ..."

They were off to the races. Their dialog turned into a barrage of complaints about each other, spiced with examples from the increasingly longer past. There were no pauses long enough for me to fit a word in edgewise. I could feel my blood pressure soar from the stress as I tried to compose a response. The contrast between the cooperation I saw when I entered and rancor I was hearing was stunning beyond understanding, until I realized that they weren't arguing with each other. They were playing to an audience of one, wanting me to declare who was right. Their volume level continued to rise until I snapped.

"STOP!" I yelled.

The anger in my voice startled even me, and left me chagrined. A deadly silence followed for an eternity lasting a few seconds before I started rattling off my judgment.

"The trouble with both of you is that you are too much alike. You are both talented and hard working perfectionists. It is good to hold high standards for yourself, but I hear you each demanding that the other one be perfect, and nobody can do that. The court can't change that. Ben, your parents have done far more for you than the law requires, and Mr. Schultz, your son has developed the skills and knowledge that will let him succeed in college and in life. You should be proud of each other. I hope you learn to appreciate each other, but I can't make you do that. I'm not helping by being here, especially if you are saving up complaints to tell me. You were working well together before I got here, so you don't need my services. When I get back to the office, I am going to close your case. You can work things out yourselves. I wish you both the best."

They were both standing stock still with open mouths as I wound down. Neither said a word until after I had turned and left.

I left before I did any more damage. I had completely blown it by losing my temper in front of my clients, a major breech of professionalism. I tried to convince myself that they had needed the "shock treatment." Even if that were true, I had reacted based on emotion and not by any reasoning. I probably didn't have the legal authority to close the case before court without the complainant's consent. I'd have to be careful how I worded the final report so that it wouldn't raise any red flags or contain any lies. If Albert called the office to complain, I'd be in big trouble, but I doubted that would happen.

I tried to think about what I should have done. I thought of nothing helpful. If I had stayed calm, practicing active listening, I would have appeared to be helpful and supportive. The whole family would appreciate my efforts, but I would be encouraging them to continue to collect petty grievances to dump on me when I visited. In their case, my active listening would not get them to change their behavior.

My internal turmoil only increased as I drove toward my house. I wasn't ready to face another human, not even Judy. I took a slight detour to Cortez Park. A walk couldn't resolve my doubts about my fitness as a probation officer, but it would help me burn off some adrenalin and calm down. I started along the canal path at a brisk pace. I started feeling better physically though my mind remained stuck in a futile attempt to figure out how I should have handled Ben and Albert . After a mile, I slowed down and reversed my direction. intentionally studying the surroundings to take my mind off my problem. Back at the park, I spotted two boys throwing something at a tree. By the time I got close, they were arguing. They looked to be about nine or ten years old.

The first words I could make out were: "No way. It's not my football."

The second voice was tearful. "You're the one who threw it. You gotta get it down."

"I tried. It didn't work."

"But my Dad will kill me."

"Sorry." The first boy turned and walked away.

"Come back!" The walking turned into a run. "I'm going to kill you if you don't come back..."

I approached the remaining boy as he stood with his quivering clenched fists and tears on his cheeks. "What's the problem?"

"My friend threw my football and it got caught in the tree and then he said he could knock it down with my shoes and he got them stuck too."

"We'll have to figure out another way to get them down."

"I'm going to be in trouble for coming late."

Looking up at the tree, I saw the shoes first near the outer branches. I spotted the football near the trunk about ten feet up. The mulberry tree had been stub-cut, so lots of thin branches radiated out from the trunk, none of them sturdy enough to climb on.

"I think you can reach it if you stand on my shoulders."

"I'll fall."

I was getting irritated by his whining tone. I resisted the temptation to walk away. "I won't let you fall. Just keep one hand on the tree trunk to steady yourself." I squatted under the tree. "Climb on, piggy back."

He complied, sitting on my shoulders. I stood. "Hold on to the trunk while I help you stand." I lifted one of his feet to rest on my shoulder, then the other, holding his calves as he wobbled to stand. "Can you reach the ball?"

"I think so."

I heard a satisfying thunk. "Now for the shoes."

"I can't reach them."

"Try shaking the branches with one hand."

His legs were wobbling and my shoulders were getting tired. I heard the shoes land. The boy's dismount was awkward. He started to fall sideways, requiring a quick reach around his chest to prevent a head-first landing. As I released him, he scrambled after his shoes before looking up at me. "Thanks, Mister."

"Glad to help." Getting a smile in return, I headed back to my car. The encounter had a miraculous effect on my spirit. It restored my faith in myself as a good, effective citizen.

The next day, I concluded my closing report on the Schultz case: "Ben and his father have reached a mutually acceptable pattern of coexistence. There is no indication that further services from a counselor or probation officer would be helpful. The case can be closed without court action."

Bert approved the report without comment. As long as Mr. Schultz didn't call, I was off the hook. As the days passed, my concern eased. Still, that final scene was never far from mind until Kate's case erupted with a new crisis.

Kate – Part II

For five weeks, the phone calls with Kate and the Hightowers remained blandly routine. Kate's comments were always short and guarded. To her, I was probably just another case worker filling out paperwork. To me, she was another kid that I hadn't been able to reach, a disappointing reminder of my limitations.

The dreaded weekend page came at the end of a beautiful Saturday. Judy and I had spent the afternoon at a spring training game; the Giants beat the Cubs 6 to 4, so I was in a particularly good mood as we spent the evening listening to music and reading. I had just gotten in bed when the dispatcher rang. "I'm sorry to bother you on a Saturday night, but a girl named Kate is asking for you. She sounds drunk."

"Oh boy. Put her through."

"Come get me. I need help. Please." Kate whined rapid-fire, in an unnaturally high-pitched voice.

My body reacted to her panic with a rush of adrenaline. I needed to sound calm and not feed her hysteria. "Slow down. Where are you?"

"I'm at the Circle-K. Please hurry."

"Which Circle-K? What are the cross-streets?"

"Lower Buckeye Road and, uh, 157th." She slowed down, regaining a little control.

"Okay. Now tell me what happened."

"Some boys at the party tried to rape me but I got away and ran here."

"That's really serious. Are you alright? You don't sound good."

"I feel kind of sick. I took some pills at the party."

"What kind?" It was my turn to fight a sense of panic.

"I don't know. They were in a punch bowl. Everybody had to take some."

"Listen to me. You need help quick. It will take me an hour to reach you. You should call 911; they'll arrive in just a few minutes then I can meet you at the hospital."

"No!" She screamed. "If you call 911, they'll send cops."

"The cops will take you to an emergency room."

"No. No cops. I saw what they did to my mother. If I see a cop car coming, I'll hide in the fields and they'll never find me. I swear I'll do it."

"I believe you. I'll come as quick as I can. Hang tight."

"Hurry. Please. I'm scared."

"I'm on my way."

As I threw some clothes on, I told Judy, "Don't wait up this could take all night. I stretched the speed limits on both the Black Canyon Freeway and Buckeye Road. I had plenty to worry about in addition to watching out for cop cars. Would she be where she said she was? Would she be passed out before I got there? – Then I would have to call 911. If I did get to her, what would I do with her? I had no plan. Lower Buckeye Road was unlit and deserted. What if I encountered the thugs from the party or a couple of mean drunks. 11:30 on a Saturday night was not a safe time to be out here all alone. After I crossed 115th Avenue, the first set of lights belonged to a small bar with a bunch of motorcycles parked in front – not a reassuring sight. Finally reaching the isolated Circle-K, I spotted three men inside, the clerk and a couple of customers with beer cartons – no sign of Kate. I parked next to the phone booth on the side. It was less than forty-five minutes since the her phone call. I got out of the car and peered into the spooky darkness. A rustling sound drew my attention toward the rear. Kate staggered out of the darkness, her arms tightly folded over her stomach.

"Finally. I've been waiting forever. I'm cold." The night air was pleasantly cool, not cold enough to account for her shivering."

"Get in the car. I told you it would take a long time for me to get all the way out here."

"I know, I know."

I held the door open as she climbed in, closed it, walked around to my side and locked us in. "Fasten the seat belt." Kate fumbled unsuccessfully with the belt until I reached over and helped her click it.

"Boy, you are in really bad shape. I think we should head to the emergency room. Do you know where the nearest hospital is?"

"No. They'll call the cops."

"Every probation officer is a deputy sheriff, so that makes me a cop. So you are already in the custody of a cop."

"But you're different. I can trust you."

"I can't take you home in the condition you're in. If we don't go to a hospital, you have to go through withdrawal from the drugs cold turkey at the detention center. Is that what you really want?"

"Whooow... I don't know what to do; just no hospital and no more cops."

I was already driving east, toward the detention center.

"Do the Hightowers know where you were going?"

"No. They went out for their anniversary. They won't be back until after one."

"Is there a babysitter at home with Amy?"

Kate hesitated before answering. "No. I waited and made sure that Amy was asleep before I left. She'll be alright; she never wakes up during the night."

"So you left a five-year-old alone in their house."

"I'm sorry. I'm sorry." Kate broke down, sobbing. I kept quiet. After a minute, she spoke through her tears. "I really screwed up. Stefani and Amy trusted me. Now everybody'll hate me."

For the first time, I felt sympathy toward Kate, yet I could think of no appropriate words. We continued in an uncomfortable silence until she blurted out, "Aren't you going to say something? Lecture me on how bad I am or tell me I'm hopeless?"

"I don't think you are hopeless. You've gotten yourself into a real bad situation and I don't know what the solution is. Right now, I'm just trying to figure out how to get us through the night. I do know that you are a strong girl, and if you accept the punishment you've earned, you'll be able to turn things around in time. I'm not going to give up on you."

We had another mile of silence before reaching the detention center. Kate was shaking enough that I had to assist her in releasing the seat belt and getting out of the car. I held her elbow to support her walk to the door. The offices were locked at night; the only entrance was through a sally port, a bare concrete room with a set of lockers for police officers to stow their weapons and a Plexiglas window overlooking the dispatcher's desk at the far end. I held my badge and ID card up to the window.

The dispatcher spoke first. "Hello, Don. Is that the girl who called earlier?"

"Yes. I need to sign Kate Knowland in for violation of probation."

"She looks like she's high on drugs."

"She is."

"I can't admit her into the population in that condition. There won't be a nurse on duty until 7:00. You ought to take her to the County Hospital."

"They wouldn't accept her without a court order or legal guardian, neither of which is available. I figured that here I could at least stay with her in an interview room and talk without all that commotion around us."

"That makes sense, except the interview rooms are in the office wing. The best I can do is let you use the transient holding tank."

"That'll have to do. Can you keep an eye on her for a minute while I make a phone call."

"Sure." He buzzed me through.

I looked up Jeff Hightower in the phonebook and dialed, expecting to leave a message on their answering machine.

Jeff answered on the first ring, "Kate?"

"No, it's Don Gilbertson. Kate is with me at the detention center. I'm afraid that she went to a party and used some drugs."

"She was supposed to be watching Amy."

"I know. She told me. It's no excuse, but she said she waited until she was sure Amy was sound asleep before she left."

"Was she arrested?"

"No. She called me to pick her up."

"At least that's something. We thought we were doing fine together."

"You were. Kate was doing better with you than she had with the last foster parents."

"I guess we were naïve, thinking we could save her. I don't think we can take her back. I can't risk having drugs in the house, around Amy."

"I understand. I'm afraid Kate needs to be placed in a more restrictive program. She'll be staying in detention for now."

"I'm sorry."

"So am I. Bye."

The dispatcher had given Kate some water. I gratefully accepted the coffee he offered me when he handed me a manila envelope for her personal effects. I had Kate empty her pockets. That produced a partial pack of cigarettes, butane lighter, a house key, six dollars and thirty-seven cents. She confirmed that the key was the Hightowers, so I slipped it into my pocket while putting the rest of the stuff and her hoop earrings into the envelope. That done, the dispatcher buzzed us through and pointed out the door of the holding tank. The holding tank was a chilly, barren, dimly lit room with a door at each end and a metal bench seat built into each side wall.

"I'm cold." Kate's arms were crossed in front of her, hugging her shoulders.

"So am I, but we're stuck in here until the drugs wear off. It's probably a good idea to keep walking around the room."

Kate complied. Over the next hour, I coaxed the details of the party out of her. I never found out the names of anyone or the address of the house. "I'm no snitch, and besides, if I tell anyone, they'll beat the shit out of me." Her fear was palpable. Fighting fatigue, I worked to maintain a calming tone of voice while Kate shuffled around the room, twitching and often looking off in the distance as though she were watching the scene she was describing.

A friend's boyfriend invited them to the party at school on Friday. For a five dollar charge, there would be plenty of beer and music. The girl friend picked up Kate and drove to the party. A bunch of kids were already there, mostly in the backyard where the kegs were. A big biker dude was collecting the money as people came in. For a while, they just hung out drinking beer and smoking cigarettes. Then they brought out the punchbowl of pills, some of the kids threw in extra pills, and everybody had to take some. That's when things got crazy. One girl was too stoned to stand up; she collapsed in giggles. Three of the jocks, they were wearing their football letter jackets, carried her inside. She was only wearing her panties when she came back out. The boys who weren't making out with their girl friends started going around feeling up the other girls. That's when Kate fled.

Sitting there watching Kate and hearing her tale was painful. I felt that I should do something to get those boys punished and the biker host thrown in prison, but at best, my report would serve as an investigative lead for some detective. I hadn't read Kate her Miranda rights, so whatever she said was inadmissible in court. I tried to ease the tension by shifting the questions to her life with the Hightowers. That didn't work for long. Relating a couple of interactions reminded her of how nice they had been to her which unleashed a torrent of anger directed at herself for blowing it with them. She ended that line of conversation by stating, "I need a cigarette."

"Sorry. I can't let you have anything but water."

"I'm thirsty."

I opened the door and requested some water. The dispatcher handed me two paper cups. Kate drained them both, then asked if she could sit down for awhile. I assented and sat in the middle of one of the benches. Kate picked a spot about eighteen inches away. We sat in silence, Kate looking at the floor and me watching her.

After a long ten minutes, she jerked and screamed, "Get them off of me! Help me."

I didn't see anything except her frenzied scratching at her arms and legs. I brushed my hands down her arms. Nothing was on them, but her muscles were incredibly taut. "I don't see anything."

"Bugs are crawling all over me. They're crawling under my skin."

"That's not bugs. It's withdrawal from the drugs. Hold my hands." I slid closer to her and held out my hands, palms up. She grabbed my wrists and I held on to hers. After a moment, she tried to jerk her hands free.

"Yeow. They're in my neck. Let me go; I have to get them out."

"I'm not going to let you hurt yourself worse. Look me in the eyes and hang on." I was close to panic myself. Kate locked onto my wrists with a death grip. Her face was frozen in a grimace while tears seeped down her cheeks. I whispered, "This is the worst part. We'll get through it. You'll get better." I repeated the words as a mantra. That seemed to have a soothing effect. Her grip remained tight, but her fingernails no longer dug into my flesh. A strange sense of intimacy emerged while we sat there, looking into each other's eyes. She seemed so vulnerable, her anguish so transparent. There was no sign of the tough teenager I had known; Kate was a frightened little girl who needed comforting. Nothing I could do or say would make the withdrawal pain dissipate any faster. We fell back into silence.

I have no idea of how much time passed before she spoke. "It still hurts, but not so bad. It's so quiet, it's spooky. Say something."

"I don't know what to say. Maybe singing would help pass the time. Do you like the Beatles?"

"Yes."

I started with "Hey Jude." It was a poor rendition, but her grip relaxed. Not surprisingly, the next tune that came to mind was "With a Little Help From My Friends". "What would you do if I sang out of tune..." actually brought a small, tight smile to Kate's lips. Together we went through "Let It Be" a couple of times.

She whispered, "I have to go to the bathroom."

"Okay."

I opened the door and we walked across the lobby. Kate was steady on her feet. "I'll wait for you at the door."

"Thanks." When she went in the Ladies' room, I looked at my watch. It was 6:15.

The dispatcher had watched us cross the room. "Looks like she's sober now."

"Yeah, I think she's alright."

"I'll let you sign her in now." He held out a clipboard with the forms.

"Thanks."

When Kate came out, I asked, "How do you feel?"

"Much better. I'm just tired and hungry."

"They'll feed you breakfast in about an hour, then you can get some sleep. In the meanwhile, the matron will get you processed in, with a shower and a jumpsuit."

"Those things are ugly."

"Get over it!"

A female guard appeared and led Kate back into the detention wing. The dispatcher offered me a cup of coffee while I completed the paperwork. "Thanks, I needed that."

"No problem."

As I drove home through the quiet Sunday morning streets, I thought of little other than how peaceful it felt outside. I got home a little after 8:00.

Judy was sitting in the kitchen with a cup of coffee. "You look awful. Can I pour you a cup?"

"No thanks. I need sleep." I leaned over and kissed her. "I hope I never again have to sit with someone going through drug withdrawal. I took all night. She's going to be alright. I'm totally exhausted."

"Is there anything I can do?"

"Not really." I took a quick shower then slept until almost supper time.

I woke to the aroma of sausages and tomato sauce. The table was set, including a tossed salad and a bottle of the good wine we got for Christmas. When I sat down, Judy served a hearty plate of spaghetti and garlic toast.

"How are you feeling?"

"Much better." I quoted Carroll, "The time has come the Walrus said to speak of other things..."

Judy chatted about her day while we ate.

Kate's arraignment was scheduled for 10:00 on Monday morning, giving us plenty of time to talk before.

After ascertaining that she had gotten sufficient sleep and food, I went through the Miranda rights and the court room procedures.

Kate brought up the crux of her situation. "You're going to send me to Adobe Mountain, aren't you?"

"If you do get committed to the Department of Corrections, they'll probably keep you in Adobe Mountain for about seven months then move you to a halfway house for a few more months before moving you to a group home or foster care. I don't like that idea because it would mess up your schooling. You've always been a good student and that can be your path to success. I'm hoping to find a place you can stay until you finish high school. I can't make any promises, and it won't be a foster home with a room of your own. I haven't given up on you. I think you learned something this weekend."

"I won't screw up again. Promise."

"At least not big time. You're allowed a few minor screw ups, like smoking."

"You're not ever going to stop nagging me about cigarettes, are you?" She was smiling.

"Probably not."

"Thank you."

"For what? Nagging you?"

"For coming to get me. You really do care." I counted that statement as a major breakthrough.

"That's right. Now it's time to face the judge."

"I'm ready."

The arraignment was routine. Kate plead guilty to violating her probation. The disposition hearing was scheduled for a week from Thursday, which not coincidently was the next scheduled pick-up date for the Department of Corrections bus.

Our secretary flagged me down on the way to my office. Bert, my supervisor wanted to see me. I doubted that was good news. When I poked my head into his office, Bert said, "Come in. Have a seat. I read your report. You had quite am eventful weekend."

"Yes. It sure was unexpected."

"Were you aware that the standard procedure is to have a uniformed officer as back up when you have to take someone into custody?"

Here it comes. "Yes. My initial response was going to be a call to the Tolleson P.D., but she said she was watching the road from a field and would stay hidden if she saw a cop. Besides, I wasn't taking her into custody at that point. I was just responding to her request to meet her and to give her a ride. When I saw what shape she was in, I tried to get her to go to an emergency room. She refused, and since she could jump out of the car and escape at any time, I decided not to try to use force."

"I see. You took a big risk going out there alone."

"I know it! I was scared the whole time, but I couldn't think of any better alternative."

"So what do you plan to do with the case now?"

"Her foster parents won't take her back. I was going to recommend commitment to the Department of Corrections, but after talking to her this morning, I want to find a residential placement that will keep her through high school. She's always been a good student and she needs stability for a couple of years. That kind of rules out Adobe Mountain and the various drug rehab programs. Do you have any ideas?"

Bert paused for a moment. I wasn't sure whether he was thinking of a facility or trying to figure out a polite way of telling me I was off base. He finally said, "Girls Ranch in Scottsdale might take her. If they turn her down, I would recommend Adobe Mountain."

"Thanks. I'll give them a try. Anything else?"

"No."

As I was leaving, he added "That was really good casework, but don't do it again."

Talk about a mixed message. Good casework should be cause for a compliment. Instead, he seemed to prefer that I play it safe and not make any waves. I inferred that I couldn't count on his support if something ever went wrong.

The phone conversation with Mrs. Johnston at the Girls Ranch was much more satisfying. She sounded genuinely concerned for the long-term welfare of her charges. They did have an open bed at the moment, but she couldn't hold it open past the weekend. I rushed through the paper work, got Kate's disposition hearing moved up to Friday morning and delivered her to the Girls Ranch. Our final face-to-face conversation took place on the drive over.

"The first couple of months are going to be rough. You'll need to keep your long term goals in mind. I'm counting on you to tough it out."

"I won't let you down. You're the only one who's stood up for me."

"You're more than worth it."

The first monthly progress report from Mrs. Johnston was positive. Kate was adjusting well, only one minor infraction. A follow-up phone call gave me Kate's perspective.

"The house parents are nice. They just have too many stupid rules, like lights out at ten every night and waking you up at 6:30 in the morning, even on weekends."

"I told you it would be rough."

"Don't worry, I can handle it. I just like to bitch sometimes."

"Don't we all. Mrs. Johnston sent us a good progress report."

"She's tough, but not mean."

"Good. She's got to be tough to run that place. You can be tough and still like people and have fun."

"I guess so."

"Take care."

"You too. Bye." Kate gave me a big hug and left me standing there with my mouth open.

Numbers Game

Big John Murphy had been the Chief Probation Officer of the Juvenile Court for the past twenty-five years. He had started out as a night shift detention guard while attending college and rose through the ranks for another fifteen years before becoming the boss. He was a low-keyed boss. The few times that I saw him, his only comments were a few words of encouragement. He had already announced his pending retirement when the newspaper ran a feature decrying the number of escapes from the detention center. That article affected the Board of Supervisors' selection of his replacement.

Our new boss, Mike Miller, transferred from the Sheriff's Department where he had been the Captain in charge of the main jail. It wasn't actually a transfer. He had twenty years in law enforcement, so he retired from the force taking his pension in addition to his new civil service salary. His first day speech to all of us employees emphasized the need to improve our productivity and accountability. He did not give any hint about how case workers could become more productive, but I was pretty sure that increased accountability would mean more paperwork and less time meeting with each client.

After the speech was over, I heard nothing from the new boss disappeared from view for over a month. His attention was focused on the detention center, so it was business as usual for our group until mid-

February. The next communication from Mr. Miller arrive as memo read at our weekly staff meeting. Bert announced that in addition to our mileage, we would soon be reporting our daily activities on a standardized form to provide management with a better measure of how we spend our time. Each activity would have a point value based on the amount of time it normally required. We reacted with a chorus of groans and grumbles about being too busy already.

"This project will document how big our workload is, providing evidence that may support a budget request for additional staff." He failed to add, 'And if you believe that, I can sell you the Brooklyn Bridge.'

"Who decided how many points each activity is worth?" I asked.

"That's the good news. A committee of employees will meet with the accountant to determine the list of activities and their point values. We need a volunteer from our unit."

We all looked around the room. Not a single hand went up.

"Come on guys. Somebody has to do this."

Dead silence.

"Don, weren't you a Math major?"

"Well, yes, but ..."

"That settles it. You're our volunteer."

"Gee, thanks." I was stuck on the committee. Everyone else looked relieved.

The first meeting brought together eight unhappy probation officers and one enthusiastic accountant. At least it was a short meeting. The accountant was well prepared. He had spent a week observing and timing the staff at work, which was the basis of the draft form he handed out. The first two columns listed names of activities and the number of points assigned to it. Each point represented fifteen minutes of applied time, "just like the way lawyers track their billable hours." The remaining columns covered the days of the week and a total. Our assignment was to use the form for a week to validate it and suggest any improvements. I asked why there was no activity listed for filling out the time and mileage sheets, which I estimated would consume a half-hour each week. The accountant explained that the proper usage was to mark down each item as it happened, so there would be no separate time spent filling in forms at the end of the week. I concluded that they wanted a scorecard to pressure us to work harder rather than an accurate accounting of our time.

It was tempting to just go through the motions on this busy work assignment. Then my competitive spirit kicked in. If management wanted to play this game, I should play to win. I decided to record the full amount of time, including paperwork, involved in my intake sessions and initial contacts. Since our unit did more of these activities than the other field units, I wanted them rated highest. To be "just like the way lawyers track," I rounded each activity up to the next fifteen-minute interval, which resulted in significantly higher point values than the draft.

On the other hand, by combining three home visits to the same part of town into one trip, they took up much less time than allotted by the draft, which was based on two points for travel and two for the actual visit. At the end of the week, I left out enough phone contacts so that my activity sheet reported at total of forty-two hours, so it did not appear to be padded.

When the committee reconvened, the other probation officers were lethargic. I was loaded for bear. The accountant started off cheerfully. "I hope you found using the form wasn't so bad." Most of the group nodded reluctantly.

I spoke up. "The form is easy to use, but I ran into some issues in the point values."

"How so, exactly?" The accountant's demeanor jumped from friendly to defensive.

I explained how the three afternoon home visits to the same area took much less than the allotted time because of the reduced travel."

The accountant smiled. "That is a good thing. We want to reward efficient use of your time."

One of the other officers spoke up. "But I have one client in a foster home in Gila Bend. It takes an hour just to drive there, so I should get more points for that trip."

"You should plan your visits so that you meet other clients on the way back. Besides, you probably have other visits that take less than an hour. The form would be too complicated if we tried to take all of the special cases into account. We need to have the points reflect the average amount of time. So, we will leave it as is." He was aiming for a rubber stamp approval, and most of the group seemed willing to grant it and get back to work.

"I have a couple of more issues. The time allotted for preparing a pre-disposition report seems too short by an hour."

"The number on the form is based on the five cases where I timed senior officers including their dictation. Maybe you'll get faster with experience."

"Did your times include correcting the draft that came back from the steno pool and reviewing the final report before the hearing?"

"Well, no." I got three points added.

When I started in on the points for an Intake Interview, several of the other officers groaned. Extending the meeting was not a popular move. Still I got another two points added for Intake Interview and one point added to Staff Meeting before the revised form was unanimously approved.

The formal announcement of the Activity Reporting Form (ARF) evoked a spontaneously chorus of disdain. Bert cut off the grumbling without enthusiasm. "Griping isn't going to change anything. Just suck it up and fill in the forms."

A month later, our staff meeting started with a summary of the results of the first four weeks of activity reporting. Our unit came out as the most productive with an average of forty-six hours of credits per week. The department average was thirty-seven. I quietly smirked while Bert said that it proved that we were the hardest working group in the building and deserved to be congratulated for our dedication. I don't think he, or anyone else, realized the size of my contribution to those results. Bert also commented that the supervisors of underperforming units were under a lot of pressure to increase their productivity and keep better track of how their staff used their time.

Our big lead did not last long. By the third month, every officer was reporting enough activity to exceed forty hours each week. Since there was no increase in our actual case loads, I figured the numbers only reflected a learning curve as the employees figured out how to play the numbers game. In any case, the County Board of Supervisors passed a budget with no increase in staffing for the Juvenile Probation Department and coincidently the Activity Reporting Form was quietly discontinued.

Frankie – Part III

The first six weeks of Frankie's stay at Rainbow Acres has passed quickly for. I had plenty of other cases to worry about. The Foster Placement Coordinator was responsible for all the routine communication with the group homes, so I wasn't required to maintain contact. When I saw "Visit Frankie" on my calendar, I had second thoughts about giving up my Sunday afternoon for work. The department didn't offer overtime pay or comp time off, and I definitely wanted more down time to relax, but I had told Frankie that I would come, and besides I was still worried about him.

Mrs. Dalhart greeted me in the parking lot. She praised Frankie to the high heavens. "Frankie is such a sweet boy. He is really kind to the younger children. He does all of his assigned chores without any complaints and volunteers to help care for the animals. On top of all that, Frankie has a knack for fixing things. Our maintenance man is taking him under his wing."

That all sounded great, but she hadn't mentioned school or his happiness. I asked where I could meet him. She directed me to the second cottage on the left.

Five boys were sitting in the living room when I entered the cottage. Frankie had put on a little weight, but was still slim. He looked up and smiled. "Mr. Gilbertson."

"Hello, Frankie. How are you doing?"

"Fine. Do you want to see my room?"

"Sure."

He led me down the hall to a room that reminded me of my freshman dorm room. Split down the middle, each side had a twin bed, a desk, dresser and a door-less closet. The main difference, was that this room wasn't cluttered. I told him, "It looks neat. Aunt Bess told me good things about you. She is obviously proud of you."

He was beaming. "I knew you would come and see me."

That removed any regrets I had about giving up part of my day off. "How are you doing in school?"

"I'm getting mostly C's and B's. The math is harder than my old school, but the teachers are nicer and Uncle John helps us with our homework."

"You look happy."

"I am."

Another boy poked his head in the door. "Come on, Frank. We're leaving for the game."

"OK." Turning back to me, "We have a kickball game against Cottage 4. I'm not very good, so you don't have to stay and watch."

"Then I think I'll go home and get my yard work done. I glad I got to see you again."

"I gotta go now. Bye."

He ran out with the other kids. I drove home, feeling confident that we had done the right thing for Frankie. He was in a good place, mentally and physically. I was proud of myself. The only cloud on the horizon was the fact that some day he would have to return to his home and Nora. That was at least a couple of years away.

Frankie was still living at Rainbow Acres when I left the probation department for greener pastures. I sent him a Christmas card, but heard nothing back.

One Saturday morning six years later, the phone rang while I was making pancakes for our family breakfast. (The kids especially liked my letter-shaped pancakes that spelled their names.) My wife answered and handed me the phone.

"Are you the Mr. Gilbertson that used to be a Probation Officer?"

"Yes, but that was a long time ago."

"I'm Frank Duncan. Do you remember me?"

The image of a scrawny twelve-year-old popped into my mind; it didn't fit with the baritone voice I was hearing. "Of course. How are you doing?"

"I'm homeless. I need a hundred dollars. Can you help me?"

His plea generated a turmoil of conflicting thoughts: I was glad to hear from him, but irritated by the intrusion into my family's weekend. My curiosity was aroused. What had he been doing since I last saw him. More than anything else, though, I cared about him. Each of the kids I struggled with had somehow found a special place in my heart. After all this time, he might have hardened and just be attempting to get money for drugs. If was it a real crisis, one hundred dollars wouldn't go very far. I felt obligated to do something. "A hundred dollars is a lot of money. I'd like to help, but we need to talk first."

"OK. I'm calling from the Circle K near my mother's house."

"I can meet you at the Burger King at 27th Avenue and Bethany Home Road in half an hour."

"That works for me."

"See you there. Good-bye"

"Bye."

As I pulled up to the Burger King, I spotted at a couple of teenagers dressed in jeans and T-shirts with backpacks and a battered suit case. They were sharing a cigarette. The boy was tall and skinny with short brown hair and sharp features. The freckles had faded, but he was still recognizable as Frankie. The girl was fairly short and well-built with shoulder-length blonde hair.

"Good morning, Frank."

"Hi. This is my fiancé, Cyndi."

"I'm glad to meet you." That wasn't true. This was a major complication. They were too young and unsettled to be getting married. I had second thoughts about my agreeing to get involved. "Let's get something to eat while we talk."

Frank toted their bags to a booth in the corner while Cyndi and I went to the counter. She ordered two breakfast sandwiches with large cokes; I added a coffee for myself and paid the bill. We joined Frank at the booth.

Frank was holding a folded paper. "Cyndi's uncle owns a furniture company in North Carolina. He offered me a job making chairs if I can get there. I've been working at a restaurant and saving money. I had almost enough, but when I went to get my pay yesterday it was locked up and I couldn't get my money so now I'm homeless. Mom said she didn't have any money to lend me and wouldn't let Cyndi stay at her house, so we slept in the bushes last night. That's why I need money for a bus ticket. That's the truth. You can read the letter." The story spilled out without surprisingly little emotion.

I decided that he needed somebody to believe in him at least as much as he needed money. "I don't need to see the letter. I trust you, and I'll help you with the bus ticket."

They both lit up. Cyndi repeating, "Thank you, thank you, thank you." Frankie just said, "Really? Wow!"

Our number was called by the girl behind the counter. Cyndi went to fetch the sandwiches and add ketchup. I continued the conversation.

"It's been a long time since I've seen you. I want to hear what you've been up to. How long did you stay at Rainbow Acres.?"

"I really liked it there. They let me stay until I was almost sixteen. I was the oldest kid there. They sent me to Voc Tech for carpentry. The math and English classes were hard, but shop was fun. I wish I could have stayed until I finished high school."

"You always were good at woodworking."

"Just before my sixteenth birthday, they sent me home and I had to transfer to Phoenix Tech. I didn't have any friends there until I met Cyndi. After that, I liked it." She leaned over and kissed him.

"How did you get along with your parents?"

"I got a job bagging groceries after school. So I had enough money to pay for my food and to buy my own cigarettes. I hung out with Cyndi on the Saturdays, so Nora couldn't gripe too much. Mom said she was responsible for me until I was eighteen, but then I was on my own."

"That matches the law."

"Yeah, but I had to move out three months before graduation. I moved in with my friend Jeff. I wasn't making enough to pay my share of the rent, so he got me a job as the dishwasher at Hernando's where he was a cook. They paid in cash every week, but I had to drop out of school. I did pass the test and got my GED."

"That's good."

Cyndi took over. "My parents don't like Frank. They tried to make us break up, but it didn't work. They blamed him for my smoking, but I'm the one who got him to smoke. One night, they locked me out when I came home after midnight, so I moved in with Frank. That's when we started planning to get married. I called Uncle Bill to see if we could live with him. He said we could stay in their trailer if Frank went to work for him. So, that's what we are going to do. Frank is going to work at the factory and I'm going to babysit during the day. I love little kids. As soon as we have enough money, I'm going to have my own baby."

It didn't sound like a good plan. I doubted that parents would trust leaving their children at a trailer with such a young girl all day. But, I didn't have a good alternative to offer, so I kept quiet.

Frank spoke next. "We almost had enough money saved. This week's pay would be enough, so I told Jeff to get a new roommate. We moved out yesterday and went down to get my money. Hernando's was all locked up. A sign on the door said it was seized by the State for back taxes. There was a phone number, so I called to try to get my pay. The man who answered, said they had all the records and they didn't list me as an employee. Besides, they hadn't paid any Social Security taxes even though they had deducted it from the pay checks of the people who were employees. So, me and Jeff are both stuck. I can't even sue them."

"You really got the shaft. Even with a job, it is hard starting out."

"I know. I'm going to work really hard and we'll eat mostly ramen for dinner. I've done that before. Cyndi and me will do anything to be together."

"I wish you luck, and hope to hear good news from you."

We left. I took two hundred dollars out of my bank's ATM and drove them to the bus station. Frank pulled out a wad of bills and I handed him the stack of twenties. He got two tickets for Greensboro on a bus leaving in ten minutes. He had needed ninety-five dollars of mine, and started to hand back the rest. "I only needed one hundred, like I told you."

"I know what you had asked for. I also know that Hernando's should have paid you more than two hundred a week and you'll need some money for food on the road and to get started in North Carolina."

"Thank you. I'll pay you back."

"No need. When you become successful, I'm sure that you will repay the favor by helping someone else in need. Good-bye and safe journey."

We shook hands and Cyndi gave me a big hug. Then they were gone.

This isn't a fairy tale. I know the odds are against them having a happy and successful marriage. Still, I had given then a chance that was better than joining the homeless of Phoenix. I figure that was worth the two hundred dollar investment.

I realized too late that we had not exchanged addresses, so I doubt I will ever find out what happened to Frank. I only hope that they have finally beaten the odds.

Tyrone - Part I

"Ugh, not another truancy case from the inner city." I muttered as I read the referral. This one was only ten years old, in fifth grade. You would think that at that age, his parents could see that he got to school every morning. At least these parents responded to the citation and referral letter by making an appointment instead of being subpoenaed into court.

The complaint from Bethune School provided only minimal information. Tyrone Brown was the son of John and Luci Brown. The address was in the Matthew Henson Projects. Tyrone had twenty-three absences. Four were excused. Fifteen of the unexcused absences occurred in the last month. I'd have to dig into what had happened recently.

It was easy to pick out Tyrone in the waiting room. He was the only person there under five feet tall. He was a skinny little fellow with a complexion the color of milk chocolate and wearing a short sleeve white shirt. He was sitting between a short, plump lady and a gaunt black man with a walker in front of him.

After the introductions and procedural explanations, I settled Mr. and Mrs. Brown in the interview room. Mrs. Brown started in, "I don't know what's got into Tyrone. We keep telling him how important school is. We make sure he leaves for school on time every morning. I don't know what else we can do. His friends are leading him astray. We'd move to a better neighborhood if we could, but we don't have enough money." Anxiety permeated her voice and posture. I couldn't tell whether it was founded on fear of the court or concern for her son.

"I'm sure that you are trying to do what's best for Tyrone. These problems are usually complicated. Before I can offer any suggestions, I need to have a better understanding of Tyrone's background."

Mr. Brown answered in a soft, calm voice. "Tyrone was born in the Philippines while I was stationed at Subic Bay. We were married by then so he is an American citizen." He paused in response to his wife's glare. "Now don't get the wrong idea. It weren't no shotgun marriage. We were engaged before, er, well you know. Enlisted men had to get permission before we could marry a local. I had done all the paperwork and we kind of celebrated when it was approved."

"I understand."

"Anyway, we moved here when my enlistment was up because of all the construction. I got a good job with the pipe fitters union. By the time Tyrone started first grade, I had saved up enough for a down payment on a house, nothing fancy, but it was ours. Everything was going great until the accident."

"What kind of accident?"

"Car wreck." He whispered.

His wife explained, "He had drinks with his buddies after work on Fridays. One night he hit another car on the way home, messed up his back real bad. That's why he needs a walker." She sounded worried that I would be judgmental, but my college drinking experiences made me sympathetic.

"When did that happen?"

"Almost three years ago. I haven't had a drink since. I spent three months in the hospital and couldn't go back to work. The doctor bills drove us into bankruptcy. Luci has diabetes and a weak heart, so she can't hold a job either. That's why we're stuck living on disability."

"That's rough. Is this Tyrone's first year at Bethune School?"

"No. He started in fourth grade and was doing alright until recently."

"Can you think of anything that changed at home or school?"

They looked at each other and shook their heads.

"What's he like at home?"

Mrs. Brown brightened up. "He's just the best little helper. He does the dishes every night and he takes out the garbage and does the vacuuming and helps me with the laundry. I couldn't ask for a sweeter baby."

Her response established two things in my mind. One, she loved her child, and two, I couldn't count on her to provide the discipline that he needed. As the conversation continued, it became clear that both parents were essentially passive. Their lives consisted mainly of watching television between meals and sleeping. I would need to try to get Tyrone connected with a more positive adult influence. The case seemed headed for long term probation.

My interview with Tyrone got off to a bad start. He kept squirming while I read and explained his Miranda rights. As soon as I finished, he blurted out, "Why do I have to go to school, anyway?"

"To start with, the law requires that you attend school until you are at least sixteen years old. But mainly because you need a high school diploma for most jobs. You'll make a lot more money if you stay in school at least that long."

"Reggie's cousin makes lots of money and he didn't go to high school."

"Who's Reggie?"

"He's my best friend."

"And what kind of job does his cousin have?"

"I don't know, but he drives a new Cadillac convertible and has lots of money."

I jumped to the conclusion that this cousin was a pimp or drug dealer, definitely not a positive male role model. That was an ugly complication that I'd have to probe into later, carefully. First I needed to get a handle on his school problems. "So, why don't you like school? Is it too hard for you?"

"No. It's not hard; it's boring. I'm not stupid." His tone had switched from argumentative to belligerent. I was losing ground.

"I'm glad that you can handle the work. Are the other kids a problem?"

"No. I can take care of myself."

"Okay. So, tell me about your teacher."

"She's mean. She yells at me to be quiet and keep still. She doesn't let us do anything except sit at our desks and fill in stupid worksheets." He was back to squirming in his chair.

"You're full of energy and don't like to sit still, do you?"

"That's right."

Getting that agreement did not point to a positive path forward, so I shifted gears again. "How are things at home?"

"Okay." As I sat quietly looking at him, Tyrone's squirming increased. He didn't let the silence last long. "It was better before my daddy got hurt. Momma really loves me. She has diabetes, so she needs my help. It's not our fault we have so much bad luck."

"When I talked with them, it was clear that they love you and are trying to do what's best. Still, it must be rough on you."

He stiffened. "I can handle it."

"So, you want to keep living at home?"

"Of course. They need me."

"What they want most is to be proud of you. They need for you to stay out of trouble. As much as they want you and you want them, if you don't stay in school, you will be taken from them and put in foster care."

"I don't want no foster parents. I'll run away."

"Then the court would place you in a secure, locked institution. It's not nice, but that's the way the system works."

Tyrone glared at me, obviously scared.

I continued, "There are lots of things that are worse than having to do worksheets in the school."

"I'll be good. I really mean it. I promise."

"We'll try it. You have one last chance. It won't be easy because you've already missed so much."

"I can handle it."

"Good. We'll go over the deal with your parents."

I spend the last portion of our session laying down the law to the whole family. Tyrone would be scheduled for a formal adjudication hearing in thirty days. For everybody's sake, Tyrone would have to attend every day of school and do all of his assigned work. If he was too sick to go, they needed to call me by 9:00am and I would come by to check. I would also be checking with the school. If that didn't happen, Tyrone would be placed in foster care. Mrs. Brown started sobbing at the thought of losing her son. I hated making the threat. I much preferred to end with a message of hope, but Tyrone's attitude and comments had led me to belief that a hard line was necessary. It was one of the rare cases where I felt sorry for the parents. They seemed kindly and caring, but weak. I did suggest getting Tyrone enrolled in the Boys and Girls Club so he would have a positive activity after school. Tyrone responded, "Only wimps go there." This further reduced the prospect of a successful probation experience. Writing my notes up in the case file only deepened my pessimism.

The next morning, I met with the principal at Bethune School, Mrs. Robbins, in her cluttered office. The energetic black woman with a trace of gray in her hair greeted me with a warm smile. She accepted my card and agreed to have me notified whenever Tyrone was absent. The exchange was pleasant, so I openly asked for her help. "I didn't get much information from my meeting with Tyrone and his parents. I'm hoping you can provide me with some insight."

"Tyrone is one of those boys who is trying to be an adult too soon. He puts on a big front and won't accept any criticism because inside he's very insecure. His parents have serious health problems and Tyrone thinks he has to take care of them."

"I picked up on that attitude. What's he like in school?"

"She looked down at the file on her desk. "He's only been with us for two years. He is certainly capable of doing the work. He has a tested IQ of 108 and does adequately on the standard tests. Until this winter, the only problem was lack of attention in class. We had him tested for ADD, but the report was negative. The psychologist ascribed his behavior problems to anxiety about his family and a lack of structure at home."

"That makes sense. Do you know of any change that might have let to his truancy?"

"I don't like to blame another student, but he has become close friends with the class cut-up."

"Reggie?"

"Yes. About half of Tyrone's absences have been on days that Reggie was also absent."

"One thing that Tyrone said raised a red flag in my mind. He said that Reggie's cousin was rich and drove a new Cadillac convertible."

"I can't comment about another student's family, but a new Cadillac should raise a red flag. In this neighborhood, all the crack dealers drive Cadillacs, and they like to recruit young boys as couriers. Little kids don't arouse as much suspicion."

"I was afraid of that, but I can't act on it without hard evidence." The thought of how much my dad's dealership might be profiting from the drug traffic briefly disrupted my train of thought.

"I wish I could help you with that. We lose way too many boys to the streets." She glanced at here watch. "Do you have any other questions for me?"

I took the hint. "No. You have been most helpful Thank you."

Monday morning, I got a phone message from Mrs. Robbins about 11:00. Tyrone had not come back to class after recess. My stern lecture had been totally ineffective. She was apologetic and told me that she would increase his supervision to make sure that he didn't get another chance to sneak away from school. At least that meant that she hadn't given up on him yet. Searching for him was bound to be futile, so I ate my lunch before leaving to drive around the neighborhood. I spent close to an hour cruising the area near the school, checking out all of the playgrounds, markets and fast food places. As expected, I saw nobody Tyrone's size. My last stop was the Brown's apartment.

Mrs. Brown answered the door and invited me in. The front room was crowded with shabby furniture. The television was tuned to a soap opera. Mr. Brown looked up from his recliner. "The school already called. He's not here."

"Do you know where his friend Reggie lives?"

They looked at each other and shook their heads. "We don't know where he goes when he's not home. He doesn't talk much." Mrs. Brown sounded defeated.

Mr. Brown came to her defense. "She went to the bus stop and waited for him to get on. What more can she do?"

"I would say that you did the right thing. But, I am afraid that he may be getting involved in something more serious than just skipping school." I was trying to prepare them for a foster placement.

"Life in the projects is dangerous, but we don't have a choice. Tyrone is getting money from somewhere. He says he gets it by washing cars, but I don't know." Mr. Brown shook his head as he spoke.

"He may need to be in a different environment for a while so he can establish better habits." I was thinking about Rainbow Acres.

Mrs. Brown gasped. Mr. Brown said, "That may be for the best for him. It will be hard for us while he's away."

We were interrupted by the ringing phone. Mrs. Brown pick it up. "Yes, I'm his mother." Her facial expression while she listened led me to assume that someone had caught Tyrone. "Well, his probation officer is here right now." She handed me the phone saying, "The policeman wants to talk to you."

"The is Don Gilbertson. I'm Tyrone's probation officer."

"This is Sergeant Morris. Tyrone was stopped after he ran from an approaching officer. The officer saw him throw an envelope down a storm drain. I'm sure it was drugs, but he claims it was a candy wrapper. We'd like to have him held in detention to see if he will identify his supplier."

"I you are probably right, but he so far he has only been cited for truancy and he hasn't been to court yet, so I can't hold him for probation violation. His parents have been completely cooperative, so unless you have evidence that he is a danger to himself or others, he doesn't fit the criteria for detention."

"We don't have anything that would hold up in court. So, what do you want to do."

"I'll come down to you substation with his parents. I'd like a copy of the police report which I'll use to fast track his arraignment for truancy."

"That's probably all you can do, but try to help us identify his supplier."

"I can give you a possible lead. He has mentioned that a cousin of his best friend, Reggie, has lots of money and drives a new Cadillac. The boys go to Bethune School. Maybe the school can provide you with Reggie's last name and address."

"Thank you."

Twenty minutes later, Tyrone was released into the custody of his parents and I had a copy of the police report. Tyrone clung quietly to his mother all the way back to their apartment. He looked like a scared toddler. I asked for a few minutes to talk with Tyrone alone. We entered his disheveled room and sat side-by-side on the bed.

"So, tell me about this thing in the police report about throwing something down the storm drain."

His demeanor changed to one of defiance. "I don't have to tell you nothing."

"Who told you that?"

"Reggie's cous..." He stopped himself in mid-word.

"He's right. You don't have to tell me anything. But I bet he didn't tell you that for juveniles the law provides the same punishment for truancy as for any other offense. What the judge decides will depend more on your attitude than on the official charge. Cooperating could help you in court."

He had shrunk back into being a scared little boy, muttering "Stitches for snitches. I can't tell you anything. I'm not a narc."

"I understand. It's dangerous to get mixed up with druggies. I had to ask as part of my job. I want you to be safe. I'm afraid of what will happen to you if you continue to hang out with Reggie's cousin." Tyrone nodded, so I continued, trying to soften his resistance to a probable foster placement without sounding like a threat. "We are going to have to make some changes. We will be going to court next week. I want you to cooperate with the judge. Your parents and I want to help you develop better habits that will keep you safe and help you succeed. I don't expect you to like everything that I do, but disobeying the rules will only make your life harder. Do you understand that?"

"Yeah." I wasn't sure whether that meant he understood or that he was just done listening. I had gained an understanding of Tyrone's dilemma. He was a scared little boy who believed that he needed to pretend that he was a tough adult.

It was still early enough in the afternoon to file the paperwork to needed to get on the court docket. Armed with the police report, I was able to get the arraignment hearing scheduled for late Wednesday morning. Since I had already done both home and school visits, there was enough time, barely, to prepare a complete pre-disposition report. The memory of Danny Donovan's drug related death haunted me. Even though I didn't have enough hard evidence to file a drug charge, his involvement seemed obvious. I was thoroughly convinced that it would be necessary to find a residential placement for Tyrone before he got in any deeper. Based on my experience with Frankie, I crossed my fingers and called Mrs. Dalhart at Rainbow Acres.

"Good afternoon. This is Don Gilbertson."

"Ah yes. Frankie's P.O. He is doing just fine."

"Actually, I'm calling about a different boy. Do you have an opening for a ten-year-old?"

"We do have one bed available, but I'm not sure for how long."

I explained Tyrone's situation and got the sympathetic response that I expected. She agreed to hold the bed for me until the weekend.

Greatly relieved, I called the Browns. Luci answered. I told her the schedule and explained the likely placement at Rainbow Acres.

Luci sobbed softly, "My poor little baby."

"I know this is hard for you. You love Tyrone and wish he could stay with you, but I'm afraid of what would happen if we don't get him away from the influence of Reggie and his cousin for a while. This placement will probably last a year and you'll be able to keep in touch with him. If he gets involved with drugs, we could lose him permanently."

"I know." The sobbing eased slightly. "Thank you."

The pain in her voice filled my gut with regret about my recommendation while my head remained sure that I had made the right decision. Somehow the pathetic thank-you stung the most.

"When you come to the court on Wednesday, please bring a suitcase or bag of Tyrone's clothes and a couple of favorite things in the car's trunk. That way, if the judge makes the placement, I can take him directly to the ranch and not keep him be locked in detention overnight. You should understand that my recommendation is not the final word. The judge may ask you if you agree with my recommendation. If you don't agree with me, you and your husband could ask that Tyrone stay with you while he is on probation. I know that you want to do what is best for Tyrone, so I want you to talk it over carefully before you come to the court."

"I'll do that."

"Okay. I'll see you on Wednesday."

That Wednesday was completely overcast with a danger of thunderstorms. The weather matched my mood when I learned that the sermonizing grouch would be hearing my case. I feared that Luci would have an emotional break-down and get a guilt inducing lecture.

When the Brown's arrived, I carefully worded my explanations of the procedures to prepare them to remain calm even if the judge sounded harsh, and reminded them that the judge was the one who had the final say over the disposition of the case. Then I asked, "Have you talked over my recommendation?"

Mr. Brown answered, "Yes."

"Can you accept my decision if the judge does?" I tried to phrase the question so that Tyrone wouldn't blame his parents for his being sent away.

"Yes. It is probably the best thing to do for now."

I spent our remaining few minutes presenting a positive picture of Rainbow Acres, emphasizing how nice the house parents are and that he would be going to a school that would give him a fresh start to do well. Tyrone wasn't buying what I was selling. He sat quietly sulking, mostly looking down at his fidgeting fingers.

The first phase of the hearing went smoothly. Tyrone plead guilty to the truancy charge and was declared a ward of the court. The hearing officer paused for a couple of minutes, scanning through the file.

"I see that the Probation Officer recommends that we proceed immediately with the disposition hearing." Addressing the parents, he continued, "Has Mr. Gilbertson discussed his recommendation with you?"

"Yes sir."

"Do you concur with his recommendation?"

"Yes sir. We wish he could stay home, ..." Mr. Brown's voice trailed off.

"According to this report, you are unable to properly take care of Tyrone because both of you have health problems. Is that so?"

Mrs. Brown's tears started flowing as her husband muttered, "I'm afraid so."

The hearing officer launched into one of his stern lectures chastising Tyrone for his disobedience and lack of respect toward the school, the law, society in general, his parents in particular. I watched Tyrone as his fidgeting stopped, replaced by tense stiffness, balled fists and clenched jaw. He was on the edge of an explosion as the lecture moved on to a warning that if he didn't mend his way, he would be locked up for a long time. I winched, thinking the judge had just destroyed all my efforts to creative a positive attitude toward going to Rainbow Acres.

We finally got to the official disposition. "The court hereby orders that you be placed on probation until your eighteenth birthday and that you be transported today and placed in the custody of Rainbow Acres."

Tyrone jumped out of his seat. "No! I won't go. They need me. I'll be good."

The gavel smacked. "Sit down young man. You are in contempt of court!"

Tyrone reacted to the hearing officer's shout by clutching his mother's skirt and wailing.

"Mr. Gilbertson, remove your client from my court room."

I jumped from my seat. "Yes sir." I made the only acceptable response, approached Tyrone cautiously and whispered, "Come, let's get out of here."

"Go with him, Honey." His mother placed his hand in mine.

As I led him out the side door, my face was red from embarrassment, his from hysteria. He kept repeating, "Let me go home. I want to go home," as we went down the long corridor to the detention area. When the door buzzed open, Tyrone jerked free from my hand. I grabbed him around the waist and swung him through the door, getting kicked while I tried to restrain his flailing arms. I informed a detention officer that Tyrone needed to be held only briefly, pending transportation. He grabbed one Tyrone's arms and helped me lead him into the padded observation room. I left him there and concentrated on composing myself as I walked back to meet with his parents. I stopped on the way to make a quick call to Aunt Bess Dalhart and let her know I would be delivering Tyrone.

Mr. Brown greeted me by apologizing for his son's behavior.

"No need. The Hearing Officer is the one who should be apologizing for his fearful threats." My quick reply was honest, but decidedly impolitic. I knew I should soften the tone. "The folks at Rainbow Acres are going to treat Tyrone well. It is a big change for him, so it will take some time for him to get used to it. I know those first few weeks before he is allowed visitors are going to be rough for you, but it is necessary."

He thanked me and handed over two shopping bags from the trunk of his car containing Tyrone's clothes and a Teddy Bear. I put them in the back seat of my car and drove around to the sally port of the detention wing to pick up Tyrone.

As soon as I entered the holding room, Tyrone blurted out, "I hate you." He was pacing the floor.

"I don't blame you. The judge made it sound pretty bad." I sat on the edge of the built in cot.

"You lied. You said I wouldn't have to go away for long. He said I was sent away until I'm eighteen. That's ten years."

"He said you would be on probation until you are eighteen. He didn't say how long you would be staying at Rainbow Acres, that depends on how well you do while you are there. Many of the kids only stay about a year, and if you are good for the first six weeks then your parents will be able to visit you there. I didn't lie to you; I just didn't explain the way probation works very well. The age eighteen is the longest it can last. Many kids get off probation earlier."

"I want to stay with my Momma."

"That's not possible right now. Sorry, but that's the way it is. Rainbow Acres is the nicest place I could find for you. The lady who runs the place, Aunt Bess, is really nice."

Tyrone settled down next to me. "What if the other kids don't like me?"

"It can be hard to make new friends, but if you are nice to them and give them a chance, they'll grow to like you. I have."

"Really?" He looked up at me. "Do you like me?"

"Yes. And I want to see you do well and be happy." After a moment of silence, I stated, "We ought to get started so we can get there in time for lunch."

"OK."

He followed me out meekly to the car. I had to remind him to fasten his seat belt. The first forty minutes of the drive were quiet except for the classical radio station playing symphonic music in the background. Tyrone broke the silence with the famous question, "Are we there yet?"

"Almost. About another five minutes."

Tyrone's fidgeting returned, increasing as we approached the ranch office.

Aunt Bess greeted us with her usual cheerfulness. She explained that the other children

were all at school. She would take Tyrone to see the
school and get registered after he ate lunch and ha
gotten settled into his room. She introduced us to
Uncle Bill, one of Tyrone's house parents. Uncle Bill
didn't look any older than me. Tyrone did not return
his broad smile; instead he looked him over warily,
trying to size him up. I shook hands all around and
left.

I was struck by sudden pangs of hunger that
demanded quick satisfaction. I stopped for a cheap
Taco Bell lunch -- My sack lunch would keep until
tomorrow. I drove back to the office under a dark
cloud. My relief at completing Tyrone's placement was
overwhelmed by the sadness of his family's situation.

Chris

Chris stopped pacing around the patio of Burger King. He had confirmed that the two jocks he was looking for were inside. He reached into the pocket of his camo jacket and brought the revolver out. He broke it open, checked the cylinder and snapped it closed. He stuck his hand back into the pocket and went in the door. He moved slowly toward the back table where two teens wearing their football letter sweaters were chatting over Cokes.

"Let Maria alone. Stop following her and calling her names!" Chris spoke in a soft, quivering voice,

"You talking about the new Mess-I-can girl?" "What's it to you?"

Chris pulled out the pistol and waved it in their general direction. "She's my sister ... and nobody's gonna mess with her. You understand?"

"Calm down. We were only joking with her." The sneers were gone from the boys faces.

"I'm not joking. Leave her alone!" His voice was loud and clear.

"It won't happen again."

"It'd better not." Chris put his hand back in his pocket and strode out past the stunned customers in silence. Once outside, he tried to look nonchalant as he headed north on 59th Avenue.

I was sitting in my cubicle in the detention center trying to finish up the paperwork before leaving for the weekend, when the intake clerk called, "You're going to have to stick around for a while. The Glendale Police is bringing in one of your boys for waving a gun at two teens. There were lots of witnesses."

"One of mine? Who?" I'm only supposed to be dealing with runaways and family problems. How did I get stuck with this, and on a Friday afternoon, to boot. Why can't I just go home and relax for the weekend?

"Chris Olsen."

"OK. I'll be here with the file."

I hung up and tried to picture Chris. He was one of the long-term foster placements I had inherited. I had only seen him once, at the get-acquainted home visit back in November. (Since then, just checked in with monthly phone calls – no problems to report.) He's a tall blond, six-three or six-four, on the slim side but not skinny. Seventeen-years old with a smooth Nordic face – I doubt he has started to shave.

I had scheduled the visit for the end of the day, saving mileage by stopping by on the way home. The foster home was a non-descript tract house, pale yellow with brown trim. The garage had been closed in. An old Ford station wagon sat in the driveway. The front lawn was closely mown with a single mulberry tree. A teenage girl answered the door.

"Alice is in the kitchen. She's expecting you."

The door opened directly into the living room: two long couches – one occupied by a sprawling boy with a book, a coffee table, a couple of lamps and a bookcase and television (off) against the opposite wall. Walking on back, I entered the family-room with a breakfast bar separating it from the kitchen. A middle-aged blond was in the kitchen with another teenaged girl.

"You must be the new case worker."

"Don Gilbertson – Here's my card. I'm glad to meet you."

"My husband will be home in about ten minutes. Chris and Tyrone's shift bagging groceries at Safeway ended at 5:00, so they should appear any moment. Katie can finish fixing supper while I show you around."

Alice led me into what had been the garage. It had been divided into a bathroom and two bedrooms, plus space for the original laundry stuff. The whole floor was covered with the same vinyl tile. The bedrooms were furnished like my old college dorm, pairs of identical twin beds, desks, dressers and a door-less closet. Unlike, my dorm rooms, the beds were made and nothing was lying on the floor. A Rolling Stones poster hung over one bed, the other side had a poster of the Thunderbirds aerial team and Air Force recruiting poster – that had to be Luke's bed. Alice talked while I looked around. No need for me to ask questions; an occasional "Umm" was enough to keep her going.

"Chris is a really good kid. When he first came to us, he was withdrawn and avoided the other kids, but he hit it off with my husband right away. He would follow Tom around anywhere. He never caused any trouble and did his chores without complaining, but it took him a long time to warm up to the rest of us. He talks about how he still misses his Mom and Dad, but avoids saying anything about his other foster homes. I don't press them, but I know most of our kids have been through things they would rather forget. It has to be hard for them to learn to trust anyone."

"Umm." What is she aiming at? Is he really that good, so is there some dark side she doesn't want to discuss?

"The other kids look up to Chris. He is always willing to help them and he has his life planned out. He gets good grades. He has to study a lot, but he manages a part-time job for 15 hours a week. He puts most of his money into a savings account. He is going to join the Air

Force and then use the G.I. scholarship money to become an electrical engineer. It is lucky that he will graduate before his eighteenth birthday. The County cuts them off the day they turn eighteen – no foster payments, no insurance, nothing. Melissa's birthday is next week. We are going to keep her here as a guest until the end of the semester. After that, she'll be on her own. Her boss at the mall is happy to have her work full time, which means she'll have to go to night classes to get her diploma. It stinks, but that is the best we can do. We are trying to find her a decent place that she can afford with a roommate."

Aha! She's telling me how good she is the good guy and the bureaucrats are the bad guy. I'm tempted to join the gripe session about the system, but I'd better stay professional. So, I simply respond: "Umm."

"Tom and I always wanted a big family, but after Katie was born, the doctor said I couldn't have any more. When she entered kindergarten, we became foster parents for the Welfare Department. We started off with two kids, but it seemed like as soon as a child got settled down and saw us as family, the case worker would take them back to a relative. It broke my heart each time we had to give one up. After five years, I had to quit. Tom and I volunteered as youth leaders at our church instead. When one of the boys was orphaned, we felt we had to take him in. We were still licensed, so we got custody. He lived with us for nearly four years before he moved out for college. He still celebrates most of the holidays with us. After that, we decided we had a calling to help teenagers who weren't going to be yanked away every few months. So we remodeled the garage so we can handle the six maximum kids the foster license allows. I hear that some foster parents are in it for the money, but I don't know how that can be. The payments don't cover the costs. Tom has a good job with some flexibility in his schedule, or we couldn't do this. We love these kids and once you see them blossom like Chris has, we wouldn't have it any other way."

"Umm." She sounds sincere and caring. I'm searching for the right level of compliment when we heard a car pulling into the driveway.

"Tom's home."

Back to the living room. Tom is wearing a crisp white shirt and tie. He's an insurance agent and looks the part. Two teenagers have come in with him, so after introductions all around, Chris and I sit down and the others disappear into the back of the house.

"So you're my new case worker."

"That's right. Here's my card so you can call me if you ever feel the need. I've been hearing nothing but good things about you."

"I won't be calling you. Tom and Alice give me all the help I need. Everything is fine."

"School?"

"I'm getting an A in math and B's in everything else. I like it here, but I'm ready to take care of myself. As soon as I graduate, I'm joining the Air Force."

"It sounds like you have a good plan. So, I'll just give you a quick call once a month."

Alice entered the room. "Time for dinner," turning towards me, "You're welcome to join us. There's always room for one more at the table."

The tabletop was a plain door with big bowls of mashed potatoes and green beans, a platter of meatloaf plus ketchup, a loaf of bread and a tub of margarine.

"Thank you, but my wife is expecting me. It's been a pleasure." It was actually tempting to accept the invitation, but my wife had been home alone all day and would be waiting to talk over supper/

As of the last monthly call, Chris was just ten weeks away from graduation. He told me he had already met with an Air Force recruiter and scored well enough to enlist with a guarantee of training as an electronics specialist. It all sounded good. Less than six months until his eighteenth birthday – Assault with Deadly Weapon would probably get him remanded to stand trial as an adult. It didn't make sense; or had I misjudged the situation so badly?

Maybe I had missed something in the file. Time to review it again: Parents died in a car crash when he was twelve. No will. Only living relative, an uncle in Chicago, wouldn't accept custody, so the Department of Welfare placed in a foster home as a dependent child. Ran away after a couple of months. Moved to a different foster home. Ran away from there twice, claiming that the other boy in the home kept stealing his stuff and beat him up. Three strikes – that was enough for the case worker to turn him over to the Juvenile Court as an incorrigible. The court placed him in another foster home with Tom and Alice Woods. He's been there nearly four years and all the progress reports are brief and positive. Absolutely no history of violence or fighting.

When the call comes from Intake, I head down with the file and get a copy of the police report. Chris is locked in an interview room, so I just give it a quick read. The Burger King manager had called when he spotted a teenager loitering outside with a gun. A responding unit stopped a boy who matched the description less than a block away. The suspect offered no resistance when he was frisked. The officer found a Smith & Wesson .32 caliber revolver in the suspect's coat pocket and read him the Miranda Rights. The weapon was empty. No ammunition or other weapons were on the suspect. The only other item in his possession was a wallet with thirteen dollars, a driver's license and Glendale High School ID identifying the suspect as a juvenile named Chris Olsen, a picture of a girl and a business card from the Juvenile Probation Office. The suspect was cuffed, placed in the patrol car and driven to the Burger King parking lot. There the manager made a positive ID and described the incident in the store. The victims had left, but the officers got the names of four other witnesses. The suspect confirmed the manager's account, stating he didn't want to hurt anyone, only to scare them. The suspect said that a friend had let him borrow the gun, but refused to identify the friend. A check of the serial number had shown that the gun was registered to a Phoenix police officer who lived in Glendale and had a teenaged son. The charges were listed a simple assault and "exhibiting a fire arm other than in self-defense" – both misdemeanors. No felony meant the jurisdiction would stay in Juvenile Court. Maybe it isn't hopeless.

I entered the interview room. Chris was slumped over, arms crossed on the table, head on his arms. "Hello, Chris."

Chris looked up. His eyes were red and teary. "I'm screwed." The client's opening remarks are usually denial, "no big deal" or self-pity with a claim that he is the victim. It's hard for me to think of the guy holding the gun as the victim.

"Tell me what happened."

"I really screwed up. I ruined my whole life." Chris was barely audible. His response was unusual. The kid was in real pain and took all the responsibility on himself. We are supposed to maintain a professional objectivity but...This kid deserved my support. I didn't know what I could do, but I was hooked.

"I can agree with the first part, but not with your whole life being ruined. We'll figure out a way to get your life back on track."

"The Air Force won't take someone with a record of violence or drugs."

Is that a fact? How would the Air Force know? Kids often think that the system is more connected than it really is. "I'm not sure that this qualifies. I'll have to find out exactly what juvenile actions go on record to the military. Meanwhile, I need you to tell me what happened, starting from the very beginning."

"We got this new girl, Maria, to take Melissa's place. She's real shy and quiet. A couple of the football players started teasing her, calling her a wetback. She said she told a teacher and the teacher said to just ignore them and they would stop, but they didn't. She pointed out John and Brian to me as the leaders. They are both big jerks. She was crying after school yesterday, said she wouldn't go back to school ever. During lunch, the same guys told her they wanted to see what a real wetback looked like, so they were going to soak her and see what she looked like in a wet T-shirt. That made me really mad. I promised that I would stop them. I had no idea how, but I had to do something. I don't even know why I was so upset about her."

"Did it remind you of your other foster home?"

"Sorta. Nobody should have to put up with that."

Okay - that was a good guess, but now is not the time to delve into psychology. "So, what happened next?"

"I told my friend about it at work and he said the only way to stop them was with a gun. I told him I didn't have a gun and even if I did, I wouldn't shoot anyone. Alex said I wouldn't have to use it, just scare them with an empty gun. He said he would bring one of his father's pistols to school the next day. He handed it to me this morning and told me to give it back after school. I was scared of getting caught with a gun on campus, so I kept it in my coat. At lunch time, I followed John and Brian to Burger King. I made sure the pistol wasn't loaded and tried to just talk to them, but they were laughing about it until I pulled out the gun. I know it was wrong, but ..."

"You should have asked the counselors for help." I really didn't have a solution either.

"They wouldn't have done anything."

I didn't have an answer. Chris broke the silence. "What are they going to do to me now?"

"Since it's Friday afternoon, the arraignment won't be until Monday morning. You'll have to stay in Detention over the weekend. I have to check on some things before the hearing. The worst that could happen is that you would be committed to the State Department of Corrections until your eighteenth birthday. I don't think that should happen. I'm going to try to figure out a way for you to stay with the Woods and graduate. I have to go now and give them a call. I'll talk to you again first thing Monday morning, before court." What I didn't tell him was that release from the Department of Corrections would probably come with a menial job, shabby rented room and no prospects for the future. Ouch!

The next step was to call the Air Force recruiting office and find out, in the pose of wanting to know how to properly advise any juveniles about their prospects in the military, exactly what their rules were in respect to juvenile records. It turns out that they don't see police arrest records for juveniles, only Juvenile Court adjudications for recruits under the age of twenty-one. A conviction of any offense with a deadly weapon or drugs other than the use of marijuana would disqualify a candidate from joining the Air Force. The Sergeant helpfully suggests that the Army or Marines might still take him.

Chris's only hope is to get the gun charge dropped. I share the common attitude that lawyers are an unwelcome complication in Juvenile Court. The law states that the treatment of a Delinquent should be determined based on "the best interests of the child." I share the common attitude that lawyers are an unwelcome complication in Juvenile Court, but this time the best interests of Chris would be served by a plea bargain. I wound my way through the corridors to the Public Defender's office only to find the door locked. Time to go home for the weekend.

Saturday was a full day. By the time I finished mowing the lawn it was 95 degrees. I tell my next door neighbor, the Major, I use a push mower because it is good exercise and better for the environment. The real reason is that we don't have enough money to spare for a good power mower that would finish the chore in half the time. I have time for a beer and a little relaxation before umpiring a pair of kids' baseball games. On the field, I am completely in charge and the concentration on every pitch keeps my mind off work. That evening, we went tickets to the Phoenix Symphony. My wife is used to the Philadelphia Orchestra so it is a step down for her, but it is still the best music in town and the balcony seats are affordable. Absorbing the music as we sit together always refreshes me. Berlioz's *Symphonie Fantastique* is one of my favorites, but as I closed my eyes to listen, my mind kept drifting back to Chris.

I woke up early on Monday morning, too early but too restless to wait for the alarm, might as well go into the office early. With the arraignment at 9:30, this was one of those days where I had to wear a coat and tie. A brown bag was packed in the refrigerator. It's one of those little things that Judy does that brightens my day. I was the first one in the office. Coffee wasn't not made yet, so I started a pot and killed time with paperwork. At 7:45, I wandered down to the Public Defender's office with my second cup in hand. The door was open and one guy was there. I explained Chris's situation and asked if he'd take the case. He was sympathetic and said the Assistant County Attorney might be persuaded to go along, but he couldn't take the case unless appointed by the judge. Could he at least talk to Chris this morning?

"Sorry, that's not permitted. It would look like I was soliciting the case. If Chris wants an attorney he'll have to ask the judge for one before entering any plea."

The burden was all on my shoulders. I can explain the options, but despite my strong opinion, I can't give any legal advice. I felt like I'm on an ethical tightrope. There were still 45 minutes to wait until the detention officers finished the morning routine and I could meet with Chris. The log book showed that Tom visited on Saturday and Alice was here on Sunday afternoon. They arrived together a few minutes before 9:00 and we went to an interview room to meet with Chris.

When Chris was brought in, I commented, "You look tired this morning."

"I didn't get much sleep. There was nothing to do in here most of the time except lie around and worry."

"The waiting is rough. We only have a few more minutes before we go into court, so let me fill you in on some things I found out. I checked with the Air Force and you were only partially right about their rules. A conviction on a gun charge would disqualify you from enlisting, but they don't look at juvenile police records."

"I don't see how that helps. A lot of people saw me with the gun."

"Remember when I read you the Miranda rights. You have the right to an attorney and there is a possibility that a lawyer could get the charges changed. He might even be able to get the gun charge dropped in return for pleading guilty to the assault charge."

"That doesn't make sense. I didn't hit anybody, so why would I admit to assault?"

"If you had actually hit them, the charge would have been Assault and Battery. In legal terms, simple assault means making a credible threat and waving a gun at someone counts as a credible threat."

"Are you telling me to lie about the gun?"

"No. I don't want you to lie. I want you to always tell the truth, and I can't tell you on how much you should say in court." I felt like I'm walking on thin ice and my stomach was starting to churn.

"Why don't you just ask the judge to change the charge?"

"It doesn't work like that. I can't represent you in court for two reasons. One, I'm not a licensed attorney and two, I am an officer of the court so in the courtroom I can only speak when the judge asks me to."

"Are you sure that the lawyer would get me into the Air Force?"

"No. I am not sure of anything except that the only one who has a chance of getting the gun charge dropped is a lawyer. I can't be sure whether he could do it or not."

"A lawyer costs a lot of money."

"That's not necessarily true. The Juvenile Court assumes that a minor cannot afford a lawyer, so if you ask for a lawyer the judge will appoint a Public Defender to represent you at no cost."

"I don't know ..."

"It's a hard choice and I can't make it for you. Whatever decision you choose, you'll have to make it before the judge asks you to enter a plea. I need to explain the procedure for the arraignment hearing and then you can talk it over with Tom and Alice."

After the rote explanation of the arraignment procedure, I exited the interview room and waited five very long minutes before the case was called. The hearing started with the "oyez, oyez" ritual and a young Assistant County Attorney reading the formal charges.

The hearing officer asked Chris, "Do you understand these charges?"

"Yes."

"Do you understand your rights?"

"Yes, Mr. Gilbertson explained them to me." Chris looked back at me then continued, "and I want a lawyer."

The hearing officer was clearly annoyed. "Do you know what a lawyer would do?"

"Yes, Mr. Gilbertson explained it to me."

"Did he tell you that if you get a lawyer I'll have to keep you in detention until I can schedule a new hearing, otherwise I could release you to your foster parents today, pending the disposition hearing."

Oh, shit! I hadn't thought of that, and it isn't really true. Chris was looking back at Alice and Tom. Was Chris going to get punished because of my advice? Shit.

Chris looked back at the judge and spoke softly, "I want a lawyer."

The judge picked up a pen and looked down at the folder in front of him. "The Public Defender is appointed to represent you. Your arraignment hearing is set for 10 am Friday in front of Judge Robinson. You are ordered to remain in the custody of the court until that hearing. Mr. Gilbertson will escort you back to the detention center." He snapped his gavel down. "Court is adjourned."

"All rise!" The bailiff announced as the judge left the room.

After a moment of stunned silence, Alice came forward and hugged Chris. "I've asked Katie to get your books and homework assignments for the week. We'll bring them tomorrow. You don't want to get behind in school."

"No I don't. Besides that will give me something to do in here. I wish I could go home." Chris sighed.

"So do I. I would have sent you home, but the judge has the final say." I interject, "I'm sorry that there are no visiting hours during the week. I'll stop by your house on my way home tonight and get the assignments to Chris first thing in the morning. I'm afraid that there is nothing you can do except wait."

Alice added, "and pray. It will be a long week for all of us."

Tom stepped forward and extended his hand for Chris to shake. "Keep up your hopes. Things will work out in the end." He turned to me, "We appreciate your efforts."

During the subdued walk back to the detention area, Chris said, "That judge scared me. I don't think he'll give me a chance."

"He always speaks gruffly in court. Besides, there will be a different judge on Friday."

- 211 -

"What's he like?"

"Judge Robinson is the elected Superior Court Judge in charge of the whole Juvenile Court. I've never seen him in court, but he has a reputation of being strict but fair."

The next three days passed slowly. I had other cases to deal with, including intake on Wednesday. Chris had to sit in detention with his school books and wait.

I got a call from the Assistant Public Defender on Thursday afternoon. It was the same young lawyer I had met on Friday. "I met with Chris. He tells a good story. I need to go over a few things in your report before I talk to the prosecutor."

"Fire away."

"How did you confirm his situation with the Air Force?"

"His foster parents showed me the contract he had signed with the recruiter. It accepted him into the Air Force with a guarantee of training as an electronics specialist subject to his he graduation from high school and passing his military physical exam and background check."

"Can he pass the background check?"

I related my telephone conversation with the recruiting sergeant.

"Chris would make a good Marine," he chuckled. "But I'm going to file a motion to drop the weapons charge."

"Thank you."

Tom and Alice were waiting on Friday morning when I escorted Chris into the courtroom. The lawyers were in the judge's chambers, so we had an extra fifteen minutes of tense waiting.

When the proceeding finally started, the Public Defender stood. "I move that the charge of displaying a weapon be dropped without prejudice."

The prosecutor concurred. So far, so good.

The judge turned to Chris. "Are you aware that if I accept this motion that the charge may be refiled at any time prior to your eighteenth birthday and that dropping this charge does not change the severity of the disposition that may be imposed by the court?"

"Yes, Your Honor." Chris had been properly coached.

"Is the defendant ready to enter a plea on the charge of Assault?"

The Public Defender replied, "Yes we are, your Honor."

"The defendant will rise." Chris complied. "How do you plea to the charge of Assault? Guilty or Not Guilty?"

"Guilty, Your Honor."

"Christopher Olsen, it is the finding of this court that you are a delinquent child. It is now my duty to determine the appropriate penalty under the law. I have carefully read the case report written by your probation officer. He details what he claims are extenuating factors and that you have already learned your lesson and have shown deep remorse. It is his recommendation that you be continued on probation in the custody of Mr. and Mrs. Thomas Woods. They have been exemplary foster parents and the court commends them for their work in helping you and the other children who have been entrusted to their care. Mr. Gilbertson has a lot of faith in you. I do not share that faith. Your actions at the Burger King constitute a dangerous crime. There are no circumstances that can justify what you did. At your age, your crime merits commitment to the State Department of Corrections." The judge paused to let these words sink in. "Nevertheless, I will allow you to earn the trust that your probation officer and foster parents have shown through their support. I am placing you back on probation as a ward of the court with the following additional conditions. You are to graduate from high school in May, you are to enlist in the United States Air

Force and complete basic training by the end of August. If you fail to meet these conditions or violate any of the existing terms of your probation, you will be summoned to appear before me and the charge of displaying a deadly weapon other than in self-defense will be reinstated. Do you understand these conditions?"

"Yes sir. Thank you."

"I am not the one you should be thanking. You should be thanking your foster parents for standing by you."

"Yes sir ...Your Honor."

"Christopher Olsen, you are hereby released into the custody of Mr. and Mrs. Woods. This session of the Superior Court of Arizona is adjourned."

When we had retrieved Chris's personal property from the detention center, Alice said, "This calls for a celebration. Let's go out for lunch."

"Thanks, Mom. I really mean it, but can you drop me off at school. I have two tests this afternoon and I can't afford to mess them up."

I felt relieved, but I thought I would feel better if we won. The judge's speech worried me. What if my judgment was wrong? If I was right, why was it so hard to get the system to work in "the best interest of the child."?

Chris did graduate, with all A's and B's.

Tyrone - Part II

Tyrone had been at Rainbow Acres for just under three weeks when I got a call from Aunt Bess.

"Good morning. It's good to hear from you. How is Tyrone adjusting?"

"I'm afraid I have bad news. We may not be able to keep Tyrone."

"Whoa ..." I was completely taken aback.

"His use of disparaging and abusive language is increasing. If it were only against the staff, we could handle it, but it is affecting the other kids. Several of them are regressing. Ramon hasn't made any friends in his cottage. We don't seem to be doing him any good."

"That's most discouraging. Is he continuing to have problems with school?"

"That's the good news. He is doing very well at school. He is a bright little boy. He knows that if he doesn't do all of his school work then he won't get visits from his parents."

"Is there anything we can do that would let him stay with you? Maybe switch him to a different cottage? I would really hate to remand a child his age to the State Department of Corrections."

"I share your concern. All of the cottages are full, so I can't move him. There might be something you could do to reassure him about his parents. He seems genuinely worried about their health. He keeps insisting that they need him at home. We talked to them on the phone and they told him that they were doing fine, but that didn't help."

"Do you have a specific suggestion?" I was feeling desperate.

Aunt Bessie's voice brightened. "Would you be willing to supervise a home visit? Maybe he would calm down if he saw that they were doing well. I was thinking that since his birthday is this weekend and he has been doing so well in school that we could justify making an exception to normal no-visit period."

"It's worth a try. I'll do it."

"Good. You can pick him up at 2:00 on Sunday and bring him by 7:30. I have some passes so that his parents can take him to the zoo."

She had me in a trap. I had already agreed to the visit. How could I tell someone who spent here whole life caring for these kids that I wouldn't give up one weekend afternoon. I had to say, "OK."

"I thought I could count on you. I hope this works."

"So do I. I'll see you Sunday." I hung up, feeling resentful. The Department wouldn't reward or even acknowledge the extra time I spent on the job. Professionals don't get paid overtime, but my salary was barely enough to get by on. At least I would get paid for the extra mileage.

Tyrone bubbled over with enthusiasm when I picked him up. "I'm back home for my birthday."

"This is a special day for you. I want you to have fun during the visit with your parents and I need to bring you back on time tonight so that you can be allowed future visits."

"I know. I know. Let's go."

Aunt Bess handed me three zoo passes fanned out so that the number was obvious. When I looked puzzled, she smiled, "His parents want some time alone with him. I agreed. You deserve some free time."

"Thank you." After subtracting driving time, I would have two hours at home. Still it was better than nothing.

Once in the car, I started probing. "So, tell me about the other kids in your cottage."

"They're a bunch of wimps."

"Can you be more specific?"

"Whatcha mean?"

"Tell me a little about each boy."

"Johnny is a know-it-all suck-up. He thinks he's better than the rest of us."

"Does he say bad things about you?"

"No! He leaves me alone."

"So is he really a problem?"

"No. Jose is the real problem. He's always dis'ing me when the parents aren't around. He talks trash."

"He sounds a lot like you."

"Huh?" His mouth formed a crooked grin.

"Do you call him names?"

"Yeah. But he started it."

"Then you can end it. Just pretend that you don't care what he says and only say nice things about him." Getting no response, I assumed the message had sunk in, and pressed on. "Is there another boy?"

"Just stupid Kevin."

"Does Kevin act stupid, or is he just a slow learner?"

"He's just dumb."

"I'll bet that if you helped him understand how to do his homework that he would become a loyal friend."

"Maybe."

"What about the girls?"

Tyrone grimaced. "They're just girls."

"They'll become more interesting in a few years."

"You mean when they get boobs?"

"That too." I let the conversation end. I wasn't ready to have a sex education session with a ten-year-old.

The hand off to his parents was cheerful and quick. I returned home and got some overdue weeding done before an early dinner. It had been a warm, sunny day. As I sat down in front of the tuna casserole, I commented, "I'm tempted to grab a cold beer."

"I'll get it." Judy offered.

"Nah. I'd better stick to ice tea. I still have to deal with a client."

"One beer won't make a difference. Nobody will know."

"I will. Besides, if it wasn't taboo to see a client after having a drink, I wouldn't be tempted. Save the beer for when I get back."

I arrived at the Brown's apartment with a couple of minutes to spare. Mr. Brown opened the door. His wife was sitting in the recliner at the far end of the room. Tyrone was on the sofa with stacks of cards on the coffee table in front of him.

"Come in. Would you like a piece of birthday cake?"

"No thank you. I just ate." I entered, but remained standing. "How was your afternoon?"

Mrs. Brown answered, "We had a real good time at the zoo. Thank you for the tickets."

"I'll pass your thanks on to Aunt Bess. She's the one who provided the tickets. I'm glad you had a good time. Now its time for me to take Tyrone back to Rainbow Acres."

"I'm playing War with my Dad. We're not finished." Tyrone protested.

"That game can last forever. Say your good-byes. It's time to go."

"I don't want to go." Tyrone slipped behind his mother's chair. "I want to stay here, with Momma."

"I understand that that's what you want, but you NEED to return to Rainbow Acres."

"I NEED TO STAY WITH MOMMA. She's needs me. Don't you, Momma?" He looked up at her with his most pathetic expression.

"I wish you could stay home, but the man says you have to go. So you have to go." She spoke softly. Mr. Brown shrugged and sat down on the sofa.

"I won't leave you. I'm staying here."

I tried to suppress my rising anger with a clear stern response. "That's is not an option. If you don't go back to Rainbow Acres, I'll have to take you take you to the detention center, where they'll hold you as probation violator."

"I don't want to go to Rainbow Acres."

"Are you choosing to go to the detention center?"

"NO! If you try to grab me, I'll kick you where it hurts."

"Don't do that." His father intervened.

"I am not going to restrain you. I didn't bring any handcuffs. If you refuse to come with me, I'll call the police and have an officer take you to detention. I really think that your best choice would be to go back to Rainbow Acres."

"I'm not leaving." Tyrone yelled. He looked like a cornered wild animal peering out from behind his mother's chair.

I asked Mr. Brown, "May I use your phone?"

"Yes."

The telephone sat on an end table at the far end of the sofa. I dialed the non-emergency number of the

Phoenix Police Department. After five rings, a woman answered.

"This is Don Gilbertson. I'm a Juvenile Probation Officer and I need an officer to assist me in taking a client into custody. I am with him and his parents at their apartment." I gave her the address and repeated her response for the Browns to hear. "A police officer will be here in ten minutes."

"Why did you call the cops?" Tyrone whined.

"That's what I told you I would do if you refused to come with me. I always keep my word."

Mr. Brown added, "You should go with Mr. Gilbertson."

"I won't go. I'm staying with Momma." Tyrone ducked out of sight behind the recliner.

I moved over near the door and glanced at my watch every thirty seconds during the interminable, embarrassing wait. Nothing else was said for eight minutes. Finally, we heard a firm knock on the door. I opened the door to a pair of large policemen.

The younger one led the way. "Where is the subject?" Tyrone emerged from behind his mother.

I showed him my credentials. "I'm Don Gilbertson. This is Tyrone." The officer looked at him, then shot me a glance that added to my embarrassment. I explained, "The court has placed him at Rainbow Acres. He was granted a home visit today because it is his birthday on the condition that he return by 7:30 tonight. He has refused to go with me."

The officer addressed Tyrone. "Is that true, son?"

"Yeah."

"Has anybody hurt you or mistreated you?"

"No. I just want to stay with my Momma. She needs me."

"That's not going to happen tonight." The officer took a pair of handcuffs from his belt and his partner moved forward. "Nobody wants to see you going to jail in handcuffs, but that's what we'll do if you make us. I really think you should go with this man. He's been very patient."

"I'll go. I'll go." Tyrone was in tears.

"Where are we going, Rainbow Acres or the detention center? It's your choice."

"Don't take me to detention. Take me back to Aunt Bess. I'll be good."

"I'm glad you made that choice. Say good-bye to your parents."

He joined his mother in a tearful embrace, then shook hands with his father. The two policemen escorted us to my car. Once Tyrone was inside the car, I apologized to the officers for involving them in the scene. The officer who had done all the talking reassured me that I had done the right thing. That helped me feel a little better.

On the way back, Tyrone asked, "Are you going to tell them about calling the police?"

"I'll have to include it in your case file for the court, but nobody else needs to know the details."

"What are you going to tell Aunt Bess?"

"The truth. I'm going to tell her how much your parents appreciated the chance to take you to the zoo for your birthday, that you seemed to have had a good time, and even though you wish you could be living at home, at the end of the visit you chose to come back to Rainbow Acres with me, and that I think that you will make a real effort to do better."

Tyrone let out a deep sigh of relief. "I don't really hate you. I just get real mad sometimes."

"I know. Let the people at Rainbow Acres help you deal with your temper, and you'll do alright."

We got back to Rainbow Acres just before 8:00, late, but not enough to cause any consternation. My optimistic version of the visit was received without any apparent skepticism. I drove off full of my own skepticism about Tyrone's prognosis and doubts about the way I had handled the situation. I didn't come up with any answers about what I should have done differently. When I got home, I promptly yielded to the temptation of a cold beer.

Aunt Bess called me the following Friday. "What did you say to Tyrone on Sunday?"

"I don't exactly remember. Is there a problem?"

"Au contraire. He's really turned over a new leaf in the cottage. He's being helpful and friendly, especially with one of the boys who is having difficulty with his schoolwork."

"I'd like to take credit, but I didn't do anything special. It's just that sometimes persistence pays off."

"Amen to that. If you keep your faith in God, he'll answer your prayers."

I couldn't buy that argument, but I didn't have a better explanation for the sudden improvement.

Marta – Part II

By the end of April, Marta had turned sixteen and eligible for formal job training through CETA. My biweekly phone calls to the settlement house had brought only good news, so I scheduled a sit down meeting with her and Rosa. I foresaw the meeting as almost a graduation party.

After congratulating them both on Marta's perfect attendance and good reports from Mrs. Ramirez, I handed her the application for the county run Culinary Arts program. "The program won't cost you a thing; they even give you a free bus pass. The cooking classes are in the morning, so you get to eat your assignments for lunch. In eighteen months, you will not only have a G.E.D. diploma, but also a steady job as an assistant chef in a restaurant. I really think that this is a great opportunity for Marta."

Marta's reaction was obvious disappointment. She frowned, then whined, "Can't I stay with Carolina?"

I cringed. After all I had done for her, how could she be ungrateful? I felt that her attitude was back to what it was that first day when all she wanted to do was stay home and play with Pablo. I fought back an urge to launch into a hard-nosed lecture on the importance of preparing for her future. Instead, I asked, "How do you think you can continue doing the same things there? The child care job only pays minimum wage. You can do better than that."

"I know. I only want to stay one more year. Then I'll have my G.E.D and Pablo will go to kindergarten. I've been studying hard. I know I can pass the test. Then, I will go to Phoenix College and become a nurse. Carolina says that I can get a scholarship. Nurses get paid more than cooks."

The assertiveness in Marta's voice stunned me momentarily. She had obviously done more than mark time at the settlement house. She had found a mentor and a purpose. I recovered enough to admit, "Actually, that sounds like a better plan than mine. I'll have to confirm it with Ms. Ramirez before I write it up for the court, I'm sure that won't be a problem. Since you are doing so well, I'm only going to call on you once a month from now on, though you can call me anytime if a problem comes up."

"So, I can keep working for Carolina?"

"Yes."

"Thank you, thank you." Marta beamed with happiness.

Rosa joined in, "I'm sorry I was rude to you at first. I was wrong about you. You're the first man that ever treated me and my Marta good."

"Thank you," I sighed. I know she meant it as a compliment, but I heard it as a sad comment on her life's experience.

I'm not a Catholic, but I was ready to nominate Carolina Ramirez for sainthood. She had worked a miracle with Marta. Where the school system had pushed Marta down, Ms. Ramirez had lifted her back up.

Joe

With no kids to have an Easter egg hunt, the holiday passed quietly, just the big church service followed by a dinner with my extended family. This time we gathered at the Cork and Cleaver with Grandpa as the host. After loading up at the salad bar, Judy and I both enjoyed the filet mignon. There is an advantage to having some wealthy relatives. No one consumed more than a couple of glasses of wine, so the conversations stayed calm and pleasant, with the minor exception of Granny nagging us about the lack of any sign of a baby.

Unlike the Christmas season, there was no lull in our case loads. I really missed having a spring break, but needed to save my vacation days so we could escape the worst of the summer's heat with a week on the beach in San Diego, staying with Judy's relatives.

The weekend after Easter produced a bumper crop of new cases. I had intake duty that Monday along with my office mate. The two of us had to process eight kids who had been detained. The appointments for Tuesday through Thursday were already filled by teens who had been cited and released to their parents.

My first case involved a fourteen year-old girl who had been picked up when the police responded to a complaint of a loud party that involved alcohol. The girl was completely sober and was brought to detention because her parent was unavailable. The parent was a single mother who had been on duty as an O.R. nurse at the time. The girl was repentant and the mother was forgiving and eager to take her home. I'm sure my lecture on the dangers of her behavior was unnecessary, but it is an expected part of the probation officer's role.

The second case also involved a single mother. This one was a stressed out retail clerk whose angry sixteen year-old daughter had run away after they argued on Friday night. The girl was picked up when a beat cop spotted her sleeping in a neighbor's car early Sunday morning. After listening to them vent a myriad of complaints about their tedious and unhappy lives for nearly an hour, I was able to get them to agree to counseling and got them an appointment with Catholic Family Services.

My next interview was a twofer, fifteen year-old twin boys from Globe. They had been stopped while trying to hitchhike at three o'clock on Sunday morning. Rather than drive the ninety miles to their home or be stuck with overtime until their parents could retrieve them from his substation, the officer chose to drop them off at the detention center. Since they were residents of another county, I wasn't going to be involved in any follow up, so I wasn't going to dig for details. Their story was that an older friend had given them a ride to a rock concert. They had split up after meeting some girls at the concert and couldn't find each other afterwards. Their parents accepted the story and took them home. I dictated a letter of reprimand to be sent to their home with a copy to the Gila County Probation Department.

I felt lucky. I had completed my intake duties by noon without picking up a single addition to my case load. My office mate got stuck with two cases that would involve thirty day counseling periods and possible court hearings. My good mood was ruined when Bert poked his head into my office.

"Hey Don, you've got another intake case on the way."

"Can't you give it to somebody else? I've already filled my quota of four, so I have a pile of paperwork to deal with." I made my protest knowing that it would be futile.

"Sorry about that. We're overloaded, and you really only saw three families. Here's the referral sheet for your afternoon case."

I reluctantly reached out and accepted the form. Joseph Simmons, age seventeen, had been reported as a runaway by his father on Friday afternoon, having not been seen since leaving for school on Thursday morning. James Simmons, the father, had called the police again late this morning to report that the school said Joe was in attendance and asked for an officer to meet him at Shadow Mountain High School to take his son into custody. The school resource officer called the son to the office when the father arrived and the boy agreed to go the Juvenile Court Center with his father. I was in for a most unpleasant confrontation.

The angry pair arrived in the lobby twenty minutes later. Both were tall, about six-foot four, topped with short, dark brown hair. The teen was athletic and handsome enough to attract a gaggle of girls. The father might have been athletic once, but now had a sizable paunch. I made my usual, short introduction before leading Mr. Simmons to the interview room. That left Joe stewing in a lobby chair.

Please start by explaining the problem as you see it, Mr. Simmons."

"This is the second time Joe has run away from home. He thinks that since he's seventeen he can do what ever he wants and all he wants to do is play ball and watch TV with his friends. I have to nag him to do his chores. He won't obey me or my wife. The law says he has to follow my rules until he turns eighteen." Mr. Simmons was struggling to keep his voice calm and reasonable. "He doesn't appreciate how good he has it. Some kids have to learn the hard way. I figure that a couple of days locked up here will make him see the light and straighten him out."

I had talked to too many parents who thought that locking the kids up would teach them a lesson to try to explain that all detention taught most kids was resentment and the discovery that other kids were more rebellious than they were. Also, disrupting their school attendance for even a few days in detention, only added to their problems afterwards. My prior attempts at logical persuasion on this issue had nearly always resulted in the parent citing some anecdote of a kid who had been scared straight. So now I just fell back on explaining the law.

"Arizona law limits pre-trial detention of juveniles to cases where there is clear evidence that the juvenile is a danger to himself or others, or where there is documented cause to believe that otherwise he would not appear for his trial. Pre-trial detention cannot be used as punishment."

"He's run away from home twice. Isn't that enough reason to believe he wouldn't show up for court?"

"No, especially not since he did not skip any school while he was a runaway. That is unusual and definitely works in his favor. Has he made any threats of physically harming anyone?"

"Well, no." He had paused. I figured he was trying to think of something to get his way. "Well, no."

"Then he doesn't meet the criteria for pre-trial detention." I wanted to cut that argument short, so I moved on to describe our standard procedure, knowing that he wouldn't like it. "This juvenile court tries to arrange counseling with a community agency in cases involving runaways instead of going through the court process. If you choose to sign a formal complaint, a court date will be scheduled in about thirty days. In the meantime, I would be assigned to work with your family to try to resolve the problem without a formal court record."

"He doesn't need to be coddled by some counselor. He needs to be held accountable for his actions and forced to obey." His voice rose in anger. It was time to accept his determined right to a day in court.

"Then, we'll proceed with the formal process. Please fill in this complaint form. I'm checking the box that identifies the Arizona Revised Statute governing runaways. Where it asks for the description of the violation, it only requires the dates he was away and the fact that he did not return home on his own power. After you sign it, we'll continue with your description of the situation and its background."

He filled out the form rapidly and returned it to me without any questions.

"I need some background information for the record. You mentioned your wife. What's her name?"

"Betty."

"Is she Joe's birth mother?"

"No. Joe's mother has some mental problems. She deserted us right after the twins were born. After the divorce was final, I married Betty. She's a full time housewife. The twins need that." He answered calmly, almost mechanically. Something was missing; I would have expected more emotion, anger or bitterness about being deserted.

"How old are the twins?"

"Josh and Jake are four."

"So Joe was thirteen when the twins were born and you got divorced. That must have been a rough year for both of you."

"It was terrible, but we handled it."

"How do Joe and Betty get along?"

"He likes her just fine. Betty is a real sweet little gal and I love her, but she's a soft touch. She leaves all the discipline to me, so I'm the one that Joe gets mad at."

"You mentioned that Joe doesn't always keep up with his chores. What are his chores?"

He crossed in arms, the classical defensive body language. "He's not overworked, that's for sure. He just has to make his own bed, take out the trash, and mow the lawn and wash my car once a week. He babysits the twins when I take my wife out to dinner and a show, but that's not really a chore because they're in bed most of that time. I had it a lot rougher when I was that age, but Betty likes to do all of the cooking, cleaning and laundry herself."

"That's sounds reasonable. How does he do in school?"

"He's a good student, all A's and B's. He inherited his father's brains – ha, ha. He succeeds when he wants to. He is the star of his baseball team, and this year he made the varsity basketball team as well."

He actually sounded proud of his son. Maybe I could leverage this connection. "Do you get to many of his games?"

"I wish I could, but I have a business to run. I have to work long hours to provide for my family."

So much for the connection. "What kind of business?"

"I'm an independent insurance broker. That means no salary and I have to pay for everything myself. I have to stay on top of things and make sales calls every day."

I tried not to let my negative image of insurance salesmen affect my response. "I see. From what you say, it sounds like the best option would be for Joe to stay put until he finishes high school. If we go into court, the judge will probably place Joe on probation until his eighteenth birthday. You do need to understand that once a juvenile is adjudicated, he becomes a ward of the court and the judge has the final say over the disposition. You would be giving up some of your control."

"I realize that. I wish I didn't have to be here, but Joe needs to learn that he has to live by the rules. He is too big for me the physically control him, so if he won't listen to me, he'll have to face the judge."

"OK. I'll talk to Joe now and see what he has to say and to make sure that he understands what could happen in to him in court."

I hadn't made any headway with the father. I'd have to put the burden of reconciliation on the son. Mr. Simmons and his son traded places, and I started round two.

"So, Joe, why did you run away?"

"I can't stand him. He's such a hypocrite!" He spit out his anger without actually answering the question.

"How so?" I'd let him vent before pressing him on his own behavior.

"He always talks about how education is the most important thing, then he comes down and drags me out of school. What a total embarrassment."

"Didn't that happen **after** you ran away?"

"Yeah, but he does things like that all the time, putting me down in front of my friends, bad-mouthing my mother. He wants people to think that he's perfect, but he's not. I bet he didn't tell you about his twins."

"Josh and Jake?" I let him know I had heard about the boys with out giving away any context.

"They aren't really twins. They were born two weeks apart. Dad was making it with his secretary when he got Mom pregnant. That's why Mom divorced him. Can you believe that?"

"Yes. I don't think you could make up something like that." Almost nothing surprised me anymore. "Do you still hear from your mom?"

"She sends me a card with ten dollars in it on my birthday and at Christmas. There's no return address. I bet Dad wouldn't let me have it if there was. I think she lives somewhere in California. Betty moved in right after Mom left. He didn't even wait for the divorce. Said he needed her to take care of the babies."

"Do you resent having her?" I intentionally used the ambiguous reference to her, to see if he would choose to defend his mother or attack his step-mother. He did neither.

"Not any more. I did at first, but she's alright. She doesn't hassle me like Dad does. She really loves the babies. She treats Josh just like Jake. I don't think Mom could have done that. I just don't understand how she can stand him. He treats her like a servant. He has to be the boss of everyone."

I tried to soften the battle lines. "She's had to make some tough choices. Maybe she sees something in him that you don't. And, maybe she believes that the kids are important enough that she chooses to tolerate his faults."

Joe looked thoughtful. I had successfully planted a seed. I followed up with, "What are your long-term, important goals?"

"I'm going to be a lawyer."

"That's pretty ambitious, but doable. Your dad told me that you get good grades and do well on sports teams."

"Yeah. I made the National Honor Society and the basketball team this year, but mostly I'm into baseball."

"What position?"

"Pitcher and outfield." Some enthusiasm broke through. "I've got an eighty-five mile an hour fast ball and a good sinker, and I'm hitting over .300 so far this year. I've already talked to some college coaches. The guy from Pepperdine says he'll give me a full-ride scholarship."

"That sounds great. It would free you from your dad and his money."

"Exactly."

"Then, all you have to do in hang in there for a few more months until you turn eighteen."

"I see what you're getting at, but you don't know what its like to live with my father."

"You're right about that, but I can definitely remember being in high school and wanting to get away from my problems at home. There were some pretty miserable times, but I toughed it out until I could escape to college. Then I went to the opposite side of the country."

"Where did you go?"

"Cornell."

"You must be smart."

"I made good grades and aced the SATs, but that's not the point. Getting to college was important enough to me that I chose to lay low and accept garbage at home long enough to get what I really wanted." Joe's face showed me that I had succeeded in establishing rapport.

"I don't know if I can do that. I've got a hot temper."

"Do you have a teacher you can talk to help you cool down?"

"I can talk to David's parents. They listen."

"Good. Who's David?"

"He's my best friend from way back. He's on the baseball team. His family goes to our church, so his parents know what Dad's like. They told me I can come over whenever I want to."

"Is that where you stayed when you ran away?"

Joe paused, studying my face. "I don't want to say anything that would get them in trouble. They didn't encourage me to run."

"I understand. I hope that you understand that there is a big difference between talking to them when you need to vent your frustrations and trying to move in with them. As long as you are under eighteen, you father has the final say over where you live. That's the law."

"But doesn't the law require him to treat me right."

"The law requires him to provide you with adequate food, clothing and shelter, and there are laws against some kinds of abuse. But the law can't make people be nice and respectful of others."

"So I'm stuck."

"Until your next birthday. So, you might as well try to make the best of it. I would suggest that you start by apologizing to your father."

The anger resurfaced. "What? He should be the one who apologizes for dragging me out of school."

"I don't think you want to be spending more time in court and miss more school and baseball. That's what will happen if you keep stirring up fights with your dad. Think about what you could have done differently. Are you sorry about making Betty worry and messing up the weekend for the little guys?"

"Yeah."

"Then you can make an honest apology about that. Are you willing to stick it out at home?"

"Yeah." He let out a deep sigh. "I'll try."

That was the best I could hope for. When the three of us were seated together, I looked over at Joe. He responded to my cue.

"Dad, I want to apologize for messing up everyone's weekend. Running away was a big mistake. I'm sorry."

"I hope you've learned your lesson. We'll see how long you keep your word."

Joe opened his mouth, looked over at me, and shut it without saying a word. I stepped in to sum up the status.

"There is no magic. I don't expect everyone to live happily ever after. It will take time and effort on everyone's part to ease the conflicts at home. I would encourage you to get family counseling and will give you a list of agencies with good reputations, but I also realize that you both have full schedules, so I'll leave that option up to you." I handed the list to Mr. Simmons. "As things stand, we will have a court date scheduled thirty days from now, which will be a Wednesday, probably in the afternoon. The most likely result of that hearing is that Joe would be placed on supervised probation until his eighteenth birthday. However, I would prefer to see you work out your problems without court intervention and keep your record officially clean. I will be working with you over the next four weeks, starting with a home visit on Thursday afternoon, around 5:30. You can also give me a call if you want to talk before then." I handed each of them a business card.

"I have business commitments so I usually don't get home until six or later."

"That's OK. I'll visit with Joe and your wife until you arrive. I think we're through for today, so you can go back to your work now."

I stood. They followed suit. We shook hands and they left. I went to attack the pile of paperwork with a bad feeling in the pit of my stomach. The degree of hostility between Joe and his dad reminded me of Ben Schultz. I would have to be especially attuned to keeping my own emotions under control.

The following Thursday, I pulled up to their house near Shea Boulevard at 5:25 pm. It was a non-descript ranch with simple landscaping and a neatly mown lawn. A faded blue Ford station wagon occupied one side of the driveway. Joe answered the door.

"How's it going, Joe?"

"OK, I guess." He sounded discouraged.

"That sounds like 'not so good.' "

"I've tried not arguing with my Dad, like you said, but he won't let up. He keeps hassling me. He hasn't changed. If anything, he's gotten worse."

"I remember him expressing doubt about you really changing, wondering how long you'd keep your word. So I'm not surprised that he's testing you. It's going to take time before he eases up."

"That's not fair. I'm doing my part."

"I know. It's going to take time to change the pattern. You're the one who really wants things to change. So the burden of improving falls mostly on you. Keep focused on your goal of college baseball. You can hang in there."

"I guess so."

"Where's Betty. I'd like to meet her."

"She's giving the twins a bath." He turned and yelled, "Betty, Mr. Gilbertson is here."

"Tell him to come on back. My hands are full right now."

I went down the hall until I reached the open bathroom door. My initial sight was of long blond hair flowing down the back of a blue dress.

"Hello Betty."

She turned to greet me. From her face I would guess that she couldn't be past her mid-twenties. Two little boys were in the tub. She was rinsing shampoo out of dark brown hair over an oblong face like Joe's. The other boy had blue eyes and a round face with blond hair like Betty's.

"I'm just getting everything ready for Jim to come home." She explained. "This is Jake and that is Josh."

"Hi, guys."

"Do you want to see our trains?" Josh hopped out of the tub wearing a big smile as his mother wrapped him in a towel.

"Yes. After you get dressed, I'll come in."

"Your turn." Betty held out another towel for Jake. He snuggled against her as she rubbed him dry. The boys trotted off down the hall.

"They seem like good, happy boys." I commented.

"Yes. They are both really sweet boys. They're a lot of fun at this age."

"How's Joe doing?"

"Better. He hasn't argued with his father all week. But I still worry about him. He stays in his room after supper. He says he has a lot of homework, but I think he's avoiding us. I wish he were happier."

"I'm afraid he's still carrying around a lot of anger. I think it would help if he got counseling."

"Jim would never allow that. He despises psychologists."

"I gathered that. That leaves the burden of keeping the peace on you and Joe. I can tell you that for all his sullenness, Joe does like you and appreciates you efforts."

"I'm glad to hear that. Sometimes I have my doubts. We're in a tough situation. I wish I was closer to him."

"About all I can say is just hang in there."

"Thank you. I have to get back to fixing dinner."

"I'll admire the boys' trains for a few minutes until Jim gets home."

The twins eagerly demonstrated how their toys trains ran around the wooden train track that took up most of the floor of their bedroom. The rest of the room was neat: bunk beds, a chest of drawers, toy chest and a bookshelf containing mostly Dr. Seuss.

"Do you read all of these?"

Jake gave me a quizzical look. "Joe reads them to us. I'm going to school next year so I can learn to read."

"That's good. So, now you mostly stay at home and play with your brother."

"Yes."

Josh chimed in. "We have a swing set with a slide and a swimming pool. See." He pointed out the window. The swimming pool was a blow-up model, less than two-feet deep. I remembered splashing around with my brother in one just like it. Those were fun times.

It was almost six and still no sign of Mr. Simmons. I wanted to get home to my own dinner with Judy. I knocked on the closed door down the hall.

"Come in." Joe was sitting at a student desk, pencil in hand with an open math book to one side.

"I've got to head out now. Keep up the good work. I'll stop by again next Thursday."

"I won't be here until late. We've got a game at Central next Thursday."

"Then I'll come by on Friday, and hear about the game."

"OK."

I went to the kitchen to say good-bye to Betty. "I'm sorry I didn't get to talk to your husband today."

"He often has to work late. I've learned how to keep dinner warm without drying out. He'll be sorry he missed you."

I somehow doubted that. "I'll see him when I come back around the same time next Friday."

"I'll mark it on our calendar. Good-by."

I should have been angry or disappointed that Mr. Simmons didn't show up on time. What I actually felt was relief. That man really got on my nerves. I'd much rather end the day with the happy encounter with Betty and the twins. I figured I was going to be stuck with the case for a long time. Mr. Simmons would insist of his day in court. The best I could hope for was to help Joe keep his anger in check for one more year.

The weekend was notable only for the first one-hundred degree day of the summer. That made Saturday's yard work into a two beer operation. It remained hot as I slogged through a routine week. Then as I was finishing my Friday morning coffee, I got a non-routine call.

"Jim Simmons here. Joe ran away again."

"What happened?" I was jolted into instant tension.

"He never came home from school last night. I called his friend's house. Mr. Williams said he was the winning pitcher for the baseball game but claims he hasn't seen him since. I think he's hiding Joe."

"What makes you think that?"

"He's always spending time there. That's where he went the first time he ran away."

"I see. Do you know what triggered Joe's disappearance? Did you have an argument last night?"

"We didn't argue. Joe just complained about having to babysit tonight. I guess he just decided he didn't have to meet his responsibility."

I felt sure there was more to the story, but I wouldn't get a fair account from him. "That's bad news. I guess there's no point in me visiting your home this afternoon.   If I hear from him, I'll let you know. Please let me know if you hear from him."

"Aren't you going to look for him at school today?" Mr. Simmons angrily demanded.

I wasn't going to bite. "Since he's less than twenty-four hours overdue, the police won't classify him as a runaway yet and since he's not on probation yet, I don't have any jurisdiction over him. I would suggest that you wait until dinner time. If he is not home by then, you can file a report with the police."

"Betty and I are going to the Beach Boys concert tonight. If he's not home I'll have to find a babysitter on short notice."

"That's up to you." I sighed, irritated by his selfish priorities.

"Aren't you going to do anything?"

"Not until there is a police report to act on."

He exploded. "That's bullshit!"

"I'm sorry you feel that way."

Click. He hung up, which was just as well. I was having trouble containing my anger with his attitude.

I spent the evening reading and listening to music in an unsuccessful attempt to relax. The phone rang three times, Judy's friends calling to chat. I kept expecting the next time the phone rang it would be either Joe or Mr. Simmons dragging me back into their feud.

Judy and I had spent Saturday afternoon touring model homes, one of our favorite free time diversions. We had chosen an upscale area; price is no object when you can't afford to buy anything. We were back home, just sitting down for dinner when the phone rang. This time it was for me, dispatch was forwarding a call from Jim Simmons.

"I found Joe. I filed a police report last night, so you can pick him up now."

"Where is he?"

"With the Williams. I happened to be driving past it on my way home when I spotted Joe playing basketball with Dave Williams. They ran inside when they saw me coming. I didn't want to get into a fight with them, so I came home and called you."

"I'll try to go talk to him. He might not be there by the time I arrive. Since he saw you, he may have taken off."

"He'll be there."

"OK. Let me write down the address and your home phone number. I'll see what I can do." The address he gave was tucked into a neighborhood on the other side of Shea from his own home. He wouldn't have driven past it on any route to his home; he had been prowling for his son. Nothing would be gained by confronting the issue, so I simply told him that I was on my way and ended the call.

I told Judy that I really had to go deal with this one. I waited long enough to scarf down my sloppy Joe and to drink half my glass of iced tea before heading off on what was probably a wild goose chase.

My destination was a sprawling ranch home with a long front porch on a corner lot. As I pulled up, I could see Joe through a window. He appeared to be standing at the kitchen sink rinsing dishes. He looked up as I got out of my car then quickly disappeared. A wild goose chase would have been easier to deal with. Now I would have to confront Joe with a clear plan.

A large imposing man answered the door. He looked to be in much better physical shape than Mr. Simmons.

"Good evening, Mr. Williams. I'm Don Gilbertson. I'd like to talk to Joe Simmons."

"He's not here."

I bristled at this lie. "Excuse me, but I saw him through the window. I'm his probation officer, and I need to talk to him."

"His father sent you, didn't he?"

"His father called me. If I didn't come he would have sent the police."

"Look. I've known Jim since grade school. All he cares about is himself and his money. He drives a new BMW and wears expensive clothes but won't buy anything nice for his family. Don't believe half of what he says. Why don't you just leave Joe alone?"

"I can't do that. There's a missing person report out on Joe. I need to talk to him."

"Do you have a search warrant?"

"Not yet." I bristled. My authority had been challenged; I wasn't about to back down. "I can get one by phoning the judge. He doesn't like to be called at home, but since I'm an officer of the court and an eye witness, he'll have a sheriff's deputy deliver it within an hour. Then you would be in trouble for harboring a runaway."

I visualized the scenario as I spoke. It was ugly. Joe could easily escape out the back door before any warrant could be served. I would lose any credibility with Joe. Mr. Williams was glaring at me like he was ready to punch me out. I didn't have to be a genius to know that I had screwed up.

"Wait. I'm sorry. I don't want to do that. I'm not going to do that. It would only make things worse for Joe. I'm not going to force Joe to do anything. I couldn't even if I wanted to. I don't have handcuffs or anything and if he chooses to run, I'd never catch him. I think you're right about his father, but we can't ignore him." As I backtracked, Mr. Williams eased his stance. "Do you want him to drag Joe out of school on Monday, like he did before?"

"No. What do are you going to do?"

"Just talk to Joe and get his view of his situation. I don't have a solution. I hope we can figure out a way that Joe can continue to play baseball and graduate from high school with his friends."

"He could stay with us. He's a good kid."

"Are you and your wife licensed foster parents?"

"No."

"The court can only place children into licensed foster placement and the licensing process takes at least six months. So he could only stay with you if he had his father's consent."

"That will never happen. It would hurt his reputation at church."

"Then we'll have to figure out another option. Can I use your front porch to talk with Joe?"

"I'll ask him." He closed the door.

I sat down in one of the rocking chairs on the porch and tried to think of a plan.

Joe came out. "What do you want?" He sounded more fearful than angry.

"I want to find out what you really want."

Joe sat down in the next chair. "I want my dad to leave me alone. I want to live here with Dave's family."

"I'm afraid that's not going to happen. I bet that if you stay here, you dad will have the police arrest you at school and take you to the detention center. Since you would be listed as running away while pending a court appearance, you would be stuck in detention for a couple of weeks. That would mess up both your school work and kill baseball. Even if we got you into a good placement, you would have to change high schools and couldn't play American Legion ball this summer."

"I know, I know. But anything is better than living with Dad."

"I thought you were doing alright at home."

"I tried, but Dad won't give me a chance."

"What made you decide to take off this time?"

"I had a date for the school dance on Friday. Dad and Betty knew about it and said I could go. I wanted to borrow Dad's BMW, but he won't let anyone touch it, except to wash it for him. I promised Linda I'd take her over a month ago. Then at breakfast on Thursday, Dad said there was a change of plans. A client had given him tickets to some dumb concert so he was taking Betty to dinner and the show on Friday, so I would have to stay and babysit. I wasn't going to break my promise to Linda, so I stuffed a change of clothes into my backpack when I left for school. I came home with Dave after our game."

"So now you are really in a jam."

"I'd rather get sent any place else than go back with Dad. He's a total hypocrite. Maybe you could get Dave's parents to be my foster home. I bet they'd take me."

"I know they would. But they aren't licensed, so that's not an option."

"So, I'm screwed."

"Maybe there's another option. Is there some relative that you'd be willing to stay with?"

"Aunt Margaret is nice. She doesn't live too far away, so I could still go to Shadow Mountain."

"Do you think she'd be willing to take you in?"

"Yes, but Dad won't agree."

"Maybe not, but I doubt he wants to pay for having placed in a group home either. If I'm careful, I might be able to talk him into sending you to Aunt Margaret instead. No guarantee, but I think it's worth a try."

"I could still play baseball?"

"That's right."

"Then I'll try it."

"You said that before. This time you'll have to stick with it, even when it's hard. Even if this works, you'll have to put up with a lot of shit for a while."

"I know. I guess you have to take me to detention now."

"You don't get off that easy. If I checked you into detention, you would have to be arraigned on Monday morning and then you'd be stuck in the system. Your father wouldn't be able to retract his complaint without admitting he was wrong. I don't see that happening. If you go back home, we have two weeks to try to reach an alternate solution. The bad news is that you would have to stay at home and obey your father for those two weeks."

"OK. Can I say good-bye to the Williams first?"

"Of course. I want you to let them know that I appreciate their cooperation as well."

While Joe was inside, I thought about the pending encounter with Mr. Simmons. It was going to be a delicate task. Joe's presence would only harden his stance, but Betty's presence might make him want to appear to be more accommodating. The hardest part for me would be to maintain an appearance of neutrality, or maybe I could make his concern for money work in Joe's favor.

All of the Williams came out with Joe. Both adults shook my hand. Mr. Williams said, "I know you are trying to do what is best for Joe. We wish you luck."

"I can use all the luck we can get. Joe deserves a chance to succeed."

Mrs. Williams gave Joe a parting hug. Dave carried Joe's backpack to my car. The short drive to Joe's house was deadly quiet. We were both deep in thought. I suspect Joe dreaded the next hour as much as I did. Upon arrival, I followed Joe through the front door. Mr. Simmons and Betty were watching television in the front room.

Betty looked up. "I'm glad you came home, Honey."

Joe walked right passed them toward his room. It was not a good start.

I jumped in before it could get any worse. "I thought it would be a good idea for Joe to wait in his room until I had a chance to talk with the two of you."

"So start talking. I see you caught Joe where I said he was."

"He chose to talk with me. Afterward, he volunteered to come home."

"His change of heart won't last."

"I agree with you. I don't foresee him staying home very long, even if he is placed on probation. So, if we go to court, I'll recommend that he be placed in a group home until his eighteenth birthday." Mr. Simmons' face went red at the word "if." "Group home placements cost around thirty-two hundred a month."

"That's ridiculous. You could sent him to A.S.U. for less than that."

"True. Colleges don't have to pay professionals to supervise a group of ten boys 24/7. Close supervision is expensive."

"I guess that's why my taxes are so high. Joe needs to learn that his attitude comes at a high price. He has to learn to obey the law and show respect for his parents."

"Actually, the taxpayers won't bear the full cost. You are still legally required to provide for the care and feeding of your children. The court would access you a monthly fee based on a financial statement that you file, along with copies of your tax returns for the past three years." I kept my voice soft and calm, which seemed to irritate him more.

"They can't do that. Tax returns are confidential. No one but the I.R.S. has a right to see them." I could see the blood vessels swell in his temples.

"Once again, you are right. You can choose to withhold your financial information. In that case, the court will assume that you do not need financial aid and bill you the full amount."

"That's blackmail! You can't do that." He exploded.

"Honey, Mr. Gilbertson doesn't make the rules. He's just telling us how the law works." Betty tried to soothe things over.

"In that case, to quote Dickens, the law is an ass."

"I understand your anger. The law can be harsh. I suspect that is why some parents choose to send unruly teenage sons to military school or to live with a relative. Having Joe sent to a group home would be expensive, but trying to keep him home will cause a lot of stress on everyone in the family." I had him nodding. "Do you have a relative who would take him in for the next year, until he finishes high school?"

After a moment of silence, Betty asked, "How about your sister?"

"I don't want to push my burden off on Marge."

"Her son's off at college. I bet she would like to have Joe there to take care of the yard."

"I don't know." He was wavering. "I'll have to talk to her."

"The decision is up to you. It is not an easy choice, and you still have two weeks before the court hearing. If I don't hear back from you before next Thursday, I'll come over and start the paper work and select an available group home. Unless you have other questions, I'll say good-bye to Joe and head home for a delayed dinner.

"Go on."

Betty added, "I'm sorry we interrupted your weekend."

Joe's bedroom was dark. He was lying on top of his bed, staring at the ceiling.

"Hang in there, Joe. When I asked your folks if there was a relative that you could stay with, Betty brought up your Aunt Margaret."

"Really? How did you talk him into it?"

"I didn't. If you or I tried to tell him what to do, he would say no. I only gave him some information about alternatives and left the decision up to him. He is still in charge. He hasn't committed yet, one way or another. You have to wait for him to decide. Meanwhile, don't stir up trouble. You have my phone number, so call ne if there are any new developments."

"OK. Thanks."

"Good night." I repeated the simple good night to his folks on my way out the front door.

I got home a little after 9:00. Judy asked if I wanted more dinner or something to drink.

"Maybe some ice cream after I shower. I'm bushed."

"How did it go?"

"I put out the immediate fire, but both sides are still smoldering. I don't think I've made a difference in either of their attitudes. I'm not looking forward to the next two weeks until we end up in court."

"You can't win them all."

"I know. It's just hard to be philosophical when someone is in so much pain. It gets to me every time."

"That's why you're so good. You really care."

"Thanks." I kissed Judy and went back to shower.

I received a notarized letter from Mr. Simmons the following Wednesday.

```
Mr. Gilbertson:
     This is to inform you that I am
withdrawing the complaint against Joseph
Simmons.  No further contact from your
office is needed or desired.
               Sincerely,
```

James Simmons

His missive raised more concerns than it answered. He obviously didn't like me or my proposals. I was tempted to call and find out what happened with Joe, but figured that if I made the call, Mr. Simmons would complain to my supervisor, accusing me of harassment. I'd have to try to put his spitefulness behind me.

A noon phone call from Joe eased my worries..

"Hi Joe. Where are you?"

"I'm at school. Dad let me move in with Aunt Margaret on Sunday night. He's mad at you, but at least he let me move out. I just wanted to call and thank you."

"I'm really glad things have started to work out. I'll be looking for your name in the sports pages."

"Thanks again. I've got to go to class now."

"Good-bye."

I filled Judy in over a dinner of macaroni and cheese. "I heard from the man who interrupted our dinner on Saturday. He's shipped his son off to a relative, so he won't be going to court after all."

"Is that bad?"

"It's probably for the best. At least I won't have to deal with him any more. The problem isn't really fixed. I made no progress with the dad and there are two younger brothers at home. It's just a matter of time before they become teenagers and the problems erupt again." My gut was still wound up in a knot over this case. "This job is getting to me. I'm on intake tomorrow, so I'll have to deal with three or four more crises. The needs are so urgent and the resources so limited. It's frustrating. I've got to get back into teaching before I burn out. This time, I'm going to focus on middle school openings, where coaching isn't such a big deal."

"I hope that works out. The hours will be better. You wouldn't be getting called out in the middle of the night. And you would have more time at home with the baby."

"That too. Wait – are you pregnant?"

"I saw the doctor today and confirmed it."

I was suddenly elated. "When is it due?"

"Don't call our baby an IT." Judy smiled.

"I didn't want to say 'he' or 'she' because I don't care which one it, oops, the baby is. So when is our first child due?"

"Mid-January."

"That calls for a celebration. I'm taking you out for an ice cream sundae."

Ronny – Part IV

I had just finished our tax returns on the second Saturday in April and was about to drive to the post office when I got a call. By then I groaned whenever dispatch told me that a probationer was on the line. This time is was Ronny Griffith.

"This is Mr. Gilbertson."

"Hello Don. I need you to come help me this afternoon."

"What's the problem?"

"We have to take the state math test on Friday and I don't understand some of the study questions."

That request brought instant relief. "I have appointments scheduled for all afternoon. I could come over after dinner. Would seven o'clock work?"

"That'll work. Thank you."

We had a good two-hour study session. Ron was feeling confident when I left.

During they May visit, Ron announced, "I made fifteen dollars last Saturday by helping my neighbor clean out an apartment."

"That's good. How long did you work?"

"All day. He bought me lunch at McDonalds. I did such a good job that he says he'll have more work for me all summer. He's a handyman for a bunch of apartments."

Fifteen dollars for a days work doesn't come close to minimum wage, even with lunch thrown in. Still, summer jobs in Phoenix are hard to come by, especially for a fourteen year-old. Having any job would be better for Ron than sitting around watching television all day or hanging out in the mall. I could get by with ignoring the violation of child labor laws as long as it was only hearsay, so I replied, "I hope it works out." I didn't probe further.

The final report card in June was the same as the one in January except that P.E. was up to a B. I wrote up a petition to grant Ron an early release from probation, describing his summer occupation as an internship in apartment maintenance. It got a rubber-stamped approved. I presented the decision to the Griffiths as a vote of confidence for the whole family. Ron had definitely earned it.

As far as I know, the Griffiths lived happily ever after, and neither Harvey Cartwright nor my report of his abuse were ever seen again.

Ramon

       Not every case involved a major crisis. Most of my long term probationers were simply marginal kids living in marginal situations. With them, the main job of the probation officer was to serve as a deterrent, a reminder that they needed to stay out of trouble. Providing encouragement to do good was a secondary function.

       Ramon Mendoza was one of the boys I inherited when I got the job. The only offense on his record was a single runaway incident that was precipitated by a conflict with his mother's boyfriend over a year ago. By the time I met him, that boyfriend, and the next one were long gone. The decision to place him on probation was based primarily on the instability of his mother's situation. The mother, Caroline Gomez, took up most of my time during my first visit. She explained that Ramon was no accident even though she had no intention of marrying his biological father or anybody else. She chose to give birth to her son when she was eighteen so she would have someone who loved her unconditionally. That comment set my teeth on edge. I could not image that parental attitude leading to anything but trouble with a teenage son.

       I remember my first impression of Ramon as pudgy and childish for an eighth grader. He complied his mother's request for a hug, though blushed at her extended cuddling in my presence. He was quiet and polite in her presence, but turned into a chatterbox when we were alone.

He had lived his entire life in a two-bedroom cottage in Victory Acres. Victory Acres is a subdivision of small starter homes built at the end of World War II for returning GIs. It had been his grandmother's house until she died of cancer four years earlier. His mother inherited it free and clear, so they stayed put even though the neighborhood had become the home territory of two generations of gang members. I drew suspicious glares every time I drove into the neighborhood, even in my old car. My body involuntarily tensed each time I passed a clump of the teens with their sagging pants and single-colored bandanas.

I made the trip at least every two weeks for eight months. I could count on a cheerful reception from Ramon. It wasn't that I did anything special; he just lapped up positive attention from a male. He was almost always alone in the house with the TV on, watching either cartoons or a video movie. About half the time, an open school book and homework papers would be on the floor in front of the TV. I always started off asking about school. Ramon struggled as a student, usually managing C's because he did all of his homework, so I tried to encourage him even when he failed tests. I praised him for his persistence and helped him with homework from time to time. His grades didn't improve, but at least he kept up on his work. One afternoon he was in a dither because he had a research report for history due the next day and did not have enough facts to complete a two page paper. When I offered to take him to the Tempe Public Library, he said he didn't have a library card. He was surprised when I told him that he could use books in the library without a card, he just couldn't take them home. When we got to the library, he picked a couple of books from the children's room. I spent my time reading magazines. After an hour-and-a-half, he declared that he was done and showed me his paper. It was something that would have been good in fifth grade. The only bright spot in his school week was band practice on Tuesday and Thursday. He played the alto sax, with reasonable tone and accuracy. Based on his pleading, I attended both his Christmas Concert and Spring Concert. They were quite tolerable, and might have been enjoyable if my attitude wasn't soured by the idea of having work intrude on my evenings.

The most distinctive part of our conversations was Ramon's morbid fascination with the possibility of disasters. The first round came as a response to one of my questions, "What do you want to be doing when you are thirty?"

"We'll all be dead by then. The Russians will blow us up in a nuclear war."

"I doubt that. We know enough about nuclear fallout to understand that all out nuclear war can't be won because the fallout would wipe out the whole earth."

"Still it might happen."

"I wouldn't worry about that. It is extremely unlikely and there's nothing I can do about it."

"The world's going to end even without a war." I braced for a religious argument; instead he appealed to science. "The sun is going to burn up and explode."

"That's not going to happen for another five billion years. By then people may have figured out how to travel to distant solar systems.
In any case, it's not a problem for you and me, or even our great-great-great-great-grandchildren."

That diverted the discussion to space exploration. Ramon could vividly imagine going to Mars, meeting space aliens and time travel, but he couldn't seem to picture himself as an adult.

During other visits, he expressed concern about Roosevelt Dam getting blown up and creating a flash flood that would wipe out his house with a rush of water twenty feet deep. I was able to reassure them that it would take at least eight hours for the water to make it from the dam site to Tempe, giving him plenty of time to escape. I was less successful in easing his worries of a plane crashing into his house near the Sky Harbor flight path, or another meteor hitting the earth with an impact like the one that caused the extinction of the dinosaurs, or getting hit by lightning. I didn't want to point out that none of the events were nearly as likely as getting hit by a stray bullet from a drive-by shooting in his neighborhood.

On the two occasions that his mother was home, it meant that she had lost her job. In her telling, she had quit because of unfair treatment by a male-chauvinist-pig of a boss mixed with insufficient tips. Once she informed me that she was starting evening classes to become a chef and improve her income, but when I phoned her the next month she had dropped out because the instructor was prejudiced against her. Even though Ramon met all the terms of his probation and had no negative incidents in well over a year, the uncertainty caused by his mother precluded consideration for early termination of his probation.

By the middle of May, I had completed my first round of teaching applications. My initial focus was on the big unified districts: Mesa, Scottsdale, Glendale, Paradise Valley and Gilbert. While I specified middle school mathematics as my preference, the main draw for the unified districts was that once I had seniority, I could transfer into a high school. I was preparing a slightly different version of my resume for the inner-city schools. Somehow all this effort to switch to a different job spurred a round of introspection evaluating the worth of probation services.

Ramon was a typical case in that I had built a degree of trust and probably kept his situation from worsening by encouraging his school work and serving as a sounding board acknowledging his periodic feelings of frustrations, which was probably worth the time spent, but it didn't feel rewarding. I hadn't made a significant change in his attitude nor his future prospects. If I got my way, I would be handing these cases off to another probation officer who would make a similar attempt to keep out of significant trouble until they turned eighteen.

I wasn't prepared for the twist that Ramon introduced at our next meeting. Instead of directly answering my opening question about school, he stated, "I'm thinking about joining a gang."

I swallowed the impulse to deliver a sermon on the evils of gangs. I'm sure he had been lectured about the dangers at school and wouldn't be swayed by a head on attack, so I calmly asked, "Why do you want to join a gang?"

"They aren't as bad as you hear. Some of my friends have joined. They had to prove they are tough by letting all the members pound them in. They said it hurt, but it wasn't so bad; they only used their fists and they didn't get hit in the face."

"Pardon me if I sound like a parent, but that doesn't sound like a good reason to join. What makes joining a gang sound attractive to you?"

"The guys in your gang are like your brothers. You can always count on them to stand up for you. When you're alone, you can always go to one of your brothers houses and have something to do. In high school, you need a loyal group you can hang with." His description made the gangs sound like college fraternities.

"Those reasons make sense. Being part of a group can be important."

Ramon looked surprised. "I never had any brothers. I don't even have a father. I'm getting too big to rely on my mother. If I was in a gang, I'd have people I could rely on."

"You have obviously been thinking this through. I bet you understand that many gang members get into trouble and end up spending time in jail."

"It's mostly the older guys that get arrested. Most of the younger guys are good."

"The problem is that it is easy to join a gang but hard to quit one. Have you seen 'Boyz N the Hood'?"

"No."

"It's a realistic movie about a gang member that shows both the good and bad things about gang loyalty. If you are interested, I'll rent it and we can watch it next week."

"OK."

"I also want you to think about alternatives."

"Like what?"

I felt I was making progress. At least I had his ear. "When I was in high school and college, the band was my gang. I made a bunch of good friends that I could rely on in the band and we had a lot of fun, not just playing music, but also some parties and hanging out together. We even got to on some neat trips for free. You're pretty good on the sax. Have you thought about trying out for the McClintock band?"

"They already had auditions. I didn't make the varsity band. I'm taking intermediate band next year."

"Not many freshmen make varsity band. I didn't. You'll probably make it for your sophomore year."

"That's a long time off."

"Maybe there's another way to get started. Marching bands need somebody to help with the equipment and setting things up on the field. That would be a way you could get some upperclassmen as friends. It would involve a lot of extra time and work. Would you be willing to try it?"

"Yes. Maybe."

"I went to high school with Mr. Dingham, the band director at McClintock."

"Really?"

"Yes. He's pretty cool. I'll talk to him and see if he can use your help."

"Thanks."

"Good. I'll come over on Tuesday afternoon with the movie, and we'll talk more then."

I left with a partial sense of relief. On the plus side, it was the first time I had heard Ramon discussing the future in a realistic manner and my nonjudgmental approach had kept his mind open for now. I had avoided an explosion, but was still in a mine field. I wasn't sure that I could deliver on my implied promise. Renting the movie would be no problem, but I didn't know Steve Dingham that well. He had been two years ahead of me in high school and I hadn't seen him since he graduated. Yet I didn't see any other viable alternatives to keep Ramon from getting sucked into a gang.

The next morning I called McClintock High and left a message for Steve Dingham. He returned the call while I was eating lunch.

"Are you the Don Gilbertson that went to West High?"

"One and the same. I wasn't sure you would remember me."

"You stood out. The only guy in the flute section along with seven girls. That made a lot of us a little jealous."

"It was fun while it lasted, but after you graduated another boy joined the section. Not only was he a better musician, he was better looking than me."

"Too bad. So, you're a probation officer now. Is one of my students in trouble?"

"No. I called to see if you could help keep one of my kids stay out of trouble."

"I don't have time to volunteer. My hands are really full at school."

"I understand. The boy I'm talking about is Ramon Mendoza. He's an eighth grader who plays the sax. He's scheduled to be in your intermediate band next year."

"The name is vaguely familiar. Is he short and a little heavyset?"

"That's the one." I went on to briefly explain his situation and ask Steve if he could use him as a Band

Aide. Steve sounded reluctant, but agreed to meet with Ramon after school the following Thursday and evaluate his attitude. I kept my fingers crossed over the weekend.

The next week started with encouraging news. I received a letter from the Scottsdale School District inviting me to an interview on Friday. The opening was for a math teacher at Supai Middle School. I promptly accepted and got a early afternoon slot. Though excited by the prospect, I also got an increased sense of urgency about trying to get Ramon established with a source of support outside his neighborhood.

On Tuesday afternoon, Ramon and I settled on the sofa in his living room to watch 'Boyz N the Hood.' Ramon was obviously taken by the protagonist, Trev Styles, as he and two friends became involved in a gang while in junior high. He stayed glued to the action when it jumped ahead seven years to more active gang activity including street drag racing, criminal activity and increasing violence. Trev wants to go straight but is sense of loyalty to his close friends keeps him involved. By the time the film ended, both of Trev's friends were dead and Ramon's cheeks were tear-stained. I felt that anything I might say would be an anticlimax. I simply reminded Ramon that I would pick him up in front of his school on Thursday to meet with Mr. Dingham. When I extended my hand to shake good-bye, he gave me a tight hug instead. I think we both realized how high the stakes were.

We were both nervous as we approached the McClintock band room. Steve had insisted on meeting privately with Ramon, so I sat on a chair reading a whodunit while they talked in Steve's office. They stayed in there for more than half an hour, much longer I had expected. Ramon finally emerged with a big grin, holding some paper. Not only was the accepted as a Band Aide, he had been invited to attend band camp the week before classes started. The papers included the permission slip for his mother to sign. Since he would be going as a worker, it wouldn't cost him a cent. He spent the ride home telling me what a great guy Mr. Dingham was. I was one cloud nine; sometimes the magic works.

His mother was home when we got back, sitting in the kitchen with a glass of wine and a half-empty bottle in front of her. At least she was pleased about the band camp. She signed the form, which I took to make sure that it got mailed promptly.

My good mood carried over to the job interview the next day. I was pleased with how it went. No questions about coaching, the principal did express concern about support for extracurricular activities, specifically mentioning the need for a sponsor the school newspaper. I was confident that I could handle that. He also seemed to view my experience as a probation officer as an asset for dealing with discipline problems. He ended with the usual comments about needing to interview some additional candidates and checks with my references before making a decision. I should be hearing back in a few weeks.

Jeremy

I landed the teaching job starting in mid-August. I planned to resign effective the end of the first week in August. That way there wouldn't be a gap in my paychecks when I cashed in my unused vacation time. Meanwhile, the pressure was off. I could almost coast through the summer.

June was easy. The end of school brought a rash of underage drinking cases. All of my intake assignments involved teens caught partying with beer and booze. All of them had the good sense to at least appear to be contrite. None of these cases took more than the initial session. A couple of the kids did ask, "Didn't you ever party when you were in high school?"

I answered honestly. "I went to a few parties where beer was plentiful but was afraid to drink any because I knew that my father would be waiting up when I got home and if I wasn't completely sober, I would never see the car keys again." I enjoyed watching the boys' reactions, especially the one who asked while his parents were in the room.

On the home front, I was fixing my own breakfasts. Judy was experiencing morning sickness and couldn't stand the smell of bacon. We did enjoy one stereotype of pregnancy by having ice cream every evening.

The Fourth of July weekend overfilled the Monday intake sessions. I wasn't on the schedule, but due to my recent light case load, I was drafted to handle a thirteen-year-old runaway, Jeremy Begay.

Jeremy's mother, Rachel, was the best looking parent I had encountered. She was petite with long, shiny black hair and a smooth, bronze complexion. She looked too young to be the parent of a teen, though she quickly assured me that she had completed training as a nurse before she got married and had Jeremy.

I commented, "Nursing a good profession, with decent pay."

"You're talking about the RNs. I'm an LPN at the Indian Hospital. We are at the bottom of the totem pole."

"It's still an important job." I tried to recover from my blunder. "I believe that Begay is a Navajo name."

"My husband is Navajo. I am Crow. I grew up on the reservation in Montana. I moved down here for nursing school and met Howard at a powwow. He was a great dancer and a long-haul truck driver. I didn't know that he had a drinking problem until much later. It's gotten worse the last couple of years and we started arguing a lot when he's home. He got real mad when he found out I was pregnant and took off. I don't know where he is. I heard he is sleeping with some woman in Tucson, but I don't know. Without his money, I couldn't afford the payments on the house we were in, so we had to move to a townhouse in Sunnyslope. Jeremy doesn't understand. He's mad at me for taking him away from his friends."

"When did this happen?"

"Howard left in April. He claimed that it was all my fault. I moved on the first of June."

"What about the pregnancy?"

"She's due in early November. I just found out last week that it's a girl. I had hoped that Jeremy would be happy to have a baby sister, but he seems resentful."

"You've both had a lot to deal with lately and deserve some help. I'm pretty sure that things can get better. I'll talk with Jeremy and then we'll get back together and make a plan."

"Oh thank you. I'm so worried."

My session with Jeremy started in sullen silence. He slumped down in his chair and studied the floor.

"So, Jeremy, what's been going on?"

"Nothing. I didn't do anything wrong."

"You sure have your mother worried."

"I just took a bus to see my friends and watch the fireworks with them. I left her a note."

"The report says that you were missing all the next day and then was picked at three o'clock on Sunday morning."

"I was walking home. The bus doesn't run at night."

"You were walking alone long after curfew, which is dangerous as well as being against the law. But, that's not the real problem, is it?"

"No."

"So what is the real problem."

"My parents ruined my life. Everything was fine until Mom made us move. She didn't even ask me what I wanted."

"Maybe she didn't think she had a choice financially. If she couldn't pay the rent, you'd get kicked out."

"It still stinks. There's nothing to do in Sunnyslope."

"June can be a hard time to move. It's hard to meet new friends when school is out."

"Yeah." His tone of voice was shifting from anger to resignation.

"Once school starts, you'll make some new good friends."

"I don't want to spend all summer cooped up like a prisoner."

"We'll have to work on that."

"What do you mean?"

"I don't know of any good places to hang out in that area other than the mountain preserve, but I can look into finding a program at a gym or swimming pool."

"I can't swim."

"That narrows the search. Do you have any hobbies?"

"Just playing basketball with my friends."

"That's a start."

I broke the ensuing silence. "Tell me about your father?"

He shrugged. "Dad was never around much."

"When he was around, did you do things together?"

"When I was little, he played catch with me, but that was a long time ago."

"What do you think about having a baby sister?"

Another shrug. "What do you want me to say?"

"Whatever you really feel."

"It's kind of cool, but I don't know. The baby will take a lot of attention."

"Meaning your mother won't have much time for you?"

"More like we won't have enough money. That was what Mom and Dad were always arguing about."

"It sounds like your mother was smart to switch to a place with lower rent."

"I guess so."

"It's natural to feel angry and resentful when things get worse and it's not your fault. From what I can tell, neither you or your mother are responsible for your current problems. I bet she has many of the same feelings that you do."

"Probably."

"I want to get both of you some help so you can make the best of things and enjoy each other more. Does that make sense?"

"Yes." Ramon's voice was still flat, but at least we were moving in a positive direction.

I thought I had established a good rapport with both Jeremy and Rachel. At the very least, I liked them and wanted to help them personally. If I didn't know that I'd be leaving in three weeks, I'd point them toward probation so they would have my support at least until Jeremy was established in high school. However, I'd have to careful not to over commit myself and I didn't have enough faith in the system to count on the quality of my replacement. So I ended the session with a strong recommendation that they get family counseling from the Catholic Social Services office, which was near their home. I did explain the thirty-day pre-court option, giving them my card and setting up a follow up visit at their home in a week.

Judy and I were watching a *M*A*S*H* rerun after dinner on Thursday when the call came in. The dispatcher had a call from Rachel Begay on the line.

"Jeremy and I just had a fight. He's locked himself in his room and won't talk to me. I'm so sorry. I don't know what to do."

"I'll be right over. Remind me, what is your address." The words came out of my mouth before I took time to consider any alternatives. I copied down the address, kissed Judy and headed out. It only took twelve minutes to get to her door, a short drive for me, a long wait for her.

Rachel opened the door before I knocked. "Thank you for coming. It's my fault. I got home late and the kitchen was a mess and I just started yelling at Jeremy."

"Let's sit down and you can fill me in."

She led me back to the kitchen and sat down at the dining table. I sat in the chair next to her. There was a half-empty coffee mug in front of her. "Would you like some coffee?"

"No thank you. Please tell me about your day at work."

"We were short handed, which isn't unusual, but my replacement didn't show up on time, so I was stuck on the ward on for an extra hour. Then I had to get groceries on the way home or there wouldn't be any food in the house for breakfast. Jeremy was supposed to do the laundry today but when I got home the dirty clothes were still in the basket and the kitchen was a mess. I guess he tried cooking something like an omelet but it was just a burnt blob in the frying pan. I was already tired and I lost it. I didn't even say 'hello.' I just started yelling at him for being so lazy and careless. Jeremy yelled back that I didn't care about him and stomped upstairs and slammed the door. I went up and tried to talk to him but he had the door jammed so I couldn't open it. I'm afraid he's going to climb out the window and run away again. Am I going crazy?"

"No. I'd probably lose my temper too if I had a day like yours. I'll go up and try talking with him."

The upstairs was completely dark. I flipped on the hall light and went up. I knocked on the door at the top of the stairs and got no answer. Turning the knob, the door opened easily into the master bedroom. When I knocked on the next door, I got a muffled response, "Leave me alone."

"It's Don Gilbertson. I'd like to talk with you."

"Just go away."

"Your mother called me because she is sorry about the argument and is worried about you."

"I don't need your help."

"Can I come in?"

"No. When I block the door with my dresser, nobody can come in."

I wondered what had I gotten myself into this time. I even thought about giving up and going home. That wouldn't be in the best interest of the child, but I had no idea of what would be in his best interest. Then my stubborn streak kicked in. I lay down on the floor so I could lower my voice and talk through the space at the bottom of the door.

"I'll wait. Let me know when you are ready."

"Why don't you just leave?"

"You see I met this neat kid on Monday. I don't know him very well yet, but I do care about him. So when his mother called and said he had a problem I came right over. I promised her that I would talk with you and I always do my best to keep my promises. So I'm stuck here until you let me in."

"Are you going to stay all night?"

"If I have to, even though this floor is not a comfortable bed."

I had plenty of time to ponder the folly of my ways during the silence that followed. The only sound was water running down in the kitchen; that would be Rachel cleaning up. I wondered what she would think if she saw me lying in the hall. I was embarrassed by my unprofessional posture. After ten minutes, even that sound stopped. Rachel did not come upstairs. I was left wondering if I would really stay there all night. Judy would be worried if I stayed out too late. Telling Jeremy that I would stay all night right after saying that I always kept my promises was a dumb move; I had painted myself into a corner. I was getting tired. Maybe I should take a nap. I tried unsuccessfully to relax and get comfortable.

After almost half an hour, I heard Jeremy's soft voice. "Are you still there?"

"Yes. The floor is getting uncomfortable, but I'm still here."

"I thought you'd give up."

"No. I'm not going to give up on you."

"Wait a minute." I heard shuffling and scraping. "You can come in now."

"Thanks."

I stood up and opened the door. Jeremy was standing in the middle of the dark room, stark naked.

The only light was coming from behind me in the hall,, so he probably didn't notice the shocked look on my face. I was really uncomfortable with the thought of being alone with a naked child.

He spoke first. "What do you want to say to me?" It sounded like a challenge, like he expected a lecture and wanted to get it over with.

"I don't know what to say until I understand what's been going on with you. Why don't you pull on some pants and pop back in bed? Then I'll sit down and we can talk."

"I always sleep in the nude."

"Nothing wrong with that."

He got back in bed and pulled a sheet up over his waist. I spotted a desk chair, pulled it next to the bed and sat down. I finally had some hope of making progress. "What did you do today?"

"Nothing. My life sucks."

"I remember feeling like that. That's why I know it can get better." Maybe it was my imagination, but he looked like he wanted to believe me. "So exactly what did you do all day."

"I ate breakfast with my mom, then she left. I washed the dishes and vacuumed the house and made my bed. Then I watched television and read a book. It was boring."

"What was the book?"

"*Twenty Thousand Leagues Under the Sea*."

"That's my favorite Jules Verne."

"Everybody dies at the end."

"Almost everybody. One normal guy survives to tell the tale, like in *Moby Dick*."

"Yeah."

"What did you do for lunch?"

"I made a peanut butter and banana sandwich. I made macaroni and cheese later when Mom didn't come home."

"Sounds like you're pretty good at taking care of yourself. Were you worried when she was late?"

"Not at first. It happens pretty often. I don't like it. She's tired and grumpy when's late."

"So you were expecting her to be in a bad mood?"

"Yeah. I started making an omelet for her to eat when she got here."

"So, that's what was in the pan on the stove."

"She was really late. I guess I left the stove on too high. I can't do anything right. When she opened the door, she smelled smoke and started yelling at me."

"It would scare me if I smelled smoke when I got home."

"Yeah, but she didn't have to go crazy about a burnt omelet."

"She told me that she overreacted because she was tired. I don't blame her."

"Do you blame me?"

"Not really. You made a mistake, but you were trying to do a nice thing even though you had a lousy day yourself."

"True."

"Did you tell you mother that she doesn't care about you?"

"I didn't mean it. I was just mad." He paused. "I know she loves me and works hard."

"It would be nice to tell her that once in a while."

"I do."

"Good." I felt good. We had made it through the sensitive topic without any rancor. "Have you had a chance to shoot any hoops this week."

"Mom won't let me go to the park. She says drug dealers hang out there."

"Sunnyslope Park has a bad reputation that way. I drove through the neighborhood on my way home of Tuesday. The grade school has a basketball court next to its playground. The only people I saw there were a couple of little kids on the swings. I'll suggest that to your mother."

"It would be better than being stuck here all day."

I was on a roll. I tried suggesting another way of relieving stress. "Have you gone to the Mountain Preserve yet? They have some pretty nice hiking trails."

"No. Why do you like it?"

"It's peaceful. When I feel stressed, I like to get away from the city noise and poke around. I enjoy spotting wild animals."

"Will you show me?"

I had set another trap for myself, but at least it would be a fun outing for me. "I'd like that, but It can be awfully hot at this time of year unless you go early in the morning."

"I'm up early. Mom leaves for work at 6:30. You could come at 6:15." His eyes were pleading.

"If your mother agrees, I guess we could go on Saturday."

"Cool."

"I think it's time for me to let you get some sleep. Do you mind if I tell your mother what we talked about?"

"Go ahead. And tell her I'm sorry I forgot to do the laundry. I'll do it tomorrow morning for sure."

"I'll give her the message. Goodnight."

"Goodnight. See you Saturday."

I went downstairs and briefed Rachel on the conversation, starting with Jeremy's promise to do the laundry. Next I asked if she had made a counseling appointment with Catholic Social Services.

"I meant to, but I promise I'll do it tomorrow." When I reacted with a brief smirk, she continued, "Now you know where my son gets his forgetfulness." From then on, she seemed relaxed and relieved. She hesitated before agreeing to allow Jeremy to go to the school playground while she was at work, but greeted the idea of a Saturday morning hike with appreciative enthusiasm. We ended by making an appointment for me to come by on Wednesday afternoon. Her work schedule was Thursday through Monday.

I apologized to Judy for getting home so late. She shrugged it off. "In only a couple of more weeks, we won't have to worry about any evening emergencies until the baby comes."

Saturday morning came too early. Still I made it to the Begays home by 6:30. The temperature was already in the eighties and headed toward one-hundred-and-ten. I dressed in chinos, a long-sleeve khaki shirt and a hat for sun protection. I had two canteens on my web belt and brought another for Jeremy. Jeremy answered the door in a T-shirt and shorts, which was probably OK given his bronze complexion. He was in a good mood, announcing that his mother a bought a new basketball. We bade his mother good-bye and headed out. The hike was an all-around success, We spotted jackrabbits, a bevy of Gambol's Quail with four chicks bobbing along after their mother, and a number of lizards. Jeremy tried to catch the lizards with no luck. When we turned to climb to the top of North Mountain, Jeremy led the way at a pace that had me puffing to keep up. We rested at the top for fifteen minutes, enjoying the view and pointing out landmarks to each other. We didn't get back until almost ten o'clock. I had drained one canteen. Jeremy had emptied his at the top of the mountain and drank most of the water in my spare canteen during the return. Even though it felt great to have shared the outdoors with Jeremy, I was hot and tired, ready to go home and grab a beer and something to eat. Jeremy thanked me when I left and wanted to know when we would hiking again.. I demurred, "I enjoyed it, but it was a one-time thing. I have to spend most of my weekends doing yard work and other chores."

The follow-up appointment on Wednesday went equally well. They had gone to a counseling session the day before and both Rachel and Jeremy liked the counselor. Jeremy had made three friends playing basketball. With all the good news, I suggested that if things continued the way they were going, I would close the court case at next week's meeting.

Jeremy objected, "You said you would help us for thirty days. Next week is only three weeks."

"I know that's what I said, and if you need me any time during the next couple of weeks, I'll do my best to help. But, I got a new job teaching math and next week is my last week as a Probation Officer."

"Congratulations." That came from Rachel.

"Can't we go hiking one more time?"

"I'll think about it."

Jeremy looked sullenly disappointed. "That means no."

"No. It means I'll think about it. I'll check my schedule, my wife's plans and the weather forecast, then I'll make up my mind."

"OK." Jeremy did not sound satisfied.

My last week on the job passed quietly. I made a final visit to each of my probationers and updated all their files, ready to be handed off to whoever my replacement would be. My final staff meeting included perfunctory good wishes all around. There was no celebratory farewell lunch. Remembering my own concerns about increased workloads when previous departures had left us shorthanded, I understood the muted response to my good luck. Anyways, I didn't plan to keep in touch with any of these co-workers.

I did get a truly celebratory moment that Thursday. It started with a call from the front desk. "There's an Airman here you wants to talk to you." Chris had made it!

"I just wanted to thank you for giving me a chance. I'm in town for two weeks before reporting to Electronics School at Randolph Field in San Antonio. I'm staying with a classmate because there's a new boy in my old room."

"Do you have your orders with you?"

"Yes."

"Let me make a copy for your file, so I can ask the judge to officially terminate your probation."

That task took just a minute. Then I wished him luck. We shook hands and he was on his way. That was enough to keep my spirits high through the next day, when I turned in my badge.

When I officially closed Jeremy's case, I agreed to ne final hike. I picked him up on the Thursday morning of my vacation and drove over to South Mountain. We enjoyed a cloudy day, making for a relatively cool hike through Hidden Valley. Jeremy led most of the way. On the way back, he stopped suddenly. I could hear the distinctive sound of a snake's rattle.

Jeremy froze in panic. "There's a snake!"

A good sized diamondback was coiled in the shade of a rock about fifteen feet ahead. I came up and put a hand on his tense shoulder. "Don't worry. A rattlesnake's strike can only reach as far as half the length of his body. As long as we stay at least six feet away, we are safe from even the largest rattler."

"Really?"

"Really." He picked up a rock.

"What's that for?"

"I want to kill him."

"Leave him alone. He's not trying to hurt you. If he wanted to bite you, he wouldn't have warned you with his rattle. He's part of nature."

"Aren't you scared?"

"No. I know that rattlers are dangerous, but so is electricity. As long as you understand and respect them, there's nothing to fear. I consider seeing a snake in the wild as adding a little excitement to our adventure."

"I like that idea." He dropped the rock.

We made a short detour to give the snake a wide berth and completed our hike. After stopping on the way back for Egg McMuffins and Cokes, we parted on best of terms.

Looking back, the year had been a adventure with more than its share of scary moments when I didn't really understand what I was doing. There were a number of times when I had strayed outside the agency's standard operating procedures. Bert would have disapproved of my extracurricular activity with Jeremy. He would have warned me against giving Rachel my home phone number, which I did to meet my commitment to remain available for the full thirty days. I was willing to take the risk. If you are going to live up to the court's philosophy of serving the best interest of the child, sometimes you have to go out on a limb to reach him.

Epilogue

I struggled with time management through most of my first year teaching. The classes often ended too soon or stretched out too long. The worst part was that I was taking so much work home. Between grading homework and preparing lessons and quizzes, I was averaging a good four hours a night of work at home. At least, I was home with Judy doing that work. I experience no regrets about changing jobs. Our baby, Helen, arrived during the first part of Christmas break. She was the best present we could imagine.

The second year, teaching became much easier. I was used to the district's red tape and could take advantage of my existing lesson plans and quizzes. Most days, I only spent a couple hours working at home. Having Helen consistently sleep through the night also helped.

In October, I went to the football game between Coronado High and McClintock. I enjoyed the cheerful greetings I got from some of the prior year's eighth graders. A second-half visit to John Dingham's band on the other side of the field was even more encouraging. As I glanced up into the stands I saw Ramon pointing at me. I went far enough up the aisle to ask him, "It's good to see you, Ramon. How's it going?"

"Great. It is good to see you to." That said, he turned to the girl sitting next to him and continued their conversation. John confirmed that Ramon was indeed doing well.

I was getting a kind of reward from working with kids that I could have never gotten selling cars with my father.

In the middle of February, a girl named Rose transferred into my eighth grade class. For the first two weeks, she gave me nothing but angry glares, not even a single homework assignment. While everyone else was working, Rose drew grotesque faces. On the first test, she scored 20%.

When I dug out her permanent record in preparation for calling her parents, I ran into a nearly blank wall. The folder contained no history or grades from her prior school. The only information was a health card, her birth date, and a mailing address with her guardian listed as Mrs. Martha Johnston. That name struck a bell. I look up Girls Ranch in the phone book and confirmed that it matched the mailing address.

The next day, I had Rose stay after class. As soon as the other students left, Rose blurted, "What do you want?"

"I want you to do your home work."

"I hate math. I always flunk the tests, so why bother."

"I could stop by the Girls Ranch and talk to Mrs. Johnston, but I know how tough their rules are, so I want to give you a chance to fix the problem on your own."

Rose went livid. "Who told you? Nobody is supposed to know where I live."

"Nobody told me. I just recognized Mrs. Johnston's name from a previous job. Do you know Kate Knowland? Is she still there?"

"I don't have to tell you anything. Stay out of my life."

"Mrs. Johnston will be getting a progress report soon enough. If you happen to see Kate, tell her Mr. Gilbertson sends his best wishes." I wrote out a pass and sent her on her way. Something strange was going on. I wondered if Rose was under some kind of witness protection program.

The next day, Rose came to class with her homework done. Lots of erasures, but complete. She came up to my desk at the end of the period.

"Kate says to tell you 'Hi.' She's the captain of high school soccer team and has a scholarship from the U. of A."

"That's great news. Give her my congratulations."

"Okay."

"Did Kate say anything else?"

"She said I'd better do my homework and not give you any more trouble."

"I don't mind a little trouble, as long as you are doing your work and trying to improve."

"What will you give me if I do?"

"I'll give you all the help you need. More importantly, you'll learn how to do the math and earn a decent grade."

"Is that all?"

"As long as you do the work in my class, I won't pry into the rest of your life."

"It's a deal."

Rose kept her end of the bargain, earned a grade of B minus for the semester and passed the math achievement test. So, I never found out anything about her past.

The news Rose brought has kept me inspired ever since. None of the children I have worked with seemed more deserving of the label "incorrigible" than the cynical, manipulative, rude teen named Kate Knowland. If she could turn her life around, there is hope for any child.

Author's Note

I wrote this book out of a desire to share the insights that I have gained from working with "At Risk" children. While all of the characters are fictional, the situations, attitudes and outcomes described in this book are drawn from my personal experience.

The dictionary definition of "incorrigible" is incapable of being corrected. The legal system applies the term to children who are adjudicated for offenses that would not be crimes if committed by an adult. By and large, these are children who are struggling to find a way to cope with painful living circumstances. I have never met a child that is actually incapable of correction, though far too often kids fail to find the support they need to become happy and productive citizens.

While this book is critical of the Juvenile Justice system. I have found the vast majority of its professionals to giving their best efforts to serve the best interests of their charges with extremely limited resources. The future of our children is too important to be left to overstressed professional. Often the most effective improvement in these children's lives is the result of a mentoring relationship with a community volunteer.

My narrative has been significantly improved by the feedback I received from the Sandwich Writers Group. My thanks go out to Ann Shea, Geri Rider, Laura Abbady, Susan Hayes, Heather Pannell, Alan Pilch, Elaine Tammi, and Mark Wiklund for their encouragement and suggestions.

Other Books by Richard Galbraith:

No Longer Crippled - A childhood memoir

A Gringo in Milparada - Life in a Village of Squatters